D0148531

RETHINKING
THE
CURRICULUM

Recent Titles in
Contributions to the Study of Education

Rethinking the Curriculum

TOWARD AN INTEGRATED, INTERDISCIPLINARY COLLEGE EDUCATION

EDITED BY
Mary E. Clark
and
Sandra A. Wawrytko

CONTRIBUTIONS TO THE STUDY OF EDUCATION, NUMBER 40

GREENWOOD PRESS
New York • Westport, Connecticut • London

Library of Congress Cataloging-in-Publication Data

Rethinking the curriculum : toward an integrated, interdisciplinary
 college education / edited by Mary E. Clark and Sandra A. Wawrytko.
     p.   cm. — (Contributions to the study of education, ISSN
 0196–707X ; no. 40)
     Based on a conference held in San Diego, Calif., June 19–23, 1989.
     Includes bibliographical references.
     ISBN 0–313–27306–5 (lib. bdg. : alk. paper)
     1. Universities and colleges—United States—Curricula—
 Congresses.   2. Curriculum change—United States—Congresses.
 3. Education, Higher—United States—Aims and objectives—Congresses.
 I. Clark, Mary E.   II. Wawrytko, Sandra A.   III. Series.
 LB2361.5.R45   1990
 378.1'99'0973—dc20   89–78404

British Library Cataloguing in Publication Data is available.

Copyright © 1990 by Mary E. Clark and Sandra A. Wawrytko

All rights reserved. No portion of this book may be
reproduced, by any process or technique, without the
express written consent of the publisher.

Library of Congress Catalog Card Number: 89–78404
ISBN: 0–313–27306–5
ISSN: 0196–707X

First published in 1990

Greenwood Press, 88 Post Road West, Westport, CT   06881
An imprint of Greenwood Publishing Group, Inc.

Printed in the United States of America

The paper used in this book complies with the
Permanent Paper Standard issued by the National
Information Standards Organization (Z39.48–1984).

10 9 8 7 6 5 4 3 2

Copyright Acknowledgments

The editors are grateful to the following for permission to use copyrighted materials:

To the *American Journal of Physics* for extensive excerpts, several tables, and an illustration that
appeared in Albert A. Bartlett's, "Forgotten Fundamentals of the Energy Crisis," *American Journal
of Physics*, volume 46, September 1978, 876–88 (quoted in Chapter 14 of this volume).

To *L & S Magazine* of the University of Wisconsin for use of an adapted version of Russell
Peterson's contribution, "Why Not a Separate College of Integrated Studies?" (Spring 1988)
(Chapter 16 of this volume).

To the memory of
Charles Michael Helmken
whose creative artistry served the cause of
higher education for more than three decades

CONTENTS

ILLUSTRATIONS

FIGURES

TABLES

PREFACE

The conference, "Rethinking the Curriculum," on which this volume is based, was held in San Diego, California, June 19-23, 1989, with 250 faculty, students, and administrators attending. Plans, however, began nearly two years earlier among a group of Southern California faculty concerned over the disparity between what is being taught in colleges and universities and what is actually happening in the world. Representatives from five campuses—California State Polytechnic University at Pomona, Glendale Community College, San Diego State University, University of California at San Diego, and University of San Diego—met frequently over this period, identifying the conference themes and planning a format that would permit wide participation by all attending, as well as exposure to some outstanding global thinkers.

The themes drew on a preceding conference with similar concerns, "Sanity, Science, and Global Responsibility," held at Brock University, St. Catharines, Ontario, in July 1988. Each morning, three or four speakers addressed the day's theme in plenary session, and during the afternoons, seminars led by various participants permitted a less formal period for exchanging ideas and sharing experiences. During the conference, there was considerable interest in ongoing future meetings, and an organization, Responsibility International, emerged under the leadership of Robert Malone of the Philosophy Department at Brock University. Clearly, there is widespread interest among North American faculty in rethinking what higher education should be about. We trust that this volume will provide important stepping-stones along that path.

We would like to take this opportunity to acknowledge the many individuals who made this remarkable conference possible. This cadre of diverse individuals miraculously was able to mesh into an interdisciplinary unity, thereby serving as a veritable model of the new vision we are all seeking. Special thanks go to Anne Wright and the entire staff of the SDSU College of Extended Studies; Bill Leasure, stalwart on-site chair; Steve Roeder, for his yeoman service throughout the conference; and Sharon Scull of Glendale Community College for her efforts in publicizing the conference.

Thanks also are due to the more than eighty presenters of afternoon seminars, who explored the myriad dimensions of the morning themes, engaging their colleagues in wide-ranging dialogues. Lastly, and most importantly, our thanks go out to each of the conference participants, who made up the receptive and responsive audience to which these papers were directed. We only regret that we have been unable to record all of the insights that emerged from this dynamic meeting of minds.

M. E. C. and S. A. W.

RETHINKING
THE
CURRICULUM

1   INTRODUCTION

Mary E. Clark and Sandra A. Wawrytko

"RETHINKING THE CURRICULUM"

This book presents the major addresses at a very remarkable conference, one that we believe could well revolutionize what is taught in our universities and colleges. To most of us in academe, "curricular change" has become a ho-hum phrase, on the order of a magnitude 3.0 tremor on the Richter scale of our intellectual horizons, scarcely arousing us to more than momentary diversion from our scholarly routines.[1] The frequency and inconsequential nature of these little jolts lulls us into ignoring them; we become dangerously habituated, forgetting that repeated small tremors indicate significant faults in the underlying territory that will one day totally rearrange the academic landscape. In our view this conference was a quantitatively different order of magnitude warning, an intellectual jolt of order 6.0 or 7.0—portending sweeping, indeed cataclysmic changes in the near future.

Under the overall theme "Rethinking the Curriculum," the conference discussed the intellectual changes needed to bring the academic world into meaningful touch with today's global realities. The consensus was that this cannot occur by the usual imperceptible adjustments in our mental landscape—our disciplinary territories. Rather it demands literally toppling many of the shaky pillars on which the conventional disciplines are based and erecting from the rubble, sounder, more functional visions of reality. As in preparing for earthquakes, we have the options of foresight: an orderly dismantling and reassembling of our intellectual architecture, or of waiting until the ineluctable tectonic forces of global reality climax, collapsing the academic world into an unserviceable heap of useless intellectual masonry.

The message of the conference—and of this book bearing its title—is that most of what passes for liberal studies and general education is so out of touch with today's world that it is simply beside-the-point. The curriculum bears little connection to contemporary reality, and even when it does, it is in such a fragmented form that little useful understanding is possible. Students, intuitively aware that this is the case, tend to treat general education requirements merely as meaningless hurdles to be gotten over by any means possible. Since fewer and fewer faculty are interested in teaching these courses, quality is in rapid decline on both sides.

However, on nearly every campus a few determined and concerned faculty are trying to change things. For the most part they are isolated, often ignored in terms of conventional rewards, and find themselves swimming alone against a mighty, slowly moving river of outdated but institutionalized pedagogy. These people, who made up the vast majority of participants at the conference, are struggling to make sense of the world for themselves and for their students. Working alone or in small groups, they develop courses uniting disciplinary labels as divergent as biology and religion, or history and engineering, all addressing a common question: What are the multiple forces that have brought the world to its present precarious state and what are the necessary changes in our thinking and acting that will help to resolve or at least ameliorate some of the crises that are to come?

Like Cassandra, they have been ignored by the mainstream of academe, although not by students. Yet because they act in such isolation, it is difficult for them to undertake the breadth of research and discussion that would strengthen their own understanding and improve what they can offer students. Most are overburdened with excessive teaching assignments in more stereotypical classes and cannot afford the time for their own continuing education. Thus, a major function of this conference was to gather these faculty together from across North America and bring speakers with contemporary global insights to interact with them, initiating a dialogue of far-reaching curricular change. This volume reflects that initial effort, and it is the editors' hope that the mind-shaking ideas that suffused the conference and empowered its participants have been captured here for all who share similar concerns.

The opening keynote address by Ernest Boyer provided a central motif for the entire conference: "Making the Connections." What is it, he asked, that all people on Earth share in common, albeit in diverse ways, and how can we help our students to grasp in the most profound way the essential components of this commonality? What we teach now no longer matches the realities of life; a gulf has opened between the "real world" our students experience and what is taught on our campuses. As a result, we now must tear down defective structures, rethink those that remain serviceable, and so reconstruct the curriculum, with priority being given to the values implicit in what we teach.

While "connections" became the overall motif of the conference, there were a number of recurring insights, some concerned with existing flaws and others with what needs to be done. Chief among the flaws was the inadequacy of current disciplines to deal with the inherent "messiness" or complexities of real world issues: hunger, conflict, pollution, and so on. This was ascribed in part to the intellectual fragmentation of over-specialization, the old story of the blind men describing an elephant. Beyond this simple fragmentation, which might be cured by forcefully re-integrating the disciplines (bringing the blind men to a more complete understanding through combining their specialized knowledge), was the repeated assertion that many disciplines, particularly among the social sciences, are founded on faulty assumptions, and require major surgery. Perhaps the following statement, made by Richard Rubenstein, best encapsulates that sentiment: "I think that we ought to show our students around these disciplines like guides showing tourists a ruined city. The point is not to live in such a place, but to take inspiration from it."[2] Indeed, it would be fair to say that much of the contemporary Western worldview was seen as in need of self-criticism and revision, leading to a major paradigm shift.

A serious consequence of the educational failure of our disciplinary fragmentation that was repeatedly pointed out is that today's decision-makers are unable to grasp the underlying causes of our global crises, catching instead at the straws of technological or social "fixes." Even if its leaders were to acquire the necessary insights, the public does not comprehend these crises sufficiently to cooperate with the needed changes in thinking. This widespread ignorance, however, does not cover up an unconscious awareness that something is seriously wrong, which has led to widespread social malaise. As Dr. Viktor E. Frankl has observed, "[t]he feeling of meaninglessness, the existential vacuum, is increasing and spreading to the extent that, in truth, it may be called a mass neurosis."[3] The young, particularly, are retreating from social and political engagement, frustrated in their hopes to create a better future.

Among the insights garnered at the conference concerning what can be done, there was a general consensus that education is inevitably political. Thus, honest and concerned educators cannot escape their duty to become activists in the political arena, providing a model for their students to follow. This does not mean engaging in the narrowly framed arguments of most politicized issues, but rather teaching students to see the political underpinnings of much that passes for "truth" and "common sense" in Western thought. The pedagogical processes recommended for this undertaking included dialogue, self-criticism, and task-oriented education, always in a cooperative framework.

Of course, cross-cultural and global thinking were important themes throughout the conference, as individuals offered us a glimpse of the rich resources, both intellectual and spiritual, that the West has tended to neglect. A balance was sought whereby global networking could be combined with a fostering of and respect for cultural diversity, to retain local political and economic autonomy. Several speakers challenged us to devise a global ethics that would bring an end to the exploitation of both our fellow human beings and our environment.

Although the conference was constructed around the following five sub-themes, each paper touched on several of them. Hence the grouping of the contributions is unavoidably arbitrary—a dilemma posed by the way our minds order and compartmentalize things, even as we were striving for integration!

THEME I: ASSUMPTIONS ABOUT THE "PROGRESS" OF KNOWLEDGE

While thinking people now acknowledge the existence of major global problems of crisis proportions and seek comprehensive and globally just solutions, there are two quite distinct philosophical approaches to such solutions. One of these relies on the application of an expanded human intelligence to our problems; the other, to a revision of our beliefs and values. The first is the heritage of the Enlightenment era, with its unabashed faith in linear "progress" and the ongoing evolution of human intelligence, with its divine spark of reason, as the pinnacle of all life forms. The corollary is that the more intelligent we are, the greater will be the benefits for ourselves as well as the rest of the world. Inherent within this approach is the expectation that technology is a key source of the answers we need. By contrast, the other approach views most of our global mess as due to the misuse of our intelligence. Accordingly, what is needed is not simply *more* information, cleverness, and technology, but rather an altogether different species of knowledge involving reflection, self-criticism, and wisdom.

The conference champion of the first approach is George Bugliarello, who proposes the conscious development of a computerized global intelligence network linking literally millions of us into an instantaneously interacting system. This technological feat, Bugliarello argues, will create a new mental imagery of the global whole—a "hyperbrain" possessing "hyperintelligence."

Opposition to the view that technology is the means by which we can become "smarter" and thereby solve our problems comes in the rebuttal of Mary Midgley, spokesperson for the alternative philosophical approach. What we really need, says Midgley, is to reconsider our fundamental assumptions about the place our species occupies in evolutionary time and ecological space. In particular, she examines the way in which our own intelligence has become an object of worship, using the physicists' latest cosmology, the Strong Anthropic Principle, as an example of the sort of homocentrism that gets us into trouble. While cleverness and technology have their uses, she warns, we had better be certain we know what they are. Hyperintelligence untempered by everyday wisdom is unlikely to be an evolutionary breakthrough.

Cyberneticist William Reckmeyer provides some insights into the ways we formulate our understandings of the world and construct the cognitive paradigms by which we live and act. Nowadays, Reckmeyer argues, we rely too heavily on multiple but unconnected perceptions arising from the disciplines—which once served us well, but are now inadequate for dealing with the increasingly complex world in which we live. In their place, or as supplement for their inadequacies, we need integrated or "systems" paradigms that explain the multiple internal feedbacks governing complex phenomena. Students today need this kind of holistic perception of reality if they are to deal with our global crises. He offers his own recommendations on how to broaden our cognitive perceptions. The related question of the values—the wisdom—that guide us to seek certain kinds of knowledge and ignore others is addressed in Theme III.

THEME II: A CRITICAL LOOK AT THE DISCIPLINES

"Critical thinking" has become a national buzzword that covers almost anything educators want it to cover. During the conference, however, contributors focused *their* critical powers on analyzing the traditional disciplines, both in terms of the adequacy of their underlying assumptions and of their ability to address major global problems. There was agreement that the rigid institutionalization of specialized disciplines is a barrier to both creative thinking and curricular change. Their monolithic domination of the university scene is largely responsible for the deep inadequacies of the curriculum in relation to today's world.

Of particular concern to conference contributors is the inability of the social sciences adequately to describe—let alone solve—any of our major global problems. Two contributors—Richard Rubenstein and Hazel Henderson—tackle this issue head-on. Rubenstein shows that not only is political theory inadequate for understanding, not to mention predicting or explaining, human conflict, but moreover so is any *combination* of contemporary disciplines: sociology, psychology, history, law, political science, economics, and so on. Each is fundamentally flawed; they do not fit together, and so they cannot form an interdisciplinary answer to this crucial global problem. Indeed, the field has become *adisciplinary*, with the most useful contributions coming from scholars who are "least bound by the methods and assumptions of their disciplines of origin."[4]

Likewise, in the field of economics, independent economic analyst Hazel Henderson is unencumbered by traditional assumptions about humans as "rational economic beings" or about economies as static entities seeking some "equilibrium state." Accordingly, Henderson is able to lay bare the serious flaws in modern economic theory. Both Nature and society are emitting serious distress signals that demand the kind of paradigm shift in thinking that Reckmeyer recommends. In her analysis, Henderson goes a step beyond Rubenstein. Whereas conflict analysts are still struggling to develop an adequate theory, new-age economic thinking already possesses much of the necessary framework. What is needed now are mass conversions so the theory can flourish, develop, and replace its inadequate predecessor.

Robert Costanza then carries the argument for escaping from the "overspecialization trap" of current disciplines one additional step. Acknowledging the intellectual trap of the disciplines described by Reckmeyer, which prevents us from envisioning new ways of seeing the world, Costanza asks: What happens to those who indeed have new visions and want to pursue them? The trap he addresses is not mental, but institutional. Academics who "hear a different drummer" are in fact not free to pursue their inner voices, especially if they transgress the boundaries of the discipline in which they are "expert." He cites a number of current opportunities for such mavericks, while pointing out the limitations associated with each, and offers ways for broadening the rewarded options available to academics along both teaching and research dimensions.

Contributing a view from the perspective of the administrator, university president Terrence White offers some suggestions for restructuring the academic world to create a more integrated, cross-disciplinary curriculum that can better address our global problems. White confronts the practical

problems associated with fulfilling the university's twofold task of dis-
seminating existing knowledge while generating new knowledge, and
specifically the knowledge needed to meet the challenges of contemporary
life. In this sense White's paper brings closure to Theme II, as well as
serving as a harbinger of the fifth and final theme, Developing Integrated
Programs.

THEME III: THE VALUE CONTENT OF EDUCATION

A vague presumption has come to pervade the public's understanding
of education, namely that its content should somehow be apolitical and
value-free. If values are not explicitly addressed in the classroom then what
is taught are simple "facts"—unadulterated and value-neutral. Henderson
had earlier noted in her paper that conventional economic theory is based
more on the values of economic theorists and their wealthy sponsors than
on actual observation of real economies.[5] Not only economics, but *everything* that is taught bears the stamp of someone's values—whether those
of a legislator, a teacher, a textbook writer, or a group of academic theorists.
Value-neutrality is one of the most pervasive misconceptions of modern
education. The curriculum is *not* unbiased, and students are *not* left to
"form their own opinions"! Whatever is taught bears the imprint of the
values implicit in society, and if by chance those values are part of the
cause of a society's problems, then it becomes necessary to address them
openly and critically in the educational curriculum. This, of course, is the
real meaning of "academic freedom," something that the American public
has yet to accept.

Values, however, are not a separate category of the mind, but arise, part
and parcel, out of our total understanding of reality, our worldview. It is
this realization that three of our contributors bring to bear, each in a
different way, on the problems of the contemporary curriculum. For
Huston Smith, the central curricular issue of our age is the degree to which
scientific methodology has come to dominate not only all the disciplines,
but the whole of our lives. As a consequence we are left both alienated and
bereft of alternative ways of seeking reality. Smith takes issue with the
attempt of all scholars to mimic science as the only reliable path to "truth."
For him, restructuring the curriculum does not mean trying to integrate the
disciplines as they *now exist*, but rather, seeking an altogether new
worldview—what he calls a new "anthropology." His point is that we need
to relegitimize talk of values, meaning, and purpose in the curriculum in
order to create a more adaptive and accurate vision of the world.

The problem of what set of values, what sort of vision of humankind, we could put in place of—or at least use to modify—our present faulty vision is taken up by Charles Wei-hsun Fu in a brilliant analysis of the distinctions between two of the world's dominant worldviews: the Eastasian and the modern Western. Fu skillfully juxtaposes the Confucian and Judeo-Christian understandings, pointing out the social and political consequences of each, and especially their inherent weaknesses. More specifically, he contrasts their respective bases in personal morality and social responsibility on the one hand and in law and contractual relationships on the other. Fu concludes with a proposal for interweaving these two approaches which, if introduced into the Western curriculum, could serve simultaneously to correct our destructive tendencies toward alienation while softening our pretensions of moral superiority. His arguments seem to us to feed well into those of Johan Galtung, who discusses the path to global peace under the next theme.

The process by which change is to be accomplished likewise is addressed by Frances Moore Lappé, as she critiques our political value system. Too often, Lappé argues, the curriculum teaches only superficial explanations for society's problems, relying upon the unexamined assumptions of single disciplines, which are often graced with the label of "common sense." She calls for the introduction of dialogue into the curriculum to force us to delve deeper into the underlying causes of problems, thus revealing their true complexity. Such dialogue ultimately demands the critical self-evaluation of values and a sense of political engagement that she believes are essential for an active, informed, truly democratic citizenry.

THEME IV: ALTERNATIVE VISIONS NOT CURRENTLY TAUGHT

Having addressed the fundamental deficiencies inherent in our current teaching—the general lack of a philosophy to match our technology; the many questionable assumptions of our Western worldview, especially about human nature and about the universal applicability of the scientific method; and the failure of our overspecialized disciplines to tackle obvious global problems—we now turn to the remedies. In this section, contributors deal with what is missing from the curriculum; in the next, with the institutional changes needed to implement a new curriculum.

Robert Malone, deploring the consequences of reductionist thinking that pervades the Western *Zeitgeist*, especially as they pertain to our understanding of our global environmental crises, outlines the theoretical basis of the new curricular imperative. Our failure as educators, as Malone sees it, lies in continuing to teach the economists' faith in the "marketplace," while studiously ignoring the connections between this misplaced faith and our growing ecological disasters. "It is sheer *hubris* to suppose that we can exist outside of Nature's laws."[6] The solution lies in incorporating *moral action* into the very process of education itself; in other words, educators must become activists.

Albert Bartlett then points out that we are failing to make meaningful even the necessary theory that we *do* teach. Despite compulsory mathematics education for all Americans, the nation as a whole, including its political leaders and economic "experts," seems not to have understood the exponential function: what continuous growth really means. Bartlett clearly demonstrates its relentless logic and suggests that until people internalize what growth entails, nations will fail to deal with such exponentially growing global problems as resource depletion, population, and pollution.

Given the nature of "growth," Johan Galtung moves us to a better understanding of the nature of peace. His emphasis is on our failure to perceive peace as something beyond the narrow horizon of disarmament and treaties. In a truly sweeping essay he deftly unfolds for us the multiple military, economic, cultural, and political understandings that must be simultaneously brought into being if a new age of permanent peace is to begin. Perhaps no other contribution illuminates so lucidly our pressing need for an eclectic, truly integrated interdisciplinary curriculum.

Making the connection between the new visions that are needed and the means for achieving them is Russell Peterson. Himself an interdisciplinarian by life experience, he argues that our nation needs not only the highly trained specialists universities are now designed to produce, but also a cadre of rigorously trained generalists: women and men who, like Renaissance thinkers, can grasp the entire global picture. Until many more such people are available, decisions will remain piecemeal and unsatisfactory. The way to generate them, he argues, is by creating separate Colleges of Integrated Studies, replete with broadly trained faculty and awarding degrees at all levels.

THEME V: DEVELOPING THE NEW CURRICULUM

Peterson and others have argued that the disciplines need to be integrated, and in some cases seriously reformed, indicating that this will require considerable restructuring of our educational institutions. The question remains of how to proceed with this task. Although the multiple problems involved—funding, disciplinary territoriality, administrative tangles, and the need for professional recognition for generalists—could not all be addressed at the conference in detail, the contributions here clearly show that *change is possible*.

David McFarland and Benjamin Taggie give a detailed analysis of the factors involved in their successful inauguration of an undergraduate interdisciplinary program at Central Missouri State University. Prior to providing a step-by-step history of their own experiences, the authors look at the hurdles involved from the perspectives of both faculty and administration. Their insightful formula may well afford a useful model for other institutions wishing to follow suit.

Representing the widely praised Interdisciplinary General Education Program of California State Polytechnic University at Pomona, James Manley and Nancy Ware describe and assess its structure. They conclude that creating a truly integrated curriculum entails the intellectual development of faculty as much as that of students, such that the two groups become reciprocal members of a shared, mutually self-critical learning community. Ware explains IGE's innovative approach to assessing the outcomes for both faculty and students, while Manley provides an historical account of how the faculty component evolved from a loosely knit group of "concerned" teachers into a cooperative, albeit continuously probing team.

Finally, William Newell, one of the nation's first leaders in integrated education, offers a summary of what the conference has accomplished and where we should go from here. The concrete means of legitimizing interdisciplinary studies and their faculty are addressed as a way to set in motion the curriculum we have rethought.

It is our sincere hope that these presentations will serve to stimulate educators and administrators to extend and implement the insights they contain, as well as to encourage those who have been laboring at what had heretofore seemed a Sisyphean task. Let us work together, then, to undermine the kind of system that allowed Mark Twain's biting taunt, "I have never let my schooling interfere with my education," and instead be inspired by the vision of John Dewey: "Education is a social process. . . . Education is growth. . . . Education is not a preparation for life; education is life itself."[7]

NOTES

1. The Richter scale of Earth tremors is a 1–10 logarithmic scale, with tremors of magnitude 4.0 being ten times those of 3.0 and so on. Thus, 6.0 is a thousand times greater than 3.0

2. Richard Rubenstein's comment occurs in Chapter 6 of this volume.

3. Viktor E. Frankl, *The Unheard Cry for Meaning: Psychotherapy and Humanism* (New York: Touchstone Books, 1978), p. 25.

4. Rubenstein, Chapter 6.

5. See, for example, Nobel economist Wassily Leontief's plaintive comments regarding the absence of any real data to underpin most of his colleagues' theories in his letter to *Science*, 217 (1982), 104–7.

6. Robert Malone, Chapter 13 of this volume.

7. Donald O. Bolander, Dolores D. Varner, Gary B. Wright, and Stephanie H. Greene, *Instant Quotation Dictionary* (Little Falls, New Jersey: Career Publishing, Inc., 1981), p. 97.

SELECTED BIBLIOGRAPHY

Clark, Mary E. *Ariadne's Thread: The Search for New Modes of Thinking*. New York: St. Martin's Press, 1989.

Commission on the Global Environment. *Our Common Future*. New York: United Nations, 1987.

Wawrytko, Sandra A. "Beyond Liberation: Overcoming Gender Mythology from a Taoist Perspective," *Movements and Issues in World Religions: A Sourcebook and Analysis of Developments Since 1945*. Ed. Charles Wei-hsun Fu and Gerhard E. Spiegler. Westport, Conn.: Greenwood Press, 1989.

2 MAKING THE CONNECTIONS
THE SEARCH FOR OUR COMMON HUMANITY

Ernest L. Boyer

THE NEED FOR CONNECTIONS

I wish to begin with a story some of you have heard. In 1972, I was sitting in my office in Albany, New York. It was a dreary Monday morning and to avoid the pressures of the day I turned instinctively to the stack of third class mail I kept perched precariously on the corner of my desk to create the illusion of being very, very busy—it is an old administrative trick.

On top of the heap was the student newspaper from one of the nation's most distinguished higher learning institutions. The headline announced that the faculty had re-introduced a required course in Western Civilization, after having abolished all requirements just three years before. (Bear in mind, this was 1972.) The students, I discovered, were mightily offended by the faculty's brash act, and in a front page editorial declared that to require a course is an "illiberal act." And they concluded with this blockbuster question: "How dare they impose uniform standards on non-uniform people?"

At first I was amused, and then troubled, by that statement. I was troubled that some of America's most gifted students, after fourteen or more years of formal education, still had not learned the simple truth that while we are non-uniform, we still have many things in common. They had not discovered the simple truth that while we are autonomous human beings, with our own aptitudes and interests, we are, at the same time, deeply dependent on each other.

This brings me to the central theme of my remarks this morning. I happen to believe that the most essential goals we pursue in education are best expressed by the simple word, "connections." Students, through their formal education, should celebrate their individuality; they should affirm their uniqueness and learn to live independent, self-sufficient lives. But students, during the undergraduate years, should go beyond their own private interests and put their learning in historical, social, and ethical perspective. Simply stated, they should discover themselves and they should discover their connections, and for this to be accomplished, the curriculum must become more purposeful and coherent.

CURRICULAR REFORMS IN THE TWENTIETH CENTURY

Since the turn of the century, we have had in the United States two great general education revivals. The first occurred about the time of World War I. In 1914, President Alexander Meiklejohn of Amherst College introduced a survey course entitled "Social and Economic Institutions." In 1919, Columbia University launched its celebrated Contemporary Civilization program, perhaps the longest-running general education sequence in the country. Dartmouth and Reed Colleges soon followed suit with survey courses. But the most hotly debated experiment of this period was the University of Chicago's reform movement with a four-year, required course of study built around the great books.

The second general education revival of the twentieth century came on the heels of World War II. Germany, known as the center of scholarship and erudition, had spawned monstrous inhumanity at Buchenwald and Auschwitz that seemed to mock decades of lofty rhetoric about education's ennobling and civilizing power. Against this somber background, American educators began to ponder, once again, the place of general education in modern life. In 1942, Dennison University offered a course entitled "Problems of Peace and Post-war Reconstruction." Later, Wesleyan in Connecticut introduced a freshman general education seminar on values.

But it was the 1945 Harvard report, *General Education in a Free Society*, that symbolized higher learning's renewal. "The Redbook," which called for more curriculum coherence, became the Bible on campuses from coast to coast. I was then a freshman dean, trying to give curriculum guidance to the faculty and we studied it word for word.

These two great curriculum revivals were products of traumatic times. The academy was responding, not consciously perhaps, to the tragic disintegrations caused by two global wars, and reformers sought to move both the university and the nation away from fragmentation, toward community and coherence. The effort was to revive, through the curriculum, a sense of national awareness and reaffirm the values and traditions—the sense of bondedness—that give meaning to a culture.

This brings me to the theme of this volume, "Rethinking the Curriculum." On most campuses today there is a growing mismatch between the requirements of undergraduate curriculum and the realities of life. Almost all colleges now have a requirement for general education, but all too often this so-called distribution sequence is little more than a grab-bag of isolated courses. Undergraduates complete the required credits, but what they fail to see are connections that would give them a more coherent view of knowledge and more authentic, more integrated view of life.

Albert Einstein wrote on one occasion that all religions, all arts, all sciences, are branches of the same tree.[1] But for most students, it is unlikely that this discovery is ever made. Frank Press, as president of the National Academy of Sciences, captured this same spirit when he suggested several years ago that scientists are, in some respects, artists, too. To illustrate the point, he observed that the magnificent double helix, which broke the genetic code, was not only rational, it was beautiful as well.

When I read Frank's speech, I reflected on those occasions when I watched the early lift-offs at Cape Kennedy. As the countdown moved from 10 to 9 to 8 to 7, the television cameras would zoom in on the scientists and engineers and capture the anxiety on their faces. But when the countdown reached "zero," followed by a successful lift-off, you could see the worry drain from their faces, replaced by a great burst of satisfaction. As I read their lips, the scientists would never say, "Well, our formulas worked again." Without exception, they would say, "Beautiful!" They chose an aesthetic term to describe a technological achievement. Yet on most campuses, the science and art departments live in two separate worlds.

Barbara McClintock, the Nobel Prize-winning geneticist, said on one occasion that everything is one. She said there is no way you can draw a line between things. I wonder if Professor McClintock has looked at a college catalog in recent days. And when Victor Weiskopf, the world-renowned physicist, was asked what gave him hope in troubled times, he replied that it was Mozart and quantum mechanics.

Today's students live in a world that is economically, politically, and environmentally connected. The protective ozone layer is endangered. Our shorelines are polluted, and the tropical rain forests are being destroyed at the rate of 100,000 square kilometers every year. I worry that education in this country is becoming increasingly parochial at the very moment the human agenda is more global. Students are not becoming sufficiently well-educated about the world they will inherit.

Several years ago at the Carnegie Foundation, we surveyed high schools in the nation and found that only two states required a course in non-Western studies. Later, when we looked at undergraduate education, we found that nearly one-third of today's college students say they have nothing in common with people in underdeveloped countries. They simply do not see their connections to those whose lives are less privileged than their own.

This parochialism was painfully expressed by Lewis Thomas when he said at a meeting of the American Association for the Advancement of Science, "These are not the best of times for the human mind." Thomas went on to say that "I cannot begin to guess at all the causes of our cultural sadness, not even the most important ones. But I can think of one thing that is wrong and eats away at us. We do not know enough about ourselves. We do not know about how we work, about where we fit in, and most of all," he said, "we do not know enough about the enormous, imponderable system of life in which we are all embedded as working parts." Thomas concluded by saying that if this century does not slip forever through our fingers, it will be because learning will have directed us away from our "splintered dumbness" and helped us focus on our common goals.[2]

I am convinced that, once again, we need a general education revival in this country. But this time the imperative is not just national; it is global. What we urgently need today is a curriculum that helps students move beyond the "splintered dumbness," see themselves as a part of a large human community, and gain a perspective that places them in larger context. But how is this more integrated world view to be accomplished?

THE COMMON HUMAN EXPERIENCE

Several years ago, Art Levine and I, in a little book entitled *Quest for Common Learning*, suggested that we organize the core curriculum, not on the basis of the disciplines and departments, but on the basis of what we called *the human commonalities*—those universal human experiences that are found among all people and all cultures on the planet.[3] What we proposed was a sequence of study that would help undergraduates discover their interdependencies and better understand the integrative nature of their existence, using the disciplines to reveal larger, more integrative ends. But what are these experiences that "non-uniform people" have in common?

First, at the most basic level, is survival—the universal human experiences of birth and growth and death. The sad truth is that most of us in Western societies go through life without reflecting seriously on the mystery of our own existence, not understanding conception, not considering the sacredness of our own bodies, not learning about how to sustain wellness, or pondering the imperative of death.

Recently I brought my mother, who is 89, to live with us in her final years. She is in need of the most basic care, and as we attend her, I am reminded of the cycles of our existence. I am also reminded how, in our modern age, we have turned life's most basic functions over to institutions. We are no longer together at the time of birth. We are no longer required to meet the basic needs of others. Dying and death become remote and children go through school rarely reflecting on their own existence.

I am suggesting that the new core curriculum might begin with a look at life itself, bringing the disciplines of biology, physiology, and geriatrics together, to help students understand the miracle of life. And perhaps, if we all knew more about ourselves we would respond more reverentially to the world around us.

This leads me to commonality number two. Beyond birth and growth and death, all people on the planet communicate with each other. We reach out to make connections, using a symbol system we call language to express our feelings and ideas. But again, do we understand the majesty of the spoken and written words which connect us, but which, like breath itself, we all too often take for granted?

Consider the miracle of this very moment. I stand here vibrating my vocal folds. Molecules are bombarded in your direction. They hit your tympanic membrane; signals go scurrying up your eighth cranial nerve, and there's a response deep in your cerebrum that approximates, I trust, the images in mine. But do you realize the audacity of this act?

It is language—the exquisite use of symbols—that makes us truly human, and I would like to see a core curriculum in which students study the origins of language—not just parts of speech. I would also like to see students consider how symbol systems vary from one culture to another, how language can be shared, and perhaps all students should become familiar with a language other than their own, so they can step outside their own language skin to understand better the nature of communication. And surely a course of study on the centrality of language would include mathematics, which is a universal symbol system. Finally, students should learn that good communication means not just clarity of expression; it means honesty as well. If we cannot trust the integrity of the message, it is—as the Sophists would have it—"saying nothing well."

Third, all human beings respond to the aesthetic. This condition is found in all cultures on the planet, and students, in the new core curriculum, should study the universal language we call art. Dance is a universal language; architecture is a universal language; music is a universal language; painting and sculpture are languages that can be understood all around the world. Salvadore Dali's painting, "The Persistence of Memory," can be understood by everyone haunted by the passage of time. And when Picasso confronts the unspeakable agonies of war, the dismembered child, the scream of a bereft mother, the shattered home, and puts them on a huge canvas called "Guernica," he makes a universal statement about destruction that can be felt in the heart of every human being.

I am suggesting that for the most intimate, most profound, most moving experiences, we need subtle symbols, and students should learn how different cultures express themselves through the universal language of the arts.

Fourth, all human beings have a capacity to recall the past and anticipate the future, and so far as we know, we are the only species on the planet that can put itself in time and space. T.S. Eliot wrote that time present and time past are both present in time future, and time future is contained in time past. And yet how often we squander this awesome capacity to look in both directions. We live only in the present.

In preparing students for the twenty-first century, we need a curriculum that provides historical perspective, focusing on both Western and non-Western studies, on the role of women as well as men in developing human knowledge, and also on the role of minorities who have been so shockingly oppressed. The study of our shared sense of time surely should be part of the new common core.

Fifth, almost everyone holds membership in groups and institutions— from families to nations. Organizational structures are found in every culture, from the simple to the most complex, and the new curriculum should include a study of how different cultures organize to carry on their lives, drawing heavily on the work in sociology and anthropology, for example.

Our son, Craig, lives in a Mayan village with his Mayan wife and two children. So far as we know, Craig is the only non-Mayan to live in that village for 1,000 years, and when we visit him each year and sit around the fire and go bathing in the stream, I am struck that the social structures used to maintain community life in Santa Cruz, Belize, are both remarkably unique and strikingly familiar. In the new curriculum, students should be asked to pursue cross-cultural studies to better understand the universal web of institutions. I would like to see, for example, a student compare Santa Cruz, Belize, with Santa Cruz, California, and understand the commonalities and the differences among their human institutions.

Sixth, we share with all people on the planet a relationship with nature. All life forms are inextricably interlocked and no education is complete without students understanding the ordered, interdependent nature of the universe in which, as Lewis Thomas said, "we are all embedded as working parts."

When I was United States Commissioner of Education, Joan Cooney, the brilliant creator of "Sesame Street," came to see me one day. She said they wanted to start a new program at Children's Television Workshop on science and technology for junior high school students, so they could understand a little more about their world and what they must understand to live. It subsequently was funded and called "3-2-1 Contact." In doing background work for that project, they surveyed some junior high school pupils in New York City, and asked such questions as: "Where does water come from?" A disturbing percentage said "the faucet." And when asked, "Where does light come from?" they said "the switch." And when asked, "Where does garbage go?" they replied "down the chute."

Incidentally, this last question was asked before that garbage barge floated endlessly offshore. I frankly regretted that a place was found to dump that junk. I was hoping that every night at six o'clock during dinner, Americans would have to stare at that garbage-without-a-country, drifting aimlessly up and down the Eastern shore, reminding us of the consequences of our endless producing and consuming, and that in the future, one of our urgent problems will be "discarding." I am suggesting that in the new curriculum, students, through the study of science, must learn about their connectedness to Nature and about the urgent need to protect the ecosystem of which we are all inextricably a part.

Finally, we all live by values and beliefs. Students should learn that all people search for meaning in their lives. Undergraduates should examine various belief systems, reflect on the values they hold, and, in their general education studies, learn how religion consequentially has shaped human history. Students cannot know the history of art without discovering religious inspiration, from Hindu cave paintings and Buddhist art, to the majestic cathedrals of the Middle Ages that so inspired Henry Adams and Monet and Chagall. Students cannot know literature without knowing how religion has shaped great writers, from Homer and Euripides, to T. S. Eliot, John Updike, and I. B. Singer. Students cannot know music without grasping the power of religion, from the amazingly gifted Benedictine nun of the twelfth century, to Leonard Bernstein's celebrated mass.

To propose the study of religion provides an occasion to make a central point about the core curriculum typology I have just proposed: to suggest that we have experiences that are universal does not suggest that we all agree. Indeed, people have often gone to war to protect their own approach to the human commonalities. So when I talk about connections, I do not suggest uniformity of behavior or a common life-style. Rather, I suggest a study of the deepest drives that make us truly human.

These, then, are the commonalities that are universal:

we all experience life,
we all communicate with others,
we all respond to the aesthetic,
we all recall the past and anticipate the future,
we all organize ourselves into societies,
we all are embedded in Nature,
and we all seek to give meaning to our lives.

Could these essential experiences produce a framework for a new core curriculum, one in which the disciplines would be used to illuminate larger, more integrated insights? Is it possible that such a study could help students better understand who they are and where they fit, and prepare them to live, with civility, in an interdependent world?

THE CENTRALITY OF VALUES

I have one final observation. In shaping the new curriculum, knowledge alone is not sufficient. A value system is required, one in which students learn that knowledge should be directed toward humane ends.

George Steiner, the contemporary British philosopher, reminded us that a person who is intellectually advanced can, at the same time, be morally bankrupt. "We now know," Steiner said, "that such a man can listen to Bach and Schubert at sundown, he can read Goethe in the evening, and the next day go to his daily work at the concentration camp to gas his fellow man." Steiner then asks: "What grows up inside literate civilization that seems to prepare it for barbarism?"[4] Well what grows up, of course, is information without knowledge, knowledge without wisdom, and competence without conscience.

When all is said and done, students must make a connection between what they learn and how they live—between the courses that they study and the realities of life. I do not have a magic formula by which such linkages can be made, but I do believe time must be taken in the classroom to explore the moral issues—the ethical questions—that the human community now confronts and how knowledge can be most appropriately applied to pressing human questions.

These questions include: Where will we get our food and how can it be equitably distributed? What about our energy supply? How can it be sustained? How can we reduce the poisons in the atmosphere? Can we have a proper balance between population and life support systems? And how can we care compassionately for the very old and very young? The goal of such an inquiry is not to impose a single set of values on all students, but to raise authentic questions and to make honorable the quest.

Nearly fifty years ago, Mark Van Doren wrote, "The connectedness of things is what the educator contemplates to the limit of his capacity." Van Doren said, "No human capacity is great enough to present a vision of the world as simple, but if the educator does not aim at that vision, no one else will, and the consequences are dire when no one does." Van Doren concludes by saying that "the student who can begin early in life to see things as connected has begun the life of learning."[5] And this, it seems to me, is the imperative of curriculum reform.

NOTES

1. Albert Einstein, *Out of My Later Years* (New York: Philosophical Library, 1950), p. 9.

2. Lewis Thomas, *The Medusa and the Snail: More Notes of a Biology Watcher* (New York: Viking Press, 1979), p. 174.

3. The ideas in this article are articulated in detail in Ernest Boyer and Arthur Levine. *A Quest for Common Learning* (Princeton: Princeton University Press, 1981).

4. George Steiner. *Language and Silence* (New York: Atheneum, 1967), p. ix.

5. Mark Van Doren. *Liberal Education* (New York: Henry Holt, 1943), p. 115.

SELECTED BIBLIOGRAPHY

Boyer, Ernest, and Arthur Levine. *A Quest for Common Learning*. Princeton: Princeton University Press, 1981.

Van Doren, Mark. *Liberal Education*. New York: Henry Holt, 1943.

I Assumptions About the "Progress" of Knowledge

3 HYPERINTELLIGENCE
HUMANKIND'S NEXT EVOLUTIONARY STEP

George Bugliarello

This chapter is about a new evolutionary step in human society made possible by information technology and telecommunication. My purpose is not to focus on the pertinent technology, as it has been discussed elsewhere,[1] but to reflect on the meaning of this step—in particular to education.

THE EMERGING GLOBAL NETWORK

Let me start by describing the emerging global communication network, comprising multiple interconnected "nodes"—where a node is defined as a human being with a computer. The nodes can be of many kinds, such as an ordinary citizen with a personal computer, a professional with an advanced computer-based expert system, a librarian and a major data bank, or a scientist with a computer-accessible laboratory. We have today, thanks above all to the personal computer, potentially about 10 million such nodes. The number is expanding very rapidly, so that we can expect in the not-too-distant future to see hundreds of millions of these nodes.

As a point of reference, in American elementary and secondary schools alone there are now 2.25 million computers—an order of magnitude increase from the 250,000 in 1983.[2] As the global network constituted by these nodes comes into being, it offers us some unprecedented opportunities. In the first place, it enables us to have what can be called "affinity" networks—that is, networks linking nodes engaged at any given time in the same kind of activity. Through these networks, for instance, we can sense globally, that is, we can instantaneously gather all sorts of information from around the globe. We can also market, design, consult, model, do assessments of technologies, and make forecasts. We can socialize. If we are interested in Ottoman history, we can communicate with people across the globe who have the same interest. We can cooperate scientifically. Above all, we can teach and learn. We can do all these things globally. Of course, we are already doing some of this through existing networks, but the organized global network that I believe is emerging represents a technological jump, both in quality and in extension.

A global affinity network of the sort I envision will extend around the world, with millions of sensing nodes. Unlike today's networks, however, which not only are much smaller, but generally link together only simple recording devices (seismographs, posting of monetary exchange rates, and the like), each sensor in the *new* network will be a "node"—a computer linked to a person. Thanks to its multiple human-computer synergisms, such a network will enable us to do things that now are impossible. It will enable us to sense instantaneously from all over the globe all sorts of physical and social parameters, with immediate feedback from millions of nodes. It will enable us to sense weather and probably improve on the current meteorological sensing networks simply because it will have many more, and more powerful, sensing stations. It will enable us to sense geophysical data, earthquakes, traffic, environment, and so on.

Even greater opportunities are offered by such a global network in sensing social parameters. We can sense employment, and we can rapidly sense opinions. We can sense whatever communal activities may be of interest to us. We can sense the popular understanding of an issue. As issues arise—whether earthquakes or political events—we can immediately sense how they are perceived anywhere in the network, and globally. We can do so only because we have a machine—the computer—as part of the node. It would be impossible for a human being alone to integrate the responses of millions of other human beings. We could of course pick up a telephone and call someone else or we could depend on the media, but if we want to have a truly integrated response from all over the globe, we need those kinds of nodes.

Another application of these affinity networks comes in professional networking, for example in the design of a civil engineering structure, such as a building. The network can connect a number of team members, wherever they may be located. There may be an expert on soils, one on structures, one on sites, one on mechanical devices that go in a building, one on elevators, one on air-conditioning, and so on. The network also can connect these experts with data bases (for example on soils, or on water supply), with laboratories (for example, a national materials laboratory), and can also connect them with experts in other fields who may not be part of the team, such as an economist, or a sociologist. To integrate this diverse team, the network will probably require a new kind of professional coordinator.

All this may seem little different from what is already possible, but there are several important facts to be noted about such a professional network. In the first place, it can operate in real time worldwide. The soil expert can be in Tokyo, the site expert in London, the mechanical expert in San Diego. Therefore the work can be carried out globally on a twenty-four hour basis. Second, the network allows for much greater specialization. Each of the experts can be a member, simultaneously, of a number of design teams. Today, without such extensive networks, logistic limitations make this much more difficult. Thirdly, there must be compatible data bases, located anywhere in the world and accessible to any member of the team anywhere in the world.

Thus there is a cascade of effects that stem from the concept of a professional affinity network. The new professional skill that is required by an affinity network such as this is how to bring the team together—the capability to synthesize the different skills and capabilities of each element of the team.

I have used the example of a design network simply because such networks are already beginning to happen. But the same concepts apply to publishing, to research, to legal work, and most certainly, to teaching. Replace the experts and technical specialists of the previous example with teachers—of physics, chemistry, mathematics, and so on. Teaching, like engineering, becomes possible on a worldwide basis in real time, with a greater degree of specialization than is the case today, and at the same time with an unprecedented degree of interaction among teachers, students, and disciplines. The new skill required is how to integrate all these different components of the teaching process—how to transcend boundaries of classrooms, institutions and nations, and how to reshape the organization of the teaching enterprise.

The technology to make this happen is almost there. The problem is the imbalance between our technical capabilities and the social organization and practices that would enable us to take advantage of those capabilities. To be sure, the technology needs to advance further, but where we have the longest way to go is in developing the necessary social organization and practices.

This is why teaching is very important—to begin to break barriers, and to enable us to make use of those connections that technology now allows us to make.

FROM GLOBAL NETWORK TO
HYPERINTELLIGENCE

So much for the structure and application of these global networks. I turn now to their deeper evolutionary significance. Here I shall introduce the prefix "hyper" to denote a synergism of biological, social, and machine faculties or components of comparable complexity. Thus, while simple telephones are not machines of complexity comparable to that of a biological mechanism, computers are beginning to approach some aspects of that complexity.

A global network of the sort I have described not only gives us the capability to sense, market, design, and so on, but also to create a hyperlanguage resulting from the interactions among the nodes, analogously to how, we believe, the protocols for early communication among humans, whatever the reason for that communication, gave birth to language. Human language is a bio-social phenomenon that stems from the social interactions among groups of individual organisms. The hyperlanguage that will evolve has one further degree of complexity and potential. It will be a bio-machine-social language, as it will also involve communications between humans and machines, and between humans via machines.

The spoken interaction among humans was a key element in the development of intelligence, as we know it.[3] (Intelligence is defined here as the ability to use knowledge to meet new situations and solve new problems, to learn, to foresee problems, to use symbols or relationships, to create new relationships, to think abstractly.[4]) We can similarly expect that the interaction among nodes—an interaction requiring a new hyperlanguage—will give birth to some kind of hyperintelligence, a term that I shall define more precisely later.

Let me summarize the evolutionary process that is leading to hyperintelligence. When we first emerged from the trees as hominids, our intelligence was primarily biological and only to a very limited extent social. Not that we—or for that matter many other primate species—were not social, that is living and operating in groups capable of bondedness, play, reciprocal grooming, and specialization of roles; of communicating information in some form; and of inventing solutions and passing them to others in the group. But prior to spoken language, the intelligence of our ancestors was still largely instinctual and limited. The increasing social interactions that developed after the advent of language—beginning with those within clans and tribes of a few hundred members and leading eventually to interactions within cities and states, and across frontiers—

created an ever-increasing social intelligence that in turn reinforced our biological intelligence, giving birth to art, religion, science, philosophy, technology.

Our biological intelligence has remained basically unchanged for at least the past 50,000 years. However, in the last forty years, in combination with social intelligence, it has begun to give birth to computers and what can be called "machine intelligence." Machine intelligence is beginning, in turn, to reinforce our social intelligence, creating the bio-social-machine intelligence that I have called hyperintelligence.

We are now at the point in which the global networks I have described, the progressions from the brain with its billions of neurons, to the node, as I have defined it, begin to constitute a global brain. This is constructed of nodes—each a human brain with some 10^{11}–10^{12} neurons plus a computer with some 10^6–10^7 memory elements, linked via the socio-machine interconnections to 10^7–10^8 other nodes, all made technically possible in real time by fiber optics. In this global brain each element of a node—human brain, computer, and interconnections—begins to have comparable capacity, if not yet comparable complexity. We can thus begin to talk of a hyperbrain, even if it still has many fewer interconnections among its nodes and is still rather limited in its capacity to extend the human brain from which it has emerged through social intelligence, and we can begin to talk of hyperintelligence as the synthesis of biological and social intelligence made possible by their interaction with machines.

We must not fall into the error, however, of equating number of elements with intelligence or hyperintelligence. In the case of the brain and of society, we know that structure is at least as significant as capacity, that is, number of individual elements. Similarly, in the hyperbrain, computer capacity and number of network interconnections are a necessary but not sufficient ingredient of hyperintelligence. It is not only the vastness of the interconnections, but also their design, speed, and simultaneity, and the power and architecture of each node that, taken together, offer the possibility of a quantum step in bio-social intelligence that warrants the use of the term hyperintelligence.

The hyperbrain and hyperintelligence may be viewed as a new step in the evolutionary development of our species. Some of the earlier steps were bio-evolutionary: the probable symbiosis of various types of bacteria and other prokaryotes that gave birth to the first eukaryotes, organisms from which multicellular forms such as ourselves are descended; the evolution of circulatory systems that made specialized internal organs possible in large organisms; and the emergence of a brain as an organ of coordination and thought.

Other steps have been socio-evolutionary, such as, in relatively recent times, agriculture and industrialization (both requiring specialization), organized government (a form of social control analogous to a brain), and information technology (an expanded memory, logic and communication capacity). The hyperbrain and hyperintelligence combine more intimately and equally than did previous evolutionary steps—the biological, the social, and the machine—the corporeal and the extra-corporeal.

The phenomena that make the emergence of hyperintelligence possible are very complex. It is difficult today to describe what hyperintelligence will be like because it will unfold from its heuristic interaction with the hyperbrain, just as our intelligence and our brain may have evolutionarily reinforced each other.[5] Of a number of statements that can be made to describe this interaction, let me underscore only the fact that the brain of a network—the hyperbrain—resides in the network, not in a single node, just as our brain does not reside in a single neuron, but is an integration of the action of billions of neurons. Thus the hyperbrain is an entity of great complexity that is very difficult for us to grasp because we are both part of it and using it. A quote by one of the Chinese "Ancient Worthies" may help describe this best: "There ceases to be a distinction between the experiencer and the experienced."[6]

We must be careful, however, not to stretch analogies with the biological brain too far because of great and obvious differences in structure and genesis. The biological brain is an organic entity that cannot be subdivided without serious functional impairment or death. This is not the case with the hyperbrain. The most probable way in which the global brain will develop is through the joining of regional or affinity networks into a whole, just as the global telephone network developed from the joining of many separate local networks. Thus, while the hyperbrain achieves its greatest potential—and indeed becomes truly a hyperbrain—through the fusing of many small networks into a large one, it can also function in segments, albeit with corresponding reduction in the totality of its capacities. Because of this ability, elements of the hyperbrain can interact with other elements in play, competition, and business.

Thus, an element of the hyperbrain—a node—can operate autonomously from the rest of the global network or at any desired level of association with the other nodes. When the hyperbrain engages all its elements, or a substantial part of them, in an act of collective sensing or collective intelligence, it does so thanks to an ability to coordinate the entire network. To put it in another way, the global brain can enhance both the performance of its individual nodes and the intelligence of the world community. It is in this relationship between the nodes and the whole, between the particular and the general, that the peculiar value of the hyperbrain lies as augmenter of our biological brain on a global scale.

THE STRATEGY FOR HYPERINTELLIGENCE

How does hyperintelligence come into being? In essence, the strategy is simple. The first necessary step is to build regional and global networks for education, for research, for marketing, for hobbies, and so forth. Some of these networks already exist, albeit in embryonic form. They need to be strengthened, extended, and interconnected to make them more efficient and global.

In order to build these networks, we must deal with a number of issues, one being protocols. How are we going to communicate across these networks of large numbers of nodes, often cutting across nationalities, human languages, disciplines? Another need is for controls. Clearly a network must have discipline. We have discussed earlier the need for a coordinator, even in a small affinity network for engineering design. The coordination of an extended network is bound to be far more complex. Maintenance is yet another need, so that the knowledge possessed by the overall network of the rules by which it functions is maintained and constantly up-dated as human languages, computers, and networks change.

The second step toward hyperintelligence is to build intelligence capacities into the global network. These capacities will develop to a limited extent simply through use of the network. But a coherent plan with widely shared goals is needed to develop such capacities as memory, making associations, recognizing patterns, inferring, abstracting and generalizing, understanding cause and effect, defining, and making logical decisions. These are the functional elements of intelligence that must be built into the network on a global basis if we want to fully utilize its potential.

Ultimately, this is also what our education must produce—people who can remember, associate, recognize, infer, generalize and make abstractions, understand cause and effect, define (because without definitions we cannot communicate), and make logical decisions.

Development of these abilities is the most difficult task of education. It is an equally difficult task in the case of the global network. For instance, the question of memory is a complex one, given the heterogeneous nature of the nodes of the network, which range from a person with his or her personal computer at home, to a librarian coordinating a powerful data bank, to a professional with an advanced computer. The memories associated with each of these nodes differ in format, content, and in the machines that store and retrieve them, making their integration in the overall network a very difficult task.

Or consider the development of a capacity for association, that is, for connecting information—a capacity that some believe is the most important means of incorporating information about the environment.[7] As we begin to communicate preferentially with certain groups in the network with whom we have an affinity of interest, be they teachers of medieval history, engineers, or what have you, we will develop preferential connections, some form of communication shorthand, and a language or dialect that will accelerate our communication. As we do so we must be careful not to become so particularized as to lose our connections with the rest of the network. Therefore we must make the functioning of the hyperbrain one of a constant dynamic and constructive tension between particularization and universality. Achievement of that tension is also a major task for education.

Another way to express this is to argue that in the development of the hyperbrain a balance must be maintained between local culture and global culture. Thanks to that balance, groups will be able to develop or reinforce local cultures, and at the same time will be able to communicate with the main global culture in a mutually reinforcing relationship. The creation of such a relationship is what makes the hyperbrain possible. We must of course agree as to what language to use to communicate throughout the global network of the hyperbrain. The problem is not very different from what we do for instance in air traffic control. At a certain moment we must accept that in order to communicate we must have a common global language. This does not negate local languages and cultures—on the contrary. The fact that I speak English does not prevent me from communicating in my native Italian, nor does it reduce my pride in Italian culture. By speaking English, I am able to communicate that culture to other cultures, and vice versa. Thus the very variety of local languages—and of data bases—that operate in the hyperbrain are the best guarantee of preservation of cultural diversity.

Development in the network of functional intelligence capacities, like memory and association, is not sufficient, however, for the creation of hyperintelligence. We need to develop additional capacities similar to those of our human intelligence, such as an artistic capacity. It is entirely conceivable to think of "network art"—the ability of millions of people to create together, interactively, a piece of art of whatever form the technology of the network allows. This is of course a very abstract concept. It is difficult to fully fathom today the form that a piece of network art will have, and how it will manifest itself to us as the art of many—perhaps thousands or millions—collaborating across the global network.

The network also needs to generate an emotional capability, so that it not only exchanges information but also can express collective feelings about that information—its concerns, for instance, about events in China, in the Soviet Union, Canada, or America. Thus network emotions reflect the composite values of the nodes, and help generate new global values.

The use of the global network for engaging in play is another important stimulus to the development of intelligence capacities. Play—the use of the network to create make-believe situations—by releasing constraints rooted in reality, releases imagination and provides the network players with that sense of control, denied by reality outside of the play, that is so significant in the development of human intelligence. Network play can come to acquire a significance analogous to sport. We can envision, for instance, a series of network "olympics," in which a team of widely scattered people, say from San Diego, Cairo, and Seoul, would engage in games with another globally scattered team, say from New York, Sydney, and Tokyo. The possibilities are vast, and so are the implications.

Finally, in looking at the dimensions of hyperintelligence we should not overlook economic and political capabilities. Hyperintelligent economic capabilities may enable us to recast the question of cooperation versus competition, and political capabilities, such as a clearer view of global consequences of actions, may give us a new tool for resolving conflicts.

To reiterate, all these are elements of intelligence—of human intelligence, expanded through the hyperbrain. And all these, in terms of the global network and hyperintelligence, are *terra incognita*—and thus focal points for research and education.

PATHOLOGIES

Like our brain, there are two poles between which the hyperbrain can function.[8] One has been called the pole of bountiful genius, which enables us to reap the benefits of the synergies among all the nodes interconnected by the hyperbrain, whether for marketing, doing engineering, creating art, or for educating.

The other pole is schizophrenia. In terms of the hyperbrain, schizophrenia can be defined as the lack of integration of the different states of the hyperbrain. Each of these modes of usage represents a state of the network. Without integration, we have a condition in which one state of the network—say marketing or playing—overrules the other states and works against them. The functioning of the network then becomes a nightmare.

This reinforces the need to focus far more than we do today on pathologies—of the brain, of society, of the machines that expand the reach of the brain, and of hyperintelligence.

THE TIMETABLE FOR HYPERINTELLIGENCE

What is the likely timetable for the development of hyperintelligence? Our neocortex started evolving rapidly when the earliest hominids emerged some four million years ago. Social intelligence, set arbitrarily at the emergence of *Homo sapiens sapiens*, has been evolving for something between 100,000 and 150,000 years, and at an accelerated pace in the last 10,000 years, with the advent of agriculture and cities. Computers, the third component of the hyperbrain, started to be significant only forty years ago. It will probably take a hundred years or so from the beginning of the development of computers for some key features of hyperintelligence to emerge. The first signs of a truly global network, however, will begin to appear much sooner, by the year 2000, since significant elements of the network already are in existence. In addition to the growing number of personal computers, fiberoptic cables, which are key to the interconnection of nodes, are expanding very rapidly.

Achievement of comprehensive global intelligence capabilities will probably require at least another fifty years beyond the year 2000. Thus we can begin to see the emergence of hyperintelligence traits around the year 2050. Considering how slowly any educational reform occurs today, this is not a long time for education to adjust itself to this development and guide it.

THE SIGNIFICANCE TO EDUCATION

The technology of hyperintelligence is progressing rapidly and relentlessly. Society, if it wishes to remain "in charge," must consciously educate itself to do so. It is essential that people be educated to think globally—especially to think ethically in a global way. The key task for education is to develop extended socio-technological systems that are capable of synergism. This is a task of immense dimensions—obviously an extremely ambitious one. But let us not forget that it may well be the survival of our species that is at stake, as the growth of a global network without a sense of purpose and responsibility can lead to catastrophic pathologies of our society.

Hyperintelligence has truly the capacity to lead us to a common world culture. It is almost inevitable that this will occur, given the development of a global network, for two reasons. In the first place, to interconnect globally—to be able to communicate with someone in Moscow or in Timbuktu—we need a common protocol and a common language which are the basic elements of a culture. Second, hyperintelligence, thanks to the millions of intelligent human-machine nodes on which it is based, and thanks to its enhanced intelligence capacities, gives us a new power to deal with global issues, from the environment to economics, from defense to education.

More specifically, what does hyperintelligence mean to education? Let us start with the curriculum. The curriculum needs to become broader, to embrace all the key aspects of hyperintelligence indicated earlier. It must prepare the student to integrate, far better than is the case today, different elements of knowledge and different human activities. The students must also learn to interact on a global scale. However, as a global synergism develops, it is very important that we do not lose the richness of local cultures, and that we continue to look at the world from the solid base of our own culture. Finally, the students will benefit immensely from a curriculum that enables them to become directly involved in the development of the global network and of hyperintelligence, rather than just being exposed to the consequences of these developments.

The global network of the hyperbrain can lead to great improvements in how teaching is organized. Many teachers will be able to specialize more and go to a much greater depth in their areas of expertise, thanks to interconnections with other teachers of their subjects, and also thanks to curricula that make available to students courses from all over the network. Other teachers, on the other hand, will become generalists, carrying out the functions of network coordinators and helping the students integrate what they learn from specialist teachers and from other students from all over the network. Every teacher, whether specialist or generalist, will need to be intellectually open to a wide variety of subjects, to facilitate their interconnections among them in the classroom—those wide interconnections that are the great benefit offered by the hyperbrain. Teaching, furthermore, will need to place a strong priority on global ethics. Global interactions require global ethics; without ethics, hyperintelligence runs the risk of becoming a schizophrenic nightmare.

In turn, the students, to prepare themselves for the era of hyperintelligence, will learn to work on projects across the network—across geographical boundaries, and across disciplines. For instance, in writing a paper on contemporary foreign policy, a student here should be able to interact with Russian or German students and scholars, or a history student should be able to communicate with an engineering student (for instance asking the reason for the effectiveness and durability of Roman roads, bridges, and aqueducts, which were such important instruments of the empire). This will intrinsically ensure that the students will not have parochial views. Students also will learn to take advantage of interconnections with data banks, laboratories, and so forth, in order, for instance, to conduct an experiment at a laboratory 8000 miles away.

Finally, students will learn to move from one state of the network to another, say from learning, to socializing, to recreation, to doing art. In brief, they will need to learn to work and operate in several dimensions across the globe, because this is what they will be doing more and more for the rest of their lives.

How will educational bureaucracies respond to the challenges of a new way of teaching and learning? I believe that, educationally, this is the most difficult question. To redress the present imbalance between technological and social capabilities is an imperative of education, as it is for society as a whole. This demands the acceptance and encouragement of a curriculum and educational system that, thanks to the developing hyperbrain, will more and more transcend the walls of institutions. But are educational bureaucracies willing and able to design and administer a curriculum made up of components from all over the world?

An indispensable correlate of this challenge is the acceptance of international teaching, and thus of international teaching credentials. If a teacher from France or Israel or Japan is to be empowered to offer a course for credit through the global network (assuming that we still maintain the credit system as we know it now) that teacher must be accepted, and "credentialized." The problem has a parallel—albeit much less daunting—in what Europe will face after 1992, to enable professionals from its different countries to practice across their national boundaries.

CONCLUSION

These are not pipe dreams. The emerging global networks and the promise of hyperintelligence give us an unprecedented opportunity to teach, learn, and do research across the globe; to go deeper into our subjects; and to synergize more strongly with other disciplines. Whether we will succeed in taking this major step forward in the capabilities of our species will depend in very large measure on our ability and willingness to restructure education—our curriculum and our institutions.

NOTES

1. George Bugliarello, "Toward Hyperintelligence," *Knowledge: Creation, Diffusion, Utilization*, 10, no. 1 (September 1988): 67–89.
2. J. Berger, "Computers Proliferating in Classroom." *New York Times*, Education Section, August 9, 1989, p. 8.
3. Eric H. Lennenberg, "On Explaining Language," *Science*, 164 (May 9, 1969), 635–43.
4. See, for example, *Webster's Third New International Dictionary* (Springfield: Merriam, 1968).
5. See Michael A. Arbib, *Brains, Machines, and Mathematics* (New York: Springer-Verlag, 1987), p. 70.
6. Fung Yu-lan, *A Short History of Chinese Philosophy* (New York: The Free Press, 1948), p. 262.
7. See, for example, V. Breitenberg, *Vehicles—Experiments in Synthetic Psychology* (Cambridge, Mass.: MIT Press, 1984).
8. B. G. Braun, "Psychophysiological Phenomena in Multiple Personality and Hypnosis," *American Journal of Clinical Hypnosis*, 26, no. 2 (1983): 124–36.

SELECTED BIBLIOGRAPHY

Johnston, William J., ed. *Education on Trial—Strategies for the Future*. San Francisco: ICS Press, 1985.
McLuhan, Marshall. *Understanding Media: The Extensions of Man*. New York: McGraw Hill, 1964.
Wenk, Edward, Jr. *Margins for Survival—Overcoming Political Limits in Steering Technology*. Oxford: Pergamon, 1979.

4 WHY SMARTNESS IS NOT ENOUGH

Mary Midgley

THE DREAM OF REASON

I am here to deflate a dream, and that is rather an ungracious, negative sort of function. People who go about deflating dreams need both to show good reason why they do it—why those dreams really are delusive—and to explain what better, more genuine aims they think should be pursued instead. I will try to do both these things, but the destructive part has to come first.

The dream that comes in question here is the hope, which George Bugliarello so forcefully expresses, that machine-assisted intelligence is the reliable, destined chariot of human progress, and, in particular, that it is our prime means of escape from our present troubles. This dream urgently needs our attention because it is so influential today. There is at present a very strong tendency to treat computer programing as a cure-all for every intellectual difficulty that arises, and immense resources, both in money and in people, are being poured into providing more of it. This has been brought home to me lately because I have three sons. All three of them have been trying for many years to find work in some enterprise that seemed to them vital, such as ending the arms race or helping the Third World or saving the environment. But nobody would pay them to do these things. In the end, all three have settled, as so many others have had to, for employment in the only field that is still always expanding—work involving computers. They have Silicon-Valley-type jobs, and for these they are quite well paid. They still try to work on the projects they really think important in such free time as they can find, but there is not much of it. They still hope eventually to bring their skills to bear on these central projects, but they see no easy way to do so.

This situation is, I think, a typical one in which a great and increasing number of thoughtful people all over the West find themselves today. If Professor Bugliarello is right, then there is nothing wrong with such a situation. If concern with computers really is humankind's most important current interest, one so promising that it is entitled to outweigh all other urgent needs, then it is quite in order to direct all able workers into it . But (if I may say so) he had better be right. Is he?

In resisting this idea, I do not of course question that computers can be of enormous use, use that will certainly have to be continued and extended. The mess into which the human race has now got itself is a highly sophisticated technological mess, which it will need all the resources of well-applied technology to clear up. Whatever environmental problem one studies today, one finds computer calculations deeply involved both in the diagnosis and in the search for a cure. I have no wish at all to deny that these machines are wonderful tools, irreplaceable servants. What they cannot do is to constitute a new master—to save us the trouble of overhauling our own concepts. Though they can in certain ways enable us to correct our logic, they are in no position to tell us where our premises are wrong, much less what it is that is wrong with them. The assumptions they use are our assumptions, and are an artificially simplified selection from the beliefs we already use. In the very common situation where we have a calamitous gap in our thinking, computers merely mirror our inadequacies and cannot possibly help us.

The limitation I am trying to point out in computers here is in part not just a limitation of machines, but a limitation of intelligence itself. Intelligence is a tool, and like other tools it can be useless, even worse than useless, when its user does not direct it rightly. Sharp saws are not useful to people who thoughtlessly cut off the branches on which they are sitting, nor are fast cars to those who drive them as hard as possible in the wrong direction. In such cases the greater efficiency of a tool simply makes things worse. This point is obvious in the case of an external tool, but it may seem less obvious in the case of intelligence.

INTELLIGENCE, CLEVERNESS, AND WISDOM

What exactly do we mean by intelligence? Is it also simply a tool, something that has only instrumental value? If we mean simply calculating power—sharpness of mind, quickness and correctness of reasoning, what is generally called smartness—then it surely is so. We all know people who are highly intelligent in this sense, but whose lives are wasted, both in other people's opinion and in their own, because their aims are uncertain, confused, or inadequate. Sometimes these people are self-destructive. Sometimes they take to crime and destroy others as well. (There are surely some first-rate intellects, equipped with the very latest computers, employed in the Mafia.) Sometimes they devote themselves entirely to trivial obsessions; sometimes they simply frustrate their own undertakings and remain inert.

We also know other people who are much less sharp and quick, but who steadily pursue well-chosen aims and who therefore manage to be extremely valuable and effective. What these non-smart but effective people excel in is a different range of faculties, extremely important but bizarrely neglected in much recent thinking. They possess strong imaginative sensibility—the power to envisage possible goods that the world does not yet have and to see what is wrong with the world as it is. They are good at priorities, at comparing various goods, at asking what matters most. They have a sense of proportion, and a nose for the right directions of travel. All this is not just an emotional matter. It calls for quite complex powers of thought, by which various insights are weighed against each other and shaped into intelligible policies. We call people who have these capacities, and who use them effectively, *wise* or *sensible* rather than *clever* or *smart*.

What often confuses us is that the word intelligence is sometimes used in a wider sense, to include this range of faculties, and people seriously lacking in it are often called stupid. Plainly, this range of capacities for evaluating is not something to be expected of computers, and forms no part of what their designers try to build into them. Computers and their programs are not expected to be original moralists. It is interesting, for example, to ask what we would think if a computer came up with a strange new value-judgment—if originality suddenly appeared. Suppose it were to say, "The only aim that ought to occupy human beings is to avoid treading on the gaps between the paving-stones on the sidewalk" . . . ? However sophisticated that machine and its programs might be, no one is going to accept this directive as authoritative and set about reorganizing life to follow it. Instead, they would surely—and quite rightly—conclude that something had gone wrong, probably that there was a bug in the program.

What I am saying is, in the first place, that computers, in their present shape and in any other that we can now imagine, can only calculate and reason from premises; they cannot criticize premises or formulate new ones. In the second place, I am saying that people who are merely clever, but who do not manage to consider or criticize their aims, are no better off than computers when confronted with dilemmas about changes of direction.

How much this matters can be seen from a simple, very schematic example. Consider two matchstick people, COMP, who is purely competitive in his attitudes, seeing all interactions as battles to be won, and CO-OP, who is quite co-operative. These two people will not only act differently, they will also see the world differently and have widely varying beliefs about it. They will put opposite interpretations on other people's motives, and will therefore constantly make differing predictions about what is to be expected from them. In an important sense, they will live in different worlds. Their difference is *not*—as is often suggested—just a matter of taking up different emotional attitudes toward an "objective" real world that they share in common. Even when confronted by the same evidence, they will select quite different elements from it for attention, will connect them into different patterns, will suppose different things to be possible and impossible, likely and unlikely. They will therefore find different reports credible and will employ different standards of evidence. Their "facts" will, in the end, be different facts. In a quite solid and practical sense, people with different models of the world in their heads actually inhabit different worlds.

It is important to notice that this is not just a matter of one being cleverer—smarter—than the other. No increase or decrease of intelligence (in the narrow sense) will alone bring either of these people to the point of view of the other. What we have here is a difference in philosophy, a qualitative difference between points of view, between two basic conceptual schemes, between distinct emotional languages, between alternative sets of terms in which the world can be interpreted. The idea that a "purely descriptive" scientific or neutral language could iron out these differences is a delusive one. When people flatter one of these languages by calling it neutral or scientific, they are in fact only proclaiming how unthinkingly they support it. (Thus, the egoistic, competitive ethic has indeed sometimes been flattered by being called "scientific," but this is only a piece of moral propaganda.)

Worldviews, then—the mental worlds we live in—are highly diverse, are full of personal quirks, are never completely and "objectively" true, are not capable of constant spontaneous change to track changes in the outside world, and hence are in continual need of intelligent—i.e. thoughtful and insightful—re-examination.

THE IMPORTANCE OF BACKGROUND ASSUMPTIONS

It is clear, then, that the worldview we hold is a matter of selection. The problem of selecting the right topics for attention among the mass of information that continually presses in upon us is one that cannot have a neutral answer. What we select is what we deem important, and decisions about importance are value-judgments. Our habitual value-judgments determine what questions we ask, and the questions we ask determine the range of answers we can possibly get. The person (for instance) who is single-mindedly determined to see every human transaction as a competition to be won or lost will succeed in seeing it that way, asking only, "Who is fighting me here and how can I win?" Some answer can always be found, and no argument will change this habit. Now of course most of us are not simplified matchstick people of this kind, and I am not suggesting that we are isolated from one another in the way in which COMP and CO-OP would be. (Such single-minded, isolated people are found only in old-fashioned economics and in literature—for instance in the tragedies of Racine—where writers put them for quite special reasons.) Our normal condition is one where we use a large number of different conceptual schemes fairly successfully for different purposes, keeping them in a rather rough and uncertain relation with each other, and we share this loose collection more or less fully with those around us. We are, for instance, unthinkingly more or less co-operative with others for a great deal of the time—probably for most of it—and only shift into competitive gear for special purposes such as games, examinations, or business promotions. (A consistent COMP introduced into our society would actually cause a good deal of surprise.)

WHY RHINOCEROSES? WHAT HAPPENS WHEN ASSUMPTIONS CLASH

Sometimes, however, two or more conceptual schemes begin to grate intolerably on one another, forcing us to take notice and make painful and difficult adjustments. This is very disturbing, because it involves taking up the floorboards on which we normally walk about and do our mental business. A directly relevant example here is the enormously confident attitude that modern Western peoples have had, for the last three centuries, to non-human Nature. This confidence has played a great part in making our current technological miracles possible, but it has now begun to put us in real danger. H. G. Wells expressed this attitude perfectly eighty years ago in his Modern Utopia, where he called upon MAN to bring to trial every terrestrial organism, "from the rhinoceros to the tubercle bacillus," and to ask whether it gave him satisfaction. If it did not, MAN should (Wells said) either get rid of it or alter it genetically till it met his specifications. This task was laid upon us by our duty to suffering humanity, and to fail in it (he seriously added) would be merely inexcusable sentimentality.

It is very striking here how clearly the questions determine the range of possible answers. Wells's first question to the rhinoceros is simply, "Are you any good to me?" This is a question asked with full, unquestionable authority from the judicial bench, and it must be answered on standards set solely by the judge, rhinocerine values not coming into the case at all. If the answer is "No," the next question is, "Can I alter you in any way to suit my purposes?" If that proves impossible, then the issue is closed by the rifle. There will be no more rhinoceroses—thus clearing the way for suffering humanity.

Now this kind of demented human imperialism sounds so strange today that we need to remind ourselves that Wells was not a fool nor lacking in intelligence. Neither was he a big-game hunter. He was a humane, imaginative, and concerned social reformer. He was also a well-educated biologist who should have known something about ecology and the interdependence of all living species. The trouble is that he was not thinking about these things, because he was obsessed with definite, elaborate, confident plans for making human life happier. He approached this aim with concepts drawn from engineering (ignoring those from, for instance, forestry or medicine); he brought existing human institutions before his inquisitorial bench to be summarily approved, rejected, or returned to the workshop for alteration. It never occurred to him to change gears when dealing with the rest of the biosphere.

Wells was not alone. It is impossible to exaggerate the confidence with which, until quite lately, even far-sighted people presumed that the physical and biological world was invulnerable to human interference. That we ourselves might really damage it on any significant scale, or even that we could irrevocably change it at all, was unimaginable. Modern, post-renaissance MAN, when not engaged in thinking of the world in this exploitative way as his oyster, has held an older-style way of viewing it—namely, as a dangerous, powerful enemy to be warded off in a heroic, unceasing "warfare against Nature." This chronic and unchanging struggle provided a fixed background for the transience and shortness of human life. That this war might in some horrible sense be *won*—that Nature might be defeated—did not occur to people. Such was the force of the worldview assumptions—the basic mental program—widely held in the West until well into this century.

GAPS IN THE PROGRAM

When events first began to suggest faults in this program, they were frequently dismissed as trivial, or just plain wrong. A striking and immediately relevant example concerned the discovery of the hole in the ozone layer. As James Lovelock points out, this discovery was not made by Big Science, but "by a lone pair of British observers, using an old-fashioned and inexpensive instrument." But this was not because Big Science had not at that time begun to work in the stratosphere. Lovelock goes on:

It is a scandal that the vast sums spent on expensive computer models of the stratosphere, and on the expensive big science of satellite, balloon and aircraft measurement, failed to predict or find the ozone hole. Worse than this, so sure were the computer modellers that they knew all that mattered about the stratosphere, they programmed the instruments aboard the satellite, that observed stratospheric ozone from above, to reject data that was substantially different from their predictions. The instruments saw the hole, but those in charge of the experiment ignored it, saying in effect, "Don't bother us with facts; our model knows best."[1]

We do not have to draw the moral of this tale in the somewhat crude terms in which many computer people have already expressed it—garbage in, garbage out. We can put it rather more subtly and politely; limits in, limits out. What is not thought of as possible will in general not be able to find space in the program. Programs, like other artifacts, are designed to work within the conceptual schemes of the people who use them. They can certainly produce surprises, because no conceptual scheme is a fully articulated closed system, and these surprises may often be very useful. But it is in the very nature of programs to be deliberately limited—to deal with a particular range of problems, excluding for the time everything that is irrelevant. And judgments about relevance are human value-judgments, made by the programers, not in some superhuman infallible way by the machines.

WHY NETWORKS ARE (DANGEROUSLY) HARMONIOUS

Here we come to what it is that makes computer networks look so attractive, and explains why many people today would readily agree with Professor Bugliarello in hailing them as the means of our salvation. There is a very good reason why computer networks do work well. Where they exist, they naturally join together people who already agree in their aims, because they are consciously trying to solve a particular shared problem. That problem has to have its limits, which can be stated, and people who do not want to accept those limits will tend not to join the network. These are ideal conditions for co-operation for a start. Moreover, where those conditions are present, it does indeed seem true that computer networks, well-used, can often make it possible to carry that co-operation to levels that could not have been reached without them. In this particular situation, a new kind of human co-operation may indeed become possible.

This is indeed a possibility of immense use and importance for the vast and difficult efforts we must make if we are to save the environment, and I have no wish at all to appear as a machine-wrecker trying to belittle it. Its limitations, however, are obvious from Lovelock's example and from many like it that keep cropping up in this rapidly changing world. The more complete the agreement is that reigns at any given time among those who are defining a given problem, the more alarm bells should be ringing among them that they may be leaving out something of importance. Agreement is no guarantee at all of completeness or correctness. The hope that it could be such a guarantee seems to be one more form of the notion (enthusiastically promoted by prophets such as Wells and B. F. Skinner), that world affairs could be saved if only they were handed over to scientists, because scientists always work in harmony by methods clearly right and impersonally agreed on. It is not hard to see why this idea looked persuasive. Scientific work proceeds by the deliberate limitation of particular problems and the development of particular methods suitable for solving them. This means that, once a particular scientific problem has been solved, the surrounding froth and splutter of competing approaches and varying contributory ideas that actually made success possible is often forgotten, and an artificial picture of a single, inevitable "scientific method" is imposed as a retrospective celebration. But while the matter is actually in flux, scientists do not necessarily find it any easier than other people to agree, or even to know just how to phrase their disagreements.

Here again, I am anxious not to appear as a belittler, failing to appreciate scientists.[2] In fact, I think that the unreal representation of the scientific task as clear, single, and straightforward does scientists an injustice, ignoring the need for original imaginative work, and for difficult co-operation across gaps, without which they could not proceed. Many scientists also dislike this myth that elevates them into culture-heroes expected to tackle the biggest problems of the age, because they know they cannot fill that role, and rightly anticipate resentment from the public when these mistaken expectations are disappointed. Indeed, the antiscience backlash that already exists owes much of its strength to that resentment. It is surely vital that computer scientists do all they can to avoid becoming prime targets for this kind of resentful disillusionment. This will be hard for them, however, because, through no fault of their own, their work has been surrounded, from its first inception, by euphoria that has generated a great deal of peculiarly gross and dishonest hype. But this is surely a reason for scrupulously avoiding all further hype, not a reason for tolerating even the mildest forms of it.

WHAT IS EVOLUTION?

I want to end with some remarks about the link between the contemporary worship of intelligence and the idea of evolution. This cult of "intelligence" centers on the idea that human cleverness is the supreme value, not just in human life, but in the whole evolutionary process, perhaps even in the development of the entire physical universe. In this ideology, the word "evolution" stands for a single, directional process, a voyage with a fixed aim, in which the universe is held to be getting cleverer and cleverer, courtesy of us. A vast process of development is leading, on this view, through our present intellectual condition, past higher and higher stages of cerebral power, toward an indefinitely distant complete attainment of the intellectual ideals currently fashionable among scholars in the West.

Now the first thing to be said about this range of beliefs is that it is not scientific. It has no basis in biology, which is where the idea of evolution has its roots. It is a self-contained ideology, a quasireligious faith. That fact alone need not discredit it, for faiths of some kind may well be necessary, but it does mean that this way of thinking can draw no support from the prestige of the sciences. J. B. Lamarck's use of the word "evolution" for this single, straight-upward process with a fixed aim has no place in modern biology. For today's life sciences, the evolution of the biosphere is *not* a ladder, still less an escalator. It is a bush, a rich proliferation of varying life-forms branching out in different directions. Creatures have diversified to fit different evolutionary niches—and this is all that we humans have done, like any other life-form.

In that context, the hypertrophy of the human cerebral cortex can be examined as an evolutionary trait on the same terms as the expansion of the giraffe's forelegs and the albatross's wings: very useful for some purposes, a great nuisance for others. Albatrosses, if they are forced to move about on land, are hampered by their huge wings and have to use their highly inadequate feet. Giraffes that have to browse on low pasture must do so in spite of difficulties posed by their tremendously long legs.

HYPERTROPHIES AND THEIR COST

It is interesting that we are accustomed to talk confidently as if our own cerebral hypertrophy were a happy exception—as if we, unlike all other highly developed animals, did not pay a price but had remained essentially unspecialized, endowed with an all-purpose tool that could adapt itself flexibly to every situation. But we all know in daily life that this is not so. All around us, we can see people trying to solve by logical argument, or by the acquiring of information, problems that can only be dealt with by a change of heart—a change of attitude, a new policy and direction. But this is the last thing we try. Because our powers of making such changes are not much better developed than the albatross's feet, we do all we can to avoid dealing with them in the only way that can actually be effective. In contemporary culture, the passionate, quasireligious exaltation of our purely cognitive faculties is surely a defense mechanism against this awkward fact, a prime means by which we try to persuade ourselves that we do not need to switch over to this much less easy, less flattering kind of thinking. And one of the most striking forms that exaltation takes today is in a series of highly colored myths relating to evolution.[3]

The most recent and bizarre of these, which can stand as an *exemple extraordinaire* of this whole class of myths, is the Anthropic Principle, of current cosmology. In its "Strong" form, the Anthropic Principle claims that the whole universe exists for the sole purpose of producing the human intellect. The entire sequence of events from the Big Bang onward has been directed through a succession of increasingly more ordered, more complex states—each by definition embodying more and more "information"—to culminate finally in the most complex entity of all, the human cortex. The special glory of this organ is that it not only embodies huge quantities of information within its own structure, but is also capable of incorporating into itself information about the entire cosmos.

Accordingly, the theory goes on, at some ultimate point in time—the Omega Point—evolution will have progressed to the point where "life"— i.e. the human mind or its evolutionary successor—"will have spread into all spatial regions of all universes which could logically exist, and will have stored an infinite amount of information, including all bits of information which it is logically possible to know. And that is the end." In case we wonder what this means, a helpful footnote explains, "A modern-day theologian might wish to say that the totality of life at the Omega Point is omnipotent, omnipresent and omniscient."[4] At this moment, apparently, the cosmic purpose will have been fulfilled and the universe will have gained the traditional attributes of God. In this way of thinking, the goal of everything—including the human race—is, quite simply, the conscious acquiring of information.

One can only wonder what makes these theorists so confident of the centrality of intellect, still more of this particular intellectual operation, within the cosmos. The notion that the universe has a guiding purpose at all is something from which physicists, from the nineteenth century on, have been at pains vigorously to distance themselves, pointing out—as is surely plausible—that cosmic purpose did not lie within the scope of their subject. (Einstein, to be sure, sometimes talked about God, but he was a very sophisticated and well-read thinker, who could draw on many areas of speculation besides that of physics.) If some reason has indeed been found to reverse this cautious policy, we might expect it to be fully stated and defended, but it is not. Inventors of the Strong Anthropic Principle neither clarify for us their understandings of God and of purpose, nor do they ask present-day theologians to help them with these awkward topics. They simply begin to talk religion as if it were a regular and familiar part of their science.[5]

Even supposing that such a "purpose" does exist for the universe, what reason is there to think that it is this one? Humanity is an infinitesimal part of the universe, and even within human life, cleverness and well-informedness are minor ideals. What is so godlike about just possessing information? Is there nothing of greater value in human life, no other element to be cherished more than the acquiring of information? Has the biosphere, too, no other value except as an object to be absorbed and digested by the human intellect? The Strong Anthropic Principle seems to be not so much a soundly reasoned scientific proposal as yet one more uncritical extension of Wells's mindless human chauvinism. Unfortunately, such chauvinism continues to lie just under the floorboards of wide areas of contemporary Western thinking.

THE IMPORTANCE OF HARMONY

The Strong Anthropic Principle and similar myths that place the human cerebral cortex at the center of an otherwise valueless universe are in fact not much more than childish, undisciplined power fantasies. In comparison with them, the ideas of hyperintelligence that Professor Bugliarello outlines are humane, civilized, and relatively realistic. What he concentrates on is the promotion of harmony. He sees the next "evolutionary step" as involving, not some miraculous expansion of individual human powers, but a sudden, marked improvement in co-operation. I am altogether with him in thinking that this is indeed what is needed. Our present very alarming predicament does not flow from any limitation in our intellectual or physical powers, but from our gross misuse of them. And among the causes of that misuse, wasteful, foolish, idly competitive friction stands first and foremost.

What is needed, then, as both he and I believe, is an immense surge away from this idle, shortsighted bickering and toward a more co-operative attitude—not just for talking purposes but at a profound level, for action. And in this action computer networks can surely play a useful part. The question is, however, what is that part? As I have already suggested, computers can only be tools of this process, not its generators. Once people have changed their attitudes enough to want to co-operate, they can use networks to tremendous effect. But the process of actually changing attitudes—of seeing that the world is in certain ways very different from what we have come to suppose, and that we ourselves must really become different—is terribly painful and not something we can hand over to machines. It is comparable to awaking from a comfortable sleep to the ominous sound of running water or crackling flames which—as we eventually realize with horror—means that the pipes have burst or the house is on fire. It is a mind-shaking experience.

If one describes this sort of experience as an "evolutionary step," one may, I suppose, be using a legitimate metaphor and not perpetrating a pretentious piece of biological nonsense. All the same, I do not find this metaphor a very suitable one. Revolutionary changes like this cannot really be described in terms of an evolutionary development. The whole belief in a continuing, predestined, *automatic* process of human evolution is a dangerously soothing one. It seems designed to promote faith that we can go on exactly as we always have done, to convince us that we do not need to criticize our mental or practical habits. It suggests that we are simply passengers on an evolutionary escalator that will carry us where we need to go whatever mistakes we may make and however little trouble we take to understand what is happening. The presumption is that we have been "naturally selected" to "succeed," regardless of what we do. I would much rather avoid all mention of evolution here altogether.

CONCLUSION

What then must we do? What particular changes in our attitude am I calling for? First and foremost, I am saying that we have to become seriously convinced in our own minds of how bad things are. Tropical rain forests really are being destroyed at appalling speed, and the effect of that and similar losses on the world's climate really is likely to be catastrophic. The way we use automobiles really is producing greenhouse gases at a rate that will wreck our climate if we do not change it fast. We can scarcely take in the extent of it all, even when we try, and are therefore unwilling to contemplate it. Secondly, we have to shake up radically our ideas of what is politically possible and of what can be expected of us. When the pipes have burst or the house is on fire, you cannot just go and have a bath as if nothing had happened. The very local, competitive way we have thought about matters like the global economy or Third World debt will have to be radically shifted. If we do not, seriously and adequately, help tropical countries to save the rest of their rain forest, we shall only have ourselves to thank for the desertification that will follow. And so forth, over the whole spectrum of approaching dangers.

I have said nothing so far about educational implications—about the curriculum—because I have been trying to show what is wrong with certain influential beliefs that are actually held by many adults, and unless I have succeeded in showing that these beliefs are faulty, there would be no reason for changing these ideas in education. If, however, I have succeeded at all in doing this—if, as I proposed at the outset, I have to some extent exposed the worship of the intellect and of its servant machines as delusive—then the ideals that should replace it surely become clear, and it will follow that they should at once be presented to students. Instead of relying on the dream that computers will save us, we must honestly confront the frightening reality that calls on us to change our internal attitudes profoundly. Instead of devoting ourselves to an inward-looking interaction with those who are already near enough to us to join our computer networks, we need to attend to people far beyond our own community. We need above all to attend to people like the South American Indians and the Himalayan peasants who are already feeling the approaching disaster and who can point out to us the things that most need doing. Instead of worshipping the intellect of the human race, we need to remember the whole vast biosphere that sustains us, and which we have in recent times so outrageously and thoughtlessly exploited.

In conclusion: If myths about computers become latched on to the more general myth of an all-powerful and upwardly evolving intellect, they will only serve to deepen our false sense of security, to keep us in our self-constructed dream world. The house is on fire; we must wake up from this dream and do something about it. We can either use computers, after waking, to deal with the difficulties we face, or we can misuse them, like so much other technology, as a drug to sedate us further, to save us from waking. This is our choice, and we shall have to make it quickly.

NOTES

1. James Lovelock, "Stand Up For Gaia" (Schumacher Lecture 1988, in *Resurgence* 29, July–August 1988. Obtainable from Schumacher Book Service, Ford House, Hartland, Bideford, Devon, UK).

2. I have tried to discuss the fascinating problem of how we can do full justice to the importance of science without somehow losing other essential aspects of life in *Wisdom, Information and Wonder: What Is Knowledge For?* (London and New York: Routledge, 1989). Other helpful discussions of this can be found in *Pluto's Republic* by Peter B. Medawar (Oxford University Press, 1984) and, more recently, in *The Element of Fire: Science, Art and the Human World* by Anthony O'Hear (London and New York: Routledge, 1988.)

3. I have discussed the nature, meaning, and pathology of these ideas briefly in my book *Beast and Man: The Roots of Human Nature* (Washington, D.C.: New American Library Paperback, 1978) Chapters 7 and 8, and more fully in *Evolution as a Religion* (London: Methuen Inc., 1985).

4. See John D. Barrow and Frank R. Tipler, *The Anthropic Cosmological Principle* (Oxford and New York: Oxford University Press, 1986), concluding passage.

5. See, for example, Stephen Hawking, *A Brief History of Time* (London: Bantam Press, 1988), pp. 174–75: "If we do discover a complete theory [of the physical laws governing motion in the universe] it would be the ultimate triumph of human reason for then we would know the mind of God."

SELECTED BIBLIOGRAPHY

Clark, Mary E. *Ariadne's Thread: The Search for New Modes of Thinking.* New York: St. Martin's Press, 1989.

Dreyfus, Hubert L., and Stuart E. Dreyfus, with Tom Athanasiou. *Mind over Machine: The Power of Human Intuition and Expertise in the Era of the Computer.* New York: The Free Press, 1986.

Midgley, Mary. *Beast and Man: The Roots of Human Nature.* Washington, D.C.: New American Library Paperback, 1978.

———. *Evolution as a Religion.* London: Methuen, 1985.

———. *Heart and Mind: The Varieties of Moral Experience.* New York: St. Martin's Press, 1981.

———. *Wisdom, Information and Wonder: What Is Knowledge For?* London and New York: Routledge, 1989.

5 PARADIGMS AND PROGRESS
INTEGRATING KNOWLEDGE AND EDUCATION FOR THE TWENTY-FIRST CENTURY

William J. Reckmeyer

KNOWLEDGE AND EDUCATION

One of the most remarkable characteristics of *Homo sapiens sapiens* is our individual and collective ability to generate information about ourselves and our world. In part, humanity's quest for knowledge results from an apparently insatiable curiosity. Often driven by a strong desire to learn about something simply because it is there, we find that "the poetry of Earth is never dead"[1] and thus is worthy of inquiry for its own sake. Yet our quest also stems from practical necessity. Human civilization exists because people are able to carry out a great variety of complex biological, cognitive, and social actions that are essential to our survival. The basic mental architecture needed to effect many of these actions is encoded in the genetic composition of individual members of our species, as it is with other forms of life. Unlike most other species, though, few of our specific behaviors are inherited. Instead, we have evolved fairly sophisticated abilities for generating, sharing, and accumulating knowledge that enhance our innate ability to deal with our complex world.

This highlights why knowledge is power and why modern society devotes so much attention and resources to education. One of the most fundamental notions developed by humanity during the last three millennia is the idea that there is a positive causal connection between education and knowledge. We believe that education improves knowledge and, perhaps more to the point in recent centuries, that people are generally better off for having undergone some sort of formal educational process than if they had been left to their own devices. This belief lies at the heart of the current debate over the quality of the entire American educational system, especially in terms of the prevailing assumption that knowledge which is clearly useful to one generation should always be taught to the next. However, there is ample evidence that traditional forms of education are no longer as relevant as they once were. We gathered in San Diego for an innovative conference precisely because many of us were convinced that significant changes should be made in American education if we are to appropriately prepare people for life in the twenty-first century.

The central issue facing higher education today was reflected in the underlying theme of that meeting: What can we do to help our students develop a better appreciation of the inherent unity characterizing reality? Those of us who are concerned with such matters usually decry the narrow disciplinary and professional ways of doing business, which tend to emphasize the parts while obscuring the whole, and find ourselves increasingly frustrated with an educational system where people are taught to count trees while the forest burns down around them. I do not think the real problem is specialization per se, for these kinds of approaches have proven successful in helping us investigate many aspects of our world and thus have dominated our quest for knowledge since their emergence during the Scientific Revolution. Rather, the culprit seems to be overspecialization and our predilection for parochial modes of inquiry that prevent people from seeing the connections common to different situations. This is of even greater concern in an era of information overloads, where floods of data about details effectively ensure that we grow ever less knowledgeable about the big picture.

HIGHER EDUCATION FOR THE TWENTY-FIRST CENTURY

Aside from whatever intellectual interest there might be in resolving how many disciplinary angels can exist on the head of a pin, what makes "Rethinking the Curriculum" so important right now? My own reasons for advocating more integrative education range from the personal to the professional to the planetary. As the father of three children who will graduate from college (if everything goes well) during the first four years of the new millennium, I want to make sure they will be ready for the world we leave them. As a professor and scholar who has been involved in such education for the past fifteen years, I think that it is vital to the health of my profession and my field. As a human being living in a time of momentous changes, I am convinced that we cannot continue our reliance on the ad hoc, piecemeal ways in which most of us deal with the world. The mismatch between our educational experience and the realities of life grows daily and we need to take more concerted action toward rectifying the debilitating effects of excessive fragmentation.

During the last quarter-century it has become fashionable for scholars and writers to note that humanity is in the dawn of a new age, one that is already showing signs of being markedly different from the life experienced by previous generations. People have various names for it, depending on which features they find most compelling. Some call it the Post-Industrial Society, the Nuclear Age, or the Information Age; for others, it is the Solar Age, the Third Wave, or the Age of Aquarius.[2] All argue rather convincingly that we are at a major turning point in human history. Changes of this sort are not unprecedented, as anyone familiar with the Renaissance and Enlightenment would be quick to point out. Moreover, we all like to think we live in special times—a natural feeling that is heightened considerably by the impending arrival of the next millennium. Still, few doubt that the twenty-first century will be a time of extensive transformation and thus full of significant opportunities as well as dangers for the human race.

The difficulty is not that everything is changing so much, or even that the overall rate and extent of change itself have been escalating so dramatically, but that the world as a whole is far more complex than ever before. For the first time in the known history of this planet, one species has developed the ability to destroy itself as well as its environment and there are precious few of us who understand what must be done to avoid catastrophe. Higher education is a good example of Kenneth Boulding's maxim that "nothing fails like success."[3] It has done such a good job of preparing specialized people in the past that we rarely question its suitability for a complex future. Yet all is not well in paradise and we need to modify the way we educate people if society is to accommodate these evolving conditions. The challenge facing us now is how to move higher education out of the nineteenth and into the twenty-first century. I believe the answer lies neither in a nostalgic return to basics nor in the stricter enforcement of higher standards, as many critics suggest, but must involve a serious commitment to weaving a more coherent basis for knowledge and education.

MESS MANAGEMENT

In general, contemporary issues are sufficiently different from traditional ones to warrant different kinds of approaches for handling them.

Not only are they novel and more complex, but they also tend to be more volatile and dangerous. More significantly, they seldom respect the narrow disciplinary boxes we learn in school, the occupational domains we encounter at work, the ideological platforms that dominate public life, or the geopolitical boundaries we have imposed on Earth. They are not reasonably well-defined problems that can be solved once and for all, so much as they are ill-defined and constantly changing messes that must be managed over long periods of time.[4] This is especially disconcerting because the remedies we devise often lead to counter-intuitive results that are worse than the original conditions we sought to improve. The dilemma is that we know a great deal more about problem solving than we do about mess management. Consequently, people are prone to treat every issue with the same kinds of conventional approaches that have worked well in the past, even though they may be poorly suited for the situation at hand—much as the drunk does when looking for his keys under the light, since that is where he can see the best.

This does not mean we are obliged to search totally in the dark, but it does suggest that people should both accept greater uncertainty and develop better sources of light if they want to address the poorly illuminated issues that typify modern life. There are no surefire recipes for success, but we are discovering that specialized approaches encourage people to take overly narrow views of the world. To cite a related metaphor, we are like the blind men observing an elephant. Largely oblivious to everything around us, we perceive reality as trunks or tusks or tails and readily dismiss other views that may contradict our own cherished perspectives. Unaware of our ingrained blindness, we are unable to develop any real sense of the whole elephant—much less to figure out ways we can work together on managing it for our mutual benefit.

We thus seem to be witnessing an unfolding "tragedy of the commons" for society at large, in which humanity's undeniable successes in handling individual trunks and tusks and tails not only mask but unexpectedly trigger adverse consequences for the whole elephant.[5] Our normal habit is to draw up specific plans and techniques for resolving specific concerns and hope that nothing strange arises. This works fine whenever circumstances are familiar or relatively simple, but falls short when we are trying to develop a better understanding of the big picture and cannot be certain which specific knowledge will be useful. The situation seems even more pressing when we realize the world is more like a herd of thundering wild elephants than it is like one of those placid animals we are so used to seeing in our zoos and circuses. Our species has come to dominate the planet chiefly because we are a race of superb generalists. We have the ability to integrate our different specialized competencies in a timely fashion and therefore have been able to occupy a wide variety of evolving niches. American higher education should take this lesson to heart. There will always be a need for the kinds of specialized knowledge that are imperative for solving detailed problems, but the critical need right now is for integrative approaches that are indispensable for managing complex messes.

PARADIGMS

In an everyday sense, "approaches" are the ways in which we deal with life. They tend to be idiosyncratic and implicit ways of "seeing the world." We cope as best we can and rarely give much thought to how we do it. In a scientific sense, "approaches" are far more shared and explicit: they are conscious paradigms that help us perceive, understand, and act in more structured ways.[6] Without going into detail, it is important to recognize that there are three fundamental kinds of features common to all paradigms.[7] First, there are epistemological ones that are concerned with "Knowing," and illuminate how we learn about the world we experience. Second, there are ontological ones that are concerned with "Being" and include what we have learned about that world. Third there are methodological ones that are concerned with "Doing" and provide us with blueprints for interacting with the world. The degree to which these features are consciously manifested often varies from one paradigm to another and from one situation to another, but all three of them are inherent and should be made as explicit as possible.

Scholars and practitioners have constructed a diverse set of progressively sophisticated paradigms during the course of humanity's quest for knowledge, with different disciplines and professions evolving different sets of approaches for addressing their own particular interests. The more people learned, the more complex our world became and the greater the need for more refined knowledge. These paradigms, especially those developed during the last five hundred years, have dramatically increased humanity's ability to deal with virtually every aspect of reality. The predicament we face now is that current issues are severely challenging the capabilities of these specialized paradigms. It is no longer scientifically valid or socially acceptable to ignore the interconnectedness of the world or to presume that we can act with impunity in everything we do. The result of this quandary is that we are in the midst of a major paradigm shift, in which people from a mixture of fields are beginning to assess the relative merits of traditional approaches and to develop new ones that are better suited to our changing times.

Our prevailing paradigms grew out of the fascination of seventeenth-century scientists with the internal workings of simple machines and derive from the enormous explanatory and utilitarian power of approaches pioneered in the eighteenth-century physical sciences. These paradigms treat issues as wholes that are equal to the sums of their parts, and therefore tend to ignore or dismiss factors that lie outside their immediate spheres of interest. Characterized by a strong belief in the ultimate objectivity of knowledge, by an isolated and static view of the world, and by a commitment to algorithmic modes of inquiry, they generally focus on the differences between phenomena. In contrast, newly emerging paradigms are growing out of the recognition by a small but growing number of twentieth-century scholars and practitioners that the more traditional approaches are inadequate for treating complex biological and social issues, even though they have proven quite powerful with simpler physical and mechanical concerns. The new paradigms view issues as greater than the sum of their parts and thus insist on a more comprehensive perspective. Characterized by a belief in the inherent subjectivity of human knowledge, an emphasis on the interconnections among the multiple aspects of our perceived reality, and a search for more flexible modes of action, they stress the similarities common to all complex phenomena.

PARADIGM TYPES

All paradigms are not created alike, however, and over the years I have found it useful to distinguish between at least three types in order to clarify essential differences in the way we organize knowledge and education. Disciplinary approaches, the first and most common type, utilize the theoretical insights and practical skills of a single domain of inquiry to address a particular subject matter. Interdisciplinary paradigms, the second type and a general rubric that includes approaches that are sometimes called multidisciplinary or transdisciplinary, combine insights and/or skills from two or more perspectives to examine something.[8] Integrative approaches, the third and most poorly understood type, go beyond interdisciplinary paradigms by subsuming multiple perspectives within an overarching framework that synthesizes insights and skills from several fields into a unified metadisciplinary process applicable to a broad range of topics. These distinctions are not always obvious, given the manner in which disciplinary types have dominated humanity's quest for knowledge and our resulting educational system, so let me share a couple of other ways to make the same points.

One way is graphical. Disciplinary paradigms are I-types of approaches, to reflect their focus on depth, and rest on the assumption that reality can be fully understood by independently studying the nature of its constituent parts and processes. They emphasize detailed knowledge and seek to learn as much as possible about the separate kinds of trees that make up our universal forest. Interdisciplinary paradigms are H-types of approaches, to reflect their focus on depth with some breadth, and take the position that understanding requires a comprehension of the connections among different phenomena. They promote comparative knowledge, often centered around common themes or area studies, and seek to learn more about the combinations of trees that make ours such a heterogeneous forest. Integrative paradigms are Π-types of approaches, to reflect their focus on breadth with some depth, and argue that understanding is maximized when it incorporates an appreciation of principles that are isomorphic to different aspects of the world. They pursue unified knowledge and seek to learn as much as possible about the organization of the trees and the forest as a whole.

Another way of distinguishing these paradigm types is metaphorical. These three types are very similar to the three principal kinds of microcomputing systems that have appeared during the last decade. Disciplinary approaches are like the dedicated word processors and database terminals that triggered the desktop computer revolution. They are highly specialized and can carry out one kind of application quite well, but different kinds of systems are needed to accomplish different kinds of tasks and information exchange among them is virtually impossible. Interdisciplinary paradigms are like the original IBM PC and other first-generation personal computers that still dominate the market. They have the capability to perform multiple kinds of applications on a single machine—but people have to learn separate procedures for each program, are usually limited to working on one task at a time, and have difficulty pulling data together from different applications. Integrative approaches are like the MacIntosh and other second-generation personal computers. They feature a master operating system with identical procedures for unrelated programs—which means that people can quickly learn how to use these applications, are better able to simultaneously work on the full range of tasks that interest them, and can easily manipulate material between programs.

THE SYSTEMS PARADIGM

One of the most ambitious examples of an integrative approach is my own field of systems. It began emerging about forty years ago, when a few scholars in areas ranging from engineering and biology to economics and philosophy became intrigued by the nonlinear causal processes they saw as common to complex biological and social phenomena. The systems field, which at its broadest combines systems (a general science/practice of organization) and cybernetics (a general science/practice of regulation), is predicated upon the belief that reality is a unified whole. It spotlights the deeper patterns that connect all phenomena and proposes that diverse aspects of reality—physical, biological, social, technological, and nöological—can be better understood and handled when treated as systems of interdependent parts that interact with their environments in universal ways.[9] The field is developing a set of generic intellectual insights and practical tools based on these universalities, with the following distinct properties.

Epistemologically, this paradigm recognizes that cognition is a complex bio-psycho-social undertaking and that our nature as human beings affects everything we do—including what we know about ourselves and our world.[10] It views our knowledge as composed of multiple images constructed by subjective observers, whether folk or expert, not as intrinsic truths discovered through acts of "immaculate perception." Ontologically, the systems field believes that these multiple images represent a constantly changing reality of infinite connections and that everything occurs as the result of certain basic organizing principles.[11] Of special significance are the feedback processes common to all complex systems and the cybernetic abilities that enable many of them to regulate their behavior. Methodologically, systems people realize that flexible blueprints are crucial to appropriate action and that effective implementation requires toolboxes of procedures to iteratively handle changing conditions.[12] In particular, the field emphasizes a combination of systematic techniques and powerful group tools since complicated situations demand coherent collective effort.

No paradigm is a panacea, even one as comprehensive as this, but the systems field does provide a powerful antidote to overspecialization as well as some important advantages over most interdisciplinary approaches. The foremost benefit offered by such an integrated paradigm is its applicability to the entire panoply of issues that affect humanity. Resolving these issues requires expertise from every domain of human experience, but such expertise is not easy to pull together given the myopia and intransigence of most disciplines and professions or the sheer volume of detailed knowledge generated by our species during its existence. We desperately need more integrative approaches like systems science that foster greater communication and cooperation among interested parties while minimizing the attendant dangers of information overload. Because it functions as an intellectual and practical Rosetta Stone, people can use this paradigm to significantly enhance humanity's ability to comprehend and improve both the trees and the whole forest.

CONSEQUENCES FOR EDUCATION

Let me close with a few comments about the implication of the notions sketched here for the issues raised in this volume. We are not dealing with trivial concerns, in either an intellectual or a practical sense. American higher education is in serious trouble and major improvements need to be made if our students are to be satisfactorily prepared for life in the twenty-first century. The key is not simply to work harder, but to work smarter. Bureaucratic and financial remedies receive most of our attention these days, yet largely miss the mark because they treat symptoms rather than causes. Our only real hope for success, it seems to me, is to cut through all the gobbledygook and focus our attention on substantially revising the basic curricula of our nation's colleges and universities. I am not suggesting that we redesign the entire system or even undertake a complete overhaul of general education. But I do think it is desirable and feasible to demand that our educational system be demonstrably relevant to daily experience and to insist that our faculty and students have a much stronger exposure to the patterns that connect as well as the details that separate.

I am also convinced that society has the right and that educators have the responsibility to establish a clearer picture of what our general expectations are for students. At the present time, there is an overwhelming commitment to specialized competencies because that is what society rewards and what our heritage cultivates. However, there is little consensus on what common attitudes and abilities we want all of our graduates to develop. My own belief is that we will always require people who are well versed in details, but that the really pressing need in the twenty-first century will be for people who are also better generalists. Instead of training students to be epistemologically passive, ontologically fragmented, and methodologically isolated we must empower them to become better explorers, integrators, and collaborators. Our world is changing radically and society will be seeking more reflective practitioners—people with generic competencies, who can responsibly and effectively blend thought and action to wrestle with the issues of the day.[13]

Integrating knowledge and education for the twenty-first century will not be easy—translating rhetoric into reality never is and it will undoubtedly meet with considerable opposition from inside as well as outside the academy. Yet we must not shrink from the task at hand. The need is compelling and our message clear. As Robert Heinlein observes, "A human being should be able to change a diaper, plan an invasion, butcher a hog, conn a ship, design a building, write a sonnet, balance accounts, build a wall, set a bone, comfort the dying, take orders, give orders, cooperate, act alone, solve equations, analyze a new problem, pitch manure, program a computer, cook a tasty meal, fight efficiently, die gallantly. Specialization is for insects."[14] American higher education can no longer afford to put all of its eggs into traditional disciplinary baskets, but must encourage more interdisciplinary and integrative approaches so that people will be better equipped to sail the uncharted waters of the future. At the beginning of the conference, Mary Clark emphasized that the job of higher education is not just to provide students with a good picture of the way society sees itself, but to critique existing approaches and help shape new ones. I could not agree more.

NOTES

1. From "On the Grasshopper and Cricket," a poem by John Keats in *Keats's Complete Poetical Works and Letters* (Cambridge: Cambridge University Press, 1899), p. 35.

2. For example, see Daniel Bell, *The Coming of the Post-Industrial Society* (New York: Basic Books, 1973); Kenneth E. Boulding, *The Meaning of the Twentieth Century: The Great Transition* (New York: Harper & Row, 1964); Fritjof Capra, *The Turning Point: Science, Society, and the Rising Culture* (New York: Simon & Schuster, 1982); Marilyn Ferguson, *The Aquarian Conspiracy: Personal and Social Transformation in the 1980s* (Los Angeles: Tarcher, 1980); Hazel Henderson, *Politics of the Solar Age* (New York: Doubleday, 1981); and Alvin Toffler, *The Third Wave* (New York: Morrow, 1980).

3. Kenneth E. Boulding, *Ecodynamics: A New Theory of Societal Evolution* (Beverly Hills: Sage, 1978), p. 42.

4. See Russell L. Ackoff, *Creating the Corporate Future: Plan or Be Planned For* (New York: Wiley, 1981); Stafford Beer, *Platform for Change* (New York: Wiley, 1975); William J. Reckmeyer, *The Emerging Systems Paradigm* (Ann Arbor: University Microfilms, 1982); William J. Reckmeyer, "Managing Complexity in the Systems Age: A Renaissance Systems Perspective," in *A Science of Goal Formulation: Foundations of Cybernetics and General Systems Theory*, edited by Stuart A. Umpleby and Vadim N. Sadovsky (New York: Hemisphere, 1989), pp. 157–172; and John N. Warfield et al., *Generic Design*. (Fairfax, Va.: George Mason University Press, 1986).

5. This theme was popularized by Garrett Hardin and permeates much of his work, including *Filters against Folly: How to Survive Despite Economists, Ecologists, and the Merely Eloquent* (New York: Viking, 1985).

6. In particular, see Gary Cutting, ed., *Paradigms and Revolutions: Appraisals and Applications of Thomas Kuhn's Philosophy of Science* (Notre Dame: University of Notre Dame Press, 1980); Ian Hacking, ed., *Scientific Revolutions* (New York: Oxford University Press, 1981); and Thomas Kuhn, *The Structure of Scientific Revolutions*, 2d ed. (Chicago: University of Chicago Press, 1970).

7. See Reckmeyer, *The Emerging Systems Paradigm* (1982) and "Managing Complexity" (1989), for more detailed discussions of these features.

8. For interdisciplinary paradigms, see Leo Apostel, Guy Berger, Asa Briggs, and Guy Michaud, ed. *Interdisciplinarity: Problems of Teaching and Research in Universities* (Paris: OECD, 1972); Daryl E. Chubin, Alan L. Porter, Frederick L. Rossini, and Terry Connolly, ed. *Interdisciplinary Analysis and Research* (Mt. Airy, Md.: Lomond Publications, Inc., 1986); Fritz Machlup and Una Mansfield, eds., *The Study of Information: Interdisciplinary Messages.* (New York: Wiley, 1983).

9. General introductions to the systems field can be found in Peter B. Checkland, *Systems Thinking, Systems Practice* (New York: Wiley, 1981); Joel de Rosnay, *The Macroscope: A New World Scientific System* (New York: Harper & Row, 1979); Robert L. Flood and Ewart R. Carson, *Dealing with Complexity: An Introduction to the Theory and Application of Systems Science* (New York: Plenum, 1987); Machlup and Mansfield, *Study of Information*, 1983; Reckmeyer, *The Emerging Systems Paradigm*, 1982; Ludwig von Bertalanffy, *General System Theory* (New York: Braziller, 1968); and Gerald M. Weinberg, *An Introduction to General Systems Thinking* (New York: Wiley, 1975). Nöological derives from nöosphere, the realm of human thought and spirituality. Nöology is the study of the formation and meaning of ideas.

10. For epistemological features, see Gregory Bateson, *Steps to an Ecology of Mind* (New York: Ballantine, 1972); Peter L. Berger and Thomas Luckman, *The Social Construction of Reality: A Treatise in the Sociology of Knowledge* (Garden City: Doubleday, 1967); Kenneth E. Boulding, *The Image: Knowledge in Life and Society* (Ann Arbor: University of Michigan Press, 1956); Humberto R. Maturana and Francisco J. Varela, *Autopoiesis and Cognition: The Realization of the Living* (Boston: Reidel, 1980); Reckmeyer, *The Emerging Systems Paradigm*, 1982; and Heinz von Foerster, *Observing Systems* (Seaside: Intersystems, 1982).

11. For ontological features, see W. Ross Ashby, *An Introduction to Cybernetics* (New York: Wiley, 1956); Norman D. Cook, *Stability and Flexibility: An Analysis of Natural Systems* (New York: Pergamon, 1980); Peter A. Corning, *The Synergism Hypothesis; A Theory of Progressive Evolution* (New York: McGraw-Hill, 1983); Jay W. Forrester, *Principles of Systems* (Cambridge: Wright-Allen Press, 1968); Erich Jantsch, *The Self-Organizing Universe: Scientific and Human Implications of the Emerging Paradigm of Evolution* (New York: Pergamon, 1980); James G. Miller, *Living Systems* (New York: McGraw-Hill, 1978); Howard T. Odum, *Systems Ecology: An Introduction* (New York: Wiley, 1983); Reckmeyer, 1982.

12. For collective effort in systems analysis, see Thomas H. Athey, *Systematic Systems Approach: An Integrated Method of Solving Systems Problems* (Englewood Cliffs, NJ: Prentice-Hall, 1982); Checkland, *Systems Thinking*; Barry A. Clemson, *Cybernetics: A New Tool for Management* (Tunbridge Wells, England: Abacus, 1984); Hugh J. Miser and Edward S. Quade, eds., *Handbook of Systems Analysis* (New York: North Holland, 1985); Shirley A. Olsen, ed., *Group Planning and Problem-Solving*

Methods in Engineering Management (New York: Wiley, 1982); Reckmeyer, "Managing Complexity"; John P. van Gigch, *Applied General Systems Theory* (New York: Harper & Row, 1978); Conrad H. Waddington, *Tools for Thought: How to Understand and Apply the Latest Scientific Techniques of Problem-Solving* (New York: Basic Books, 1977); and Warfield et al., *Generic Design.*

13. For example, see Marion Brady, *What's Worth Teaching? Selecting, Organizing, and Integrating Knowledge* (Albany: State University of New York Press, 1989); Mike Pedler, ed., *Action Learning in Practice* (Aldershot, England: Gower, 1983); Reckmeyer, "Managing Complexity"; Donald A. Schon, *The Reflective Practitioner: How Professionals Think in Action* (New York: Basic Books, 1983); and Donald A. Schon, *Educating the Reflective Practitioner: Toward a New Design for Teaching and Learning in the Professions* (San Francisco: Jossey-Bass, 1987).

14. Robert A. Heinlein, *Time Enough for Love* (New York: Berkeley, 1986), p. 248.

SELECTED BIBLIOGRAPHY

Apostel, Leo, Guy Bergher, Asa Briggs, and Guy Michaud, eds. *Interdisciplinarity: Problems of Teaching and Research in Universities.* Paris: OECD, 1972.

Chubin, Daryl E., Alan L. Porter, Frederick L. Rossini and Terry Connolly, eds. *Interdisciplinary Analysis and Research.* Mt. Airy, Md: Lomond Publications, Inc., 1986.

de Rosnay, Joel. *The Macroscope: A New World Scientific System.* New York: Harper & Row, 1979.

Kuhn, Thomas. *The Structure of Scientific Revolutions,* 2d ed. Chicago: University of Chicago Press, 1970.

Reckmeyer, William J. *The Emerging Systems Paradigm.* Ann Arbor: University Microfilms, 1982.

II A Critical Look at the Disciplines

6 THE LIMITATIONS OF POLITICAL THEORY FOR ANALYZING CONFLICT

Richard E. Rubenstein

INADEQUACY: THE DEPTH OF THE PROBLEM

When the field of conflict resolution was first developed, many of its advocates considered it *interdisciplinary*. They hoped that focusing the light of several disciplines on human conflict would illuminate the causes, nature, and consequences of deep-rooted conflict and improve our ability to resolve serious conflicts without large-scale violence. Two problems, however, have all but shattered these hopes. First, too many of the "light beams" do not cross. There is little basis for collaboration, for example, between a psychologist who assumes that human beings are innately aggressive and a sociologist who assumes that they are infinitely "socializable". Second, even where the beams do cross, there is what one might call a problem of theoretical power failure. So inadequate has existing theory proved for anticipating serious conflict, analyzing it while in progress, or making sense of it afterward that we have been forced to start almost from scratch in an effort to develop a generic theory useful in conflict resolution. As my colleague John Burton has written, this field will either become *adisciplinary* or, like other interdisciplinary fads of recent years, it will cease to exist.[1]

What do we demand of social theory? Good theory makes sense of the world around us, explaining the connections between apparently disconnected events. It often makes nonsense of so-called common sense, demonstrating that things are not necessarily what they seem. It reevaluates changes occurring over time, illuminating the continuities and discontinuities between past and present, and indicating to what extent the present can be projected into the future. It redefines relationships between thought and its objects, and between oneself and others. And, of course, it stimulates new thinking. Perhaps prediction is not of the essence of social theory, as some believe it to be in the case of "hard science." But we are entitled to demand that social theory at least account for unanticipated events after the fact, in order to make future related events more predictable.

By none of these criteria, I am sorry to say, does social theory succeed in illuminating our understanding of conflict. Only a few studies have helped us (and then only fragmentarily) to interpret the most serious and protracted conflicts of the past two decades. The violent struggles described below have therefore come as a surprise to academic analysts as well as to policymakers and the general public. Not one of these conflicts, to my knowledge, has been satisfactorily explained or integrated into a coherent picture of world society. This theoretical failure has left the practice of conflict resolution in a quandary, for how can one resolve conflicts whose root causes, nature, and consequences are so poorly understood?

Consider the following major episodes of unanticipated political conflict during the past twenty years:

Communal Conflict. The period since the end of the Indochina War has seen a radical intensification of violent conflict between ethnic, racial, religious, and national groups in virtually every region of the world, with communal warfare rising (or sinking) to the status of number one killer of the world's peoples. A short list of nations now experiencing serious (which is to say, potentially genocidal) communal conflict includes Sri Lanka, India (Punjab), Burma, Malaysia, Israel, Lebanon, South Africa, Rwanda-Burundi, Sudan, Ethiopia, China (Tibet), Iraq (Kurdistan), the Soviet Union, Yugoslavia, Bulgaria, Spain, Northern Ireland, the Philippines, Fiji. . . . If the list were expanded to include nations in which communal conflict could erupt at almost any time, it would include a majority of the world's nations.

Religious Conflict. The outbreak and course of the Iranian Revolution dramatically illustrated the rise of worldwide conflict between the forces of "secular modernism" and "religious fundamentalism." This conflict, so at variance with contemporary social theory, has generated terrorism, state terror, rioting, and revolutionary activity throughout the Arab states, and is now felt far beyond the boundaries of the Islamic world. The experts are as astonished as any lay observers to find rebellious Polish workers marching behind icons of the Black Madonna, North Americans battling over issues like abortion and school prayer, and Latin Americans fighting (in many cases, to the death) for or against the principles of "Liberation Theology."

Internal Conflict in the Communist States. Equally unforseen was the outbreak of a struggle between "reformers" and "conservatives" that would destabilize virtually every Communist nation, unleashing a wave of ethnic and national rebellions in the Second World. The coincidence of this conflict with a period of unexpected East-West detente demonstrates that the obsolescence of older forms of conflict and the rise of new forms are opposite sides of the same coin. If one cannot account for conflict, one cannot account for collaboration, either. Moreover, well after the occurrence of events like the student uprising and massacre in T'ienanmen Square, the experts found themselves unable to agree on their significance. Was the student rebellion a mere "palace revolt" or did it herald a social revolution? Are the Communist states capable of self-reformation or are the Soviet and Chinese empires disintegrating? One looks for answers to such questions based on social theory, but finds only conclusions deduced from ideological dogmas.

Internal Conflict in the Capitalist States. A plague of drug addiction and criminal violence, accompanied by largely ineffective state repression, appeared with little warning in the capitalist world, worsening the already severe conflict between minority and poor communities and more powerful groups. In narcotics producing nations like Bolivia, Colombia, and Peru, struggles among producers, and between producers and the state, took on the character of guerrilla war, with "narco-terrorism" appearing as a new form of political violence. In consumer nations like the United States, an officially declared "war on drugs" has been experienced by impoverished minority communities as a war on *them*. The poverty of social theory in this case has left the field to advocates and practitioners of state coercion and vigilantism, with ominous implications for the social future in the industrialized nations.

Other Serious Conflicts. Notwithstanding the thawing of the Cold War, protracted class-based insurgencies (denominated "low intensity conflicts" by those who do not live with them) continue to erupt in diverse locales, including El Salvador, Peru, Guatemala, Burma, and the Philippines. Equally perplexing are the persistence of terrorism as a significant form of violent struggle on virtually every continent, and outbreaks of spontaneous "economic rioting" in urban areas from Buenos Aires to Amman. Meanwhile, new forms of communal violence continue to develop, the most recent type being the "sports violence" now plaguing the nations of Western Europe. There seems no end to the varieties of social conflict—or to the astonishment of "experts" without a theory that will explain them.

Most of the conflicts described above involve violence within a single state rather than interstate war, although (as in the Iran-Iraq war) they may spill across national boundaries. In most, the parties are "domestic" groups defined by race, religion, class, or ethnic identity, which enter into conflict with or without support from groups outside their nations of residence. Notwithstanding those various political ideologies that predict that humans will be pacified when elections are free and markets unregulated,[2] when the bourgeoisie has been eliminated and property is collectively owned,[3] or when developing nations have been "modernized,"[4] the trend toward communal violence transgresses all established theoretical categories. Intergroup warfare appears in industrial, semi-industrial, and agrarian states; in capitalist and communist polities; in imperial centers and in the nations of the periphery. Although we may still be horrified, we are no longer surprised to learn that West European soccer matches must be guarded by armed men to prevent bloody outbreaks of communal violence, or that black defendants in the United States are far more likely to be executed for murder if the victim is white than if he or she is black.

FLAWS IN POLITICAL THEORY

I want to focus for the moment on some problems of political theory, although a similar critique could be made of any of the other disciplines that have attempted to comprehend the causes and nature of conflict. In Western political theory, the individual citizen or subject is deemed to have two primary politically cognizable interests—freedom and property—whose satisfaction can be guaranteed by a properly designed state system governed by a competent elite. Capitalist theory views individual self-determination in politics and the market as a method ultimately of satisfying property interests; Communist theory sees planned distribution of property as a method ultimately of realizing individual self-determination. But the "individual" conjured up in each schema is an unrealized and unrealizable abstraction—a bundle of "rights" and "interests" whose primary political relationship is with the equally abstract state.

This heritage has left us with little understanding of the process of *political bonding*, i.e., the ways in which individuals are gathered into social groups other than the state, that mobilize their energies and loyalty. Rousseau's democratic theory and pre-Stalinist Marxism had the advantage of recognizing fundamental forms of human solidarity prior to the state. But political theory and practice in the age of the "corporate state" bear out Roberto Unger's insight that while *liberty* and *equality* became guiding principles in the West and East, respectively, *fraternity*—for which there was no true basis in either theory—was abandoned.5 This theoretical blind spot is no oversight; it reflects the overall subservience of modern scholarship to political authority. Governing elites in both major world-systems find the activities of nonstate communities (and of individuals driven to form such communities) inimical to their preferred goals.6 Despite official "recognition" of ethnic minorities, linguistic groups, worker or farmer associations, and religious communities, political leaders normally proceed as if such communities did not exist, except as a source of annoyance (and, occasionally, a source of votes). Ordinarily, they deal with such groups as aggregates of isolated individuals.7 Wittingly or not, social thinkers have reinforced this behavior by declaring nonstate communities to be "outside the social contract"—theoretical anomalies both in the "individualistic" West and the "classless" East. If they exist, state authorities conclude, it must be because their members are mad, bad, anachronistic, or supported by a foreign power. Suppression, either legal or extralegal, is their usual answer. Nevertheless, the urge toward group solidarity among such communities—even when it takes grotesque and destructive forms—has proved irrepressible.

Driven by events to acknowledge this enormous lacuna in our fundamentally authoritarian social theory, we are now at the beginning of an effort to redefine the political individual in such a way as to account for the manifold forms (and potential forms) of solidarity. One theoretical initiative that is becoming influential among certain analysts of conflict and conflict resolution is the effort to define the basic *needs*, shared by all humans, whose nonsatisfaction can be counted on to generate destructive behavior (either violent conflict or apathetic withdrawal). Rather than conceiving of humans as abstract clusters of conscious interests that can be accommodated through bargaining or suppressed by force, this new theory posits the existence of ontological or organic needs for security, identity, meaning, bonding, and development that humans *will* attempt to satisfy whatever those in authority say or do.8 The human needs approach replaces the malleable (socializable, deterrable) individual of older social theories with the *necessitous* individual—a "social animal," to be sure, but one whose ineluctable needs shape social organizations over the course of time rather than being shaped by them. It thus reveals the essential powerlessness of power, or, to be more precise, the reason that those attempting to wield power without satisfying basic human needs find the costs of this effort increasing at an exponential rate.

IMPLICATIONS OF NEEDS THEORY

The implications of this theory for practical conflict resolution are profound. For if communal conflict is generated by unsatisfied basic needs, the first task must be to develop processes by which these can be identified, the second to imagine alternative methods of satisfying them, and the third to assist the parties in conflict to make the necessary changes, even if they involve structural alterations in political and social systems. These are *not* currently acknowledged by many theorists and practitioners in the field to be the appropriate tasks of conflict resolution. Some, relying on conventional social theory, view conflict resolution as the theory and practice of power-based negotiation. Others, while recognizing the bankruptcy of that theory, define the field purely in terms of "process," advocating the virtues, say, of mediation over other forms of dispute resolution. But without a theory that explains the breakdown of inherited forms of social organization and the rise of new forms of group solidarity, processes capable of resolving deep-rooted communal conflicts cannot be deduced.

Human needs theory may serve this purpose, but only if it remains free of the assumptions that crippled earlier attempts to define "political man." I have argued elsewhere that if human needs theory becomes merely the latest version of abstract and static "natural law" philosophy, it will add little to existing social thought.[9] What we need to understand is how needs and their satisfiers are revealed over time in connection with continuous changes in the natural environment, in systems of production, and in systems of social meaning. We need to know, too, the role played by such needs in the psychological history of the individual and of the human species. On the basis of such understandings, it may be possible to identify not only those needs beginning to be recognized as germane to contemporary communal struggles (e.g., identity and recognition), but those newly emerging in the course of ongoing social transformation (e.g., the need for uncoerced associated work).[10] This could give us the capacity to foresee the development of new forms of conflict that might be resolved or restructured before they became murderous, and therefore far more difficult to deal with.

It seems clear, in any case, that the construction of new social theory capable of illuminating the causes of conflict cannot take place within the boundaries of any established academic discipline. Neither can such a theory be constructed *across* those boundaries, if that means simply combining well-established truths from several disciplines. On the contrary, we are compelled to explore diverse disciplines, including those that may not at first seem relevant to our inquiry, not so much for established truth as for the fragmentary insights and intuitions that will enable us eventually to construct an adequate picture of the human being. Those interested in the study of terrorism will understand what I mean when I say that there is more truth about terrorism in Andre Malraux's novel, *Man's Fate*, than in all the State Department reports written during the past two decades.[11]

ADVICE ON A FUTURE CURRICULUM

Rethinking the curriculum begins, it seems to me, with the admission that we are astonished by the human capacities for conflict and collaboration revealed by recent history. Clearly, neither political science nor its sister disciplines has furnished a reliable roadmap to the evolution of our nature as social beings. The failure of these disciplines either to predict or render a coherent account of the major conflicts of our time suggests profound methodological as well as contextual limitations. It may be well to remember, apropos of the current craze for "interdisciplinary" studies, that one cannot make a large truth out of a lot of small falsehoods. Indeed, in my own field of conflict resolution, those scholars who are making the most significant contributions seem to be those least bound by the methods and assumptions of their disciplines of origin.

Where to start, then, in rethinking the curriculum? I am not opposed to teaching political science, sociology, psychology, history, law, economics, and so forth; but I think that we ought to show our students around these disciplines like guides showing tourists a ruined city. The point is not to live in such a place, but to take inspiration from it. And that being so, I would certainly not reserve any area of the city (law, for example) only for tourists who already hold bachelor's degrees. Let undergraduates explore all the ruins—even that fallen temple bearing the fantastic motto, "A government of laws, not men."

But when the real-world learning starts, we ought to consider organizing students and teachers, like workers in any sensible enterprise, to perform *tasks*, their tasks as intellectuals being to answer interesting questions. At the center where I work, the primary tasks are to discover why people join together with others they define as "brethren" to dominate or destroy those they define as "strangers," and what makes them redefine these categories. A corollary task is to learn how outsiders not involved in the conflict can possibly assist in this process of redefinition. Other centers, involving students and teachers at all levels and from diverse disciplinary and experiential backgrounds, might take as their tasks such essential inquiries as these:

Why do humans love and stop loving each other? How does membership in intimate groups imprison or liberate them? How are families evolving in different societies in response to social change? What sort of interventions in these processes are possible or desirable?

Why are most of the world's people poor? To what level of comfort do they aspire? How can they reach that level without despoiling the planet?

What sorts of meaning do people crave? What sorts of transcendent experience? How does religion satisfy or fail to satisfy these needs? What is organized religion's role in human social evolution?

Why are virtually none of the organizations styling themselves "democratic" actively controlled by their members? In what areas of human life is such control possible and desirable? How can it be realized?

What sorts of work need to be done? What sorts of work do people want to do? How can humans get the work that needs to be done done, while giving people the opportunity to do the sort of work they want to do?

Under what circumstances must people abide by rules? Why do they violate rules? What ought to be done to them, or to the rules, if they do?

How do people think and act creatively? Is there a human instinct for creative expression? For play? How can opportunities for creativity be maximized on a worldwide scale?

One could continue in this vein, understanding that no such research center could hope to accomplish its tasks without (a) moving beyond disciplinary boundaries, including the boundaries separating "social science" from "the humanities," and both from "hard science"; (b) junking most received intradisciplinary truths; and (c) moving freely between theoretical and practical questions. It should also be clear that each center's tasks must be global, and that their accomplishment requires the exercise of historical, comparative, analytical, and (dare one say it?) intuitive skills.

Could a university be built around centers rather than disciplines, with tours of the ruined cities reserved for the early years of training and one's continuing education? I would ask, rather, can we afford to trust our survival and happiness as a species to the caretakers of the disciplinary (and conventionally interdisciplinary) museums? The day may come—and soon—when task-based education seems a natural extension of the idea of education itself.

NOTES

1. John W. Burton, "Conflict Resolution as a Political System" (Working Paper 1 of the Center for Conflict Analysis and Resolution, George Mason University, 1988).
2. Milton Friedman, *Capitalism and Freedom* (New York: Vintage, 1962).

3. Karl Marx and Friedrich Engels, *The German Ideology* (Moscow: Progress Publishers, 1964).

4. Samuel F. Huntington, *Political Order in Changing Societies* (New Haven: Yale University Press, 1988).

5. Roberto M. Unger, *Knowledge and Politics* (Cambridge, Mass.: Harvard University Press, 1979); see also Norman Birnbaum, *The Radical Renewal: The Politics of Ideas in Modern America* (New York: Pantheon Books, 1988).

6. Discussed in John W. Burton, *Global Conflict: The Domestic Sources of International Crisis* (London: Wheatsheaf, 1984).

7. See Richard E. Rubenstein, *Rebels in Eden: Mass Political Violence in the United States* (Boston: Little, Brown, 1970); Richard E. Rubenstein, "Group Violence in America" (Working Paper 2 of the Center for Conflict Analysis and Resolution, George Mason University, 1989).

8. See John W. Burton, *Deviance, Terrorism and War: The Process of Resolving Unsolved Social and Political Problems* (New York: St. Martin's Press, 1979); Katrin Lederer, ed. *Human Needs: A Contribution to the Current Debate* (Cambridge, Mass.: Gunn, Oelinschlager & Hahn, 1980); Roger A. Coate and Jerel A. Rosati. *The Power of Human Needs in World Society* (Boulder, Colo., and London: Lynne Rienner, 1988).

9. Richard E. Rubenstein, "Human Needs Theory: Beyond Natural Law" in John W. Burton, ed., *Conflict: Human Needs Theory* (London: MacMillan and New York: St. Martin's Press, 1990).

10. Leon Trotsky, *Literature and Revolution* (New York: Pathfinder, 1957); Herbert Marcuse. *Eros and Civilization: A Philosophical Inquiry into Freud* (Boston: Beacon Press, 1968).

11. Andre Malraux, *Man's Fate* (New York: Modern Library, 1936).

SELECTED BIBLIOGRAPHY

Burton, John W. *World Society*. Lanham, Md: University Press of America, 1987.

Burton, John W. *Deviance, Terrorism and War: The Process of Solving Unsolved Social and Political Problems*. New York: St. Martin's Press, 1979.

Camus, Albert. *The Rebel: An Essay on Man*. New York: Vintage Books, 1956.

Clark, Mary E. *Ariadne's Thread: The Search for New Modes of Thinking*. London: Macmillan; and New York: St. Martin's Press, 1989.

Coate, Roger A., and Jerel A. Rosati. *The Power of Human Needs in World Society*. Boulder, Colo., and London: Lynne Rienner, 1988.

Gurr, Ted Robert. *Why Men Rebel*. Princeton, N.J.: Princeton University Press, 1970.

Rubenstein, Richard E. *Alchemists of Revolution: Terrorism in the Modern World*. New York: Basic Books, 1987.

7 WILL THE REAL ECONOMY PLEASE STAND UP?

Hazel Henderson

THE CRISIS OF PERCEPTION IN ECONOMIC THEORY

In the past twenty years, as a citizen-activist and self-employed writer, I have come to believe that virtually all of today's crises are crises of perception, caused by our disabling dogmas and belief systems—all of those "-isms." Living in New York in the 1960s, I began to sense that the planet was dying, a very alienating set of sensibilities to be carrying around during a period when people did not even know the word "pollution." In fact, I felt very much like an extraterrestrial (and I still do)! So, instead of going to college, I decided to use my extraterrestrial view as part of my social change tool kit. This was very effective in my community organizing. I helped organize one of the first environmental groups in the United States.[1] It gave me the distance and perspective necessary to study economics and find out what was wrong with it.

Nowadays I feel less alienated, because many people do know what we mean when we criticize environmentally devastating economic policies. To initiate dialogue with economists, I tried to make them see that if industrial society continues to drift in the same direction, more and more of the people in such societies eventually would have to be employed cleaning up the mess. Additionally, more and more people in the future would need to be paid to provide those loving services we used to do freely for each other in family and community.

When I confronted economists in this way they would say, "What's wrong with this kind of society? The GNP is obviously going up and everybody is fully employed." It was back then, around the mid 1970s, that I began to realize that trying to guide complex societies by using macroeconomic policy, summed up in indicators such as the Gross National Product, was a little like trying to fly a Boeing 747 aircraft with nothing on the instrument panel except an oil pressure gauge. There was no way to tell whether the flaps were up or down, or what the altitude was, or whether the fuel tanks were full, or anything else!

My explorations into the history of economic thought were a fascinating saga in the sociology of knowledge. As I had suspected, I found that economics lacked a scientific basis and is largely deduced from extremely dubious assumptions and postulates about the world. I became aware that, on the whole, although economics paraded itself as a science, behind that façade were concealed the *values of economists*. Economics is a profession, as is the law, and economists, like lawyers, are very useful to their clients, who tend to be the powerful and the wealthy.

Looking at the values systems that guided disciplines such as economics became for me the most important device for cutting through the various mathematical formulas and the endless economic studies. Underneath all this raw data and bits of information were the guiding assumptions and models—the worldviews and paradigms that valued the services offered by day care centers, waste disposal companies, drug rehabilitation programs, etc., but did not value clean air and water, parenting, or volunteer work. Until one arrived at these basic goals, purposes, and values, one really could not assess the quality of research studies. Working in Washington D.C., as a member of the Advisory Council to the Office of Technology Assessment, I increasingly came to acknowledge the fact that the most important thing to find out about any study was simply who had paid for it! Since I was quite idealistic in the beginning, it was profoundly unsettling to learn that economics was largely politics in disguise.

One of the unrealistic postulates common in economics is the idea that the material wants of human beings are insatiable and we are all rationally maximizing our various self-interests. This assumption of rational action in line with self-interest I found challenged by psychologists such as David McClelland. It was McClelland who informed me: "Economists haven't even discovered Freud yet, let alone Abraham Maslow."[2] I found some dirty linen as well, namely the fact that the Nobel Prize that is given in economics is not a Nobel Prize at all. The $145,000 prize money for the so-called Nobel Memorial Prize was put up by the Central Bank of Sweden. It is the only prize *not* included in the will of Alfred Nobel, and was lobbied onto the Nobel Prize Committee. Gradually I pieced together what had been realized for over 200 years: that economics was an intellectual scandal. Some of the very best economists had come to the same conclusion, as I was able to document with quotations from such profound thinkers as Gunnar Myrdal, Joan Robinson, Kenneth Boulding, Barbara Ward, and Irving Fisher.[3] One gem I encountered during my research is from a 1904 lecture given in London by the economist A. C. Pigou: "Economics furnished the ungodly, blunt instruments with which to bludgeon at birth useful projects of social betterment."[4]

As I researched the history of economic thought, I wondered whether the truth would ever catch up with economics, since it is a method for stifling public choices. In other words, if you can mystify public choices as cost-benefit analysis, you can fuzz over who are the winners and losers, by averaging out the costs and benefits per capita. Only later do these confused public decisions come unravelled in political conflict over social and environmental costs incurred and displaced onto taxpayers, consumers, or future generations. One hires an economist to do a cost-benefit analysis in rather the same way that one hires a lawyer to do a brief—to put the best face on whatever policy one is promoting.

THE IMPERATIVE OF COOPERATION

Now, in the late eighties, the planet has begun to teach human beings directly, and it seems that almost everything we are being taught concerns cooperation. There is absolutely no way for us to deal with any of the problems we have created—whether acid rain, holes in the ozone layer, or anything else—until we learn to cooperate. In addition, the rate of social change is accelerating to the point where our learning processes are accelerating as well, engulfing and even shattering many disciplines, along with whole epistemologies. All of these change processes have begun to undermine economics and the sophistries of macroeconomic management.

Countries all over the world have to ride the roller coaster of world trade, as capital flows around the planet through countries in Europe, Asia, Africa, the Americas and back again. We are entering an era of global interdependence in which six great globalization forces must be dealt with. These include:

1. the globalization of technology and production;
2. the globalization of finance ("hot money," equivalent to some $500 billion, sloshes around the planet every 24 hours, while money and information merge as blips on thousands of computer screens);
3. the globalization of militarization (everywhere on the planet small-scale surrogate wars are being fought because nuclear weapons are too dangerous to risk using); and
4. the globalization of pollution.

Another very interesting process is (5) the globalization of work and "labor markets," as economists like to call them, whereby people migrate across borders looking for work while companies also migrate in search of cheaper labor forces. Finally, there is (6) the globalization of consumption and the emergence of a planetary culture.

These six globalization forces have led to a seventh, a gradual loss of national sovereignty that results from all of the feedback loops and other responses to the first six globalizations, accelerated due to their interactions. Politicians can no longer promise their citizens that they can manage the economy. Nor can they promise full employment, protection for their citizens in times of war, or protection from the effects of global pollution. Furthermore, these accelerating changes are irreversible, and they require a paradigm shift in knowledge and research methods such as we are discussing at this conference. The focus has changed from exactitude, static equilibrium, and classical reductionism to research methods and policy tools based on what might be called systems views, that is, dynamic, nonlinear, probabilistic, feedback-driven models of *dis*equilibrium. It is very interesting to watch some of my economist friends now tiptoeing to a place called the Santa Fe Institute in New Mexico or trying to find a chaos theorist to take to lunch, in an attempt to figure out what chaos models are about.

Along with the loss of sovereignty being experienced by all nation-states, we have a multiplicity of geopolitical realignments and restructurings. The shift moves us away from the old East/West, Communist-Socialist/Capitalist polarization that characterized the Cold War Era (1945–1988). Then the main game was Mutually Assured Destruction, but in fact it has turned out to be mutually assured destruction of the economies of the two superpowers. Now the move toward North/South polarization is fracturing those old alliances. Around the world countries are seeking new partners—the United States getting together with Canada, Europe-1992, a Pacific Basin-type NATO, and so on. As a result of this new, multipolar world, economic theory is falling further and further behind in mapping the kind of phenomena that it purports to help politicians deal with. The new world game is "mutually assured development," and the focus is on the meaning of this development. The new rubric is "sustainable development," a phrase that worried World Bank officials have already co-opted.

In a sense, these new economic conditions and new ways to "view the global playing field" (as the politicians talk about it) require a complete redefinition of most of the issues, largely because of the new indivisibility of economic relationships. The global economy has become a "commons," in need of new agreements concerning the rules of the game. This has changed almost every definition in the textbooks of economics. As I have detailed elsewhere, the old definitions of "competitiveness," restricted to product/economic/national, are unworkable.[5] The same is true of the old rules of comparative advantage and the old definitions of protectionism. (Almost everybody has become a "closet protectionist," a good signal that the concept has been exhausted.[6]) The old "terms of trade" used in economic theory are swamped daily by financial flows: those billions and billions of dollars in hot money sloshing across the borders, making a joke of monetary policy, fiscal management, and the old concepts about money and debt. As mentioned above, money and information have become nearly equivalent in this global casino. However, information does not behave like any other commodity—it is not scarce. If you give me information you still have it, but I have it too. Since most of the laws of economics are based on scarcity, it is no wonder that economists do not know how to deal with information and have so little to say about abundance.

NEW PARADIGMS FOR THE FUTURE

The differing assumptions held by economists, on the one hand, and futurists and system theorists, who have a humanities or broad interdisciplinary perspective, on the other, are summarized in Table 7.1. Most economists were brought up on the idea of cybernetic systems which are homeostatic and governed by *negative* feedback loops designed to bring the system back to its original form. Like the thermostat on a home heater, when the house/economy gets to a certain temperature the thermostat turns itself off. Although this model might apply to early agrarian or small-scale production economies, conceived in terms of the market-equilibrium, supply/demand theories of today, it is rarely applicable, due to the complexity of networks of production processes.

Today we are dealing with morphogenetic systems that are both internally and structurally dynamic. Such systems are characterized by rapid innovation and evolution, which includes many irreversible components and decisions, and they generate *new* structures because they are governed by *positive* feedback loops. The loops continue to amplify small and probable initial deviations, pushing the whole system and many of its subsystems over thresholds into completely improbable new states. These are precisely the systems being studied by chaos theorists, i.e., general turbulence and unpredictable systems of climate and weather prediction, hydrodynamics, and other areas.

Table 7.1
Differing Perceptions, Assumptions, Forecasting Styles

ECONOMISTS	FUTURISTS/SYSTEMS THEORISTS
forecast from past data, extrapolating trends	construct "what if" scenarios, trends are not destiny
use of optimistic, pessimistic forecasts	identify "preferred futures" plot trends for cross-impacts
change seen as <u>dis-equilibrium</u> (i.e., equilibrium assumed, if all other things are	fundamental change assumed (transformation assumed)
"normal" conditions will return	denial of "normal" conditions in complex systems
reactive (assumed control by the "invisible hand")	pro-active (focus on human choices and responsibilities)
linear reasoning reversible models	living system, organic models
focus on "hard" sciences and data	focus on life sciences, social sciences, "soft", fuzzy data
deterministic reductionist, analytical	indeterminacy, holistic, synthesis, seeking synergy
short-term focus (e.g., discount rates in cost/benefit analysis)	long-term focus, intergenerational costs, benefits and trade offs

non-economic, non-monetarized data seen as "external"
(e.g., voluntary, community sectors, unpaid production, environmental resources)

includes data on voluntary, unpaid productivity, changing values and lifestyles, environmental conditions, maps contexts, external variables (uses post-economic models, technology assessment, environmental and social impact studies)

methods tend to exemplify existing trends (e.g., Wall Street psychology, "herd instinct" in investing, technologies, economic development)

methods "contrarian" (e.g., look for anomalies, check biases in perception, cultural norms) identify latent potentialities

entrepreneurial when "market" is identified

socially entrepreneurial e.g., envision future needs, create new markets)

precise, quantitative forecasts
(e.g., Gross National Product for the next quarter of the year, annual focus)

qualitative focus (e.g., year 2000 studies, anticipatory democracy), date from multiple sources, plot interacting variables, trends in long-term global contexts

Several change models are emerging. One of the most interesting is that developed by NASA in their Earth Systems Science Program. It is widely interdisciplinary, including plate tectonics, biogeochemical and solar-driven processes, strato- and meso-spheres. It provides models of what is happening on this planet from one million through ten thousand year time scales, from one hundred year time scales to points of human intervention, such as fifty or twenty-five year scales. Catastrophe mathematics was developed by Rene Thom in Paris in 1972 and models at least seven modes in which systems change their states.[7]

Cybernetic models, based on work done by Magoroh Maruyama, envision homeostasis and metamorphosis, governed by both negative and positive feedbacks.[8] The order through fluctuation model was developed by Nobel Prize winner Ilya Prigogine.[9] Finally, chaos theorists, such as Ralph Abraham, are discussed in James Gleick's best-selling book, *Chaos*, a useful overview of the development of the theories now outflanking economics.[10] Abraham bases his model on point, periodic, and chaotic attractors which can "magnetize" systems into new states.[11]

All over the world there are economic debates—from China to the Soviet Union, the United States to Europe, and throughout the Southern Hemisphere. They are very old debates about *what is valuable*—but under new conditions. For example, the old economic theories said that air and water were free. But we now know that this is not true—they are becoming more valuable every day. Determining the extent of their value and that of other vanishing natural resources is the key point—most especially since market prices cannot predict *when* they will be exhausted. Cultures are very valuable, but no one has ever figured out how to measure their value. A culture can be seen as a highly compressed information system—a package of software, if you like—that enables a certain population to live in an ecosystem more or less successfully. In my first book, *Creating Alternative Futures: The End of Economics*, I called for an inventory of all value systems of all cultures, and their level of performance (i.e., the "outputs" of behavior and technology) in helping a population to survive in a given ecosystem over historical time frames.[12] I believe survival factors would correlate highly with behavioral characteristics of cooperation, sharing, and honesty.

Another recurring element in the debates concerns the who, what, why, when, where, and how of regulation versus deregulation. Economic dogma is not essential to decide any of these points. To have a conversation about rules, one need not use the box marked "economics" at all! Instead, one can take the much more fruitful approaches of decision sciences and game theory. Whenever the discipline of economics is used to discuss questions of regulation, one immediately gets mired in the ideological battles about whether one is a communist or a capitalist. I have had very fruitful discussions in the past few years with many of my Chinese colleagues, who actually seem ready to transcend the box marked "economics" and at long last give a decent burial to both Karl Marx and Adam Smith.

We must simply move on and realize that the issue is one of *rules of interaction* and governance in human societies which are larger and more technologically adept than any within human historical experience. These ideological debates about regulation and deregulation, and the holy war that has been waged between communism and capitalism, can be taken beyond the context of economics (Table 7.2). On the top left are what economists have referred to as markets and the private sector, with the sets of rules flowing from these designations. Futurists and systems theorists, people from other disciplines, are on the top right, and they refer to these "markets" as open systems of *divisible* resources. They work quite well with win/lose rules, the competitive rules devised by Adam Smith in *The Wealth of Nations*.[13]

Moving back to the first side, we see what economists talk about as the "commons," what they see as common *property* resources. In most textbooks on economics this concept is reduced to a mere footnote; little space

Table 7.2
Models for Describing Rules of Interaction and Value-Systems

ECONOMISTS markets	FUTURISTS/SYSTEMS THEORISTS open systems
private sector individual decisions competition "invisible hand" anti-trust laws property rights (government protection and enforcement)	divisible resources individual decisions win-lose rules Adam Smith's rules laws enforce win-lose and property rights (government protection and enforcement)
commons	**closed systems**

property of all humans (focusing on
   individual-based rules of
   interaction)(often assigns monetary
   values/shadow prices)
public sector
public choice theory
monopoly and oligopoly under regulation
consortia (cooperation)
market intervention to correct market
   "failures"
communal or "socialistic"
"mixed" economies
	individual natural resources, amenities
	   (valued by, but not necessarily the
	   property of, humans)
	arena of public decisions on resource-
	   allocation and rule-making, access
	   to tax supported goods and services,
	   win-win rules, cooperative agreements,
	   treaties, etc., to prevent lose-lose
	   outcomes (i.e., "tragedies of the
	   commons")
	communal, traditional mutual aid,
	   non-money, informal sectors of
	   production and exchange

is devoted to the theory of the commons, even though economists have realized late in the game that this is where the action has moved. The commons are obviously the property of all, i.e., *indivisible* resources, such as air and water, where rules *have* to be set up. This "public sector," as the economists call it, is considered a monopoly under regulation or as consortia. However, these concepts are clouded by their focus on private property and individual rights vis-à-vis community and social needs and rules of interaction. Contrastingly, in systems theory (on the right), the commons is viewed simply as a *closed system*; indivisible resources, requiring win/win rules, necessitate rules of cooperation and agreements. As globalization processes proceed, more and more commons are created.

Significantly, the formerly open, competitive global economy has *itself* become a most crucial commons. In spite of all the dogma and the ideology at the G-7 summit meetings about the global free market and its "competitiveness," all of these leaders and their economists are actually being forced to devise sets of win/win rules and ad hoc agreements, such as the Plaza and Louvre Accords. Simultaneously, most politicians remain captives to macroeconomic advice, what I call the politics of the "last hurrah." The advice economists give to governments is basically centered around choices between fiscal and monetary policies: the brakes or the gas pedal. The brakes use monetarism, tight money, and high interest rates to create a recession in order to "wring inflation out of the system." The gas pedal represents fiscal policies, such as forms of deregulation, investment tax credits, tax cuts, arms buildups, and so on, or monetary policies such as loosening the money supply.

Politicians are really in a terrible fix. The only way they can survive using the macroeconomic management view of the world is to somehow keep four monitors of distress—unemployment, inflation, deficits, and interest rates—within acceptable levels. In this way they can avoid a revolution or getting voted out of office. But that game is getting harder and harder to play, because each time one barometer of distress is brought down, the other three worsen. Furthermore, there is a fifth barometer, external trade deficits, which has become a factor since the domestic policies of all countries are hostage to the interactions of the global financial commons.

The reason macroeconomics no longer works, as well as the reason we need to move to what I call *post*-economic policymaking, is because the system is actually a vicious circle of fast feedback loops (see Figure 7.1). The four barometers of distress are inextricably connected with other variables. Manipulating one thus creates a whole set of effects that permeate the global economy. Additional interactions come from the corporate and sectoral economy (lower right corner) or individuals (top left corner). In the latter case, a group of individuals may decide to opt out of the whole system and initiate their own systems of barter. This so-called underground economy is the fastest growing segment of most economies.

A NEW ECONOMIC MODEL

In the mid-seventies I proposed my own economic reformulation (Figure 7.2), and I am happy to report that it is now getting into the textbooks. Since the economists are always talking about "the pie," my model is "a cake," which goes from a macroeconomics view of the world to a systems view of a productive society. In other words, the icing that tops my cake is what economists call the private sector, which many believe is the only productive sector. While very important and innovative, the private sector rests on the next layer, the public sector. Despite its being an essential infrastructure in all but extreme laissez-faire theories, many economists deny that the public sector is productive. The next layer is the underground economy, which economists are now rushing to examine, because it is throwing off all of their calculations. The two top layers correspond to the economists' pie, and generally tend to be quantified in terms of money coefficients, however erratic (the currency may be dollars, yen, rubles, pounds, or any others). However, since currencies are now widely fluctuating, a new coefficient for measuring *real* purchasing power (Purchasing Power Parity) is becoming increasingly popular.

What economists do *not* look at in any systematic way (although they are beginning to be pushed into looking at it by the rest of us) are the two lower layers of the cake. These nonmonetarized elements are still largely invisible in macroeconomic policy models. The third layer down is the nonmonetary sector: "sweat" equity reflected in do-it-yourself labor, bartering, social, familial, community structures—all of the *un*paid work involved in parenting, volunteering, subsistence agriculture, or mutual aid. This amounts to an enormous oversight since in most of the world's economies this non-monetary economy is much *larger* than the economy that is quantified in terms of money and forms the basis for the official GNP statistics. In industrial societies and the so-called developing societies, sociologists are beginning to quantify the nonmonetary sector. In France, for example, a recent study showed that 53 percent of all productive hours worked were unpaid and only 47 percent were paid. A similar study done in Sweden found a 50/50 split between paid and unpaid productivity, while a 1984 study in Canada came to the same conclusion.

Figure 7.1
Systems Model of an Economy

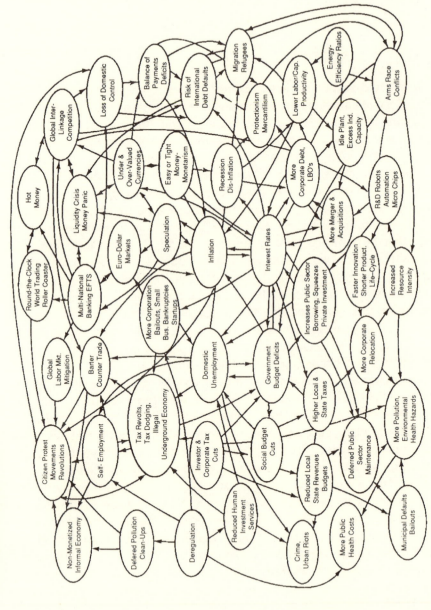

Note the existence of multiple feedback loops and reciprocal relations among various actors and sectors in the overall network.

Figure 7.2
Interactive Productive System of an Industrial Society

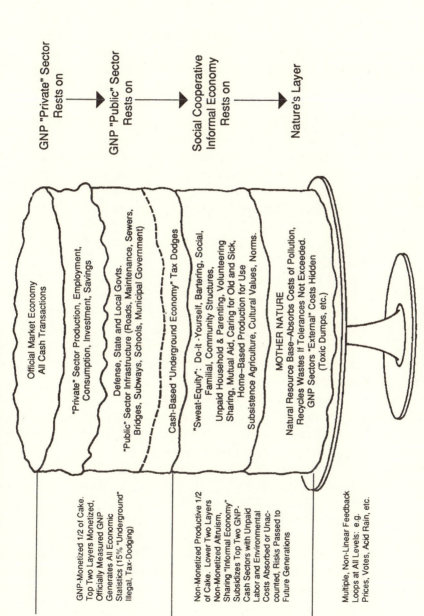

Official Market Economy
All Cash Transactions

"Private" Sector Production, Employment,
Consumption, Investment, Savings

Defense, State and Local Govts.
"Public" Sector Infrastructure (Roads, Maintenance, Sewers,
Bridges, Subways, Schools, Municipal Government)

Cash-Based "Underground Economy" Tax Dodges

"Sweat-Equity": Do-it -Yourself, Bartering, Social,
Familial, Community Structures,
Unpaid Household & Parenting, Volunteering
Sharing, Mutual Aid, Caring for Old and Sick,
Home-Based Production for Use
Subsistence Agriculture, Cultural Values, Norms.

MOTHER NATURE
Natural Resource Base–Absorbs Costs of Pollution,
Recycles Wastes If Tolerances Not Exceeded.
GNP Sectors "External" Costs Hidden
(Toxic Dumps, etc.)

GNP "Private" Sector
Rests on

GNP "Public" Sector
Rests on

Social Cooperative
Informal Economy
Rests on

Nature's Layer

GNP-Monetized 1/2 of Cake.
Top Two Layers Monetized,
Officially Measured GNP
Generates All Economic
Statistics (15% "Underground"
Illegal, Tax-Dodging)

Non-Monetized Productive 1/2
of Cake. Lower Two Layers
Non-Monetized Altruism,
Sharing "Informal Economy"
Subsidizes Top Two GNP-
Cash Sectors with Unpaid
Labor and Environmental
Costs Absorbed or Unac-
counted, Risks Passed to
Future Generations

Multiple, Non-Linear Feedback
Loops at All Levels: e.g.
Prices, Votes, Acid Rain, etc.

This three-layer cake with icing comprises the four productive segments of an economy: the private sector, the public sector, the unpaid economy, and Mother Nature. Only the first two are included in traditional economic theories.

So we see how colossal the error has been—like trying to manage a country with a map of only half the territory.

But the entire cake rests on Mother Nature. If we fail to account for the productivity of Nature we get into a terrible mess. In August 1989 I participated in a meeting hosted by Venezuelan President Carlos Andres Perez, at which recommendations were made for correcting the GNP to reflect all the hidden factors.[14] In most industrial societies the two bottom layers have been ignored, discounted, devalued, even "cannibalized." Indications of their impending destruction are being translated back onto the balance sheets as social and environmental costs. For example, in the United States we have decided that parenting our children is not a very valuable activity. So, needless to say, few people want to do it and conflicts arise as to who will do it. The market economy has picked up on this crisis and we now have day care centers traded on Wall Street—not exactly what we had in mind, but it is better than nothing. A similar solution occurred for the argument over who was going to do the cooking, and fast food companies have stepped into the unwanted role. If you want Mom to cook breakfast, you go down to MacDonald's because that is where "she's serving it up."

In a sense, the same thing has happened with Mother Nature when we overstressed her tolerance and ability to clean up and process our wastes. Nature too revolted, and now we are forced to spend over $30 billion to keep drinkable water coming out of our faucets. Some $100 billion is needed to clean up the nuclear weapons waste. These various social and environmental costs are massive and have yet to be fully quantified. They constitute almost a mirror image of the GNP.

Today all of these issues are becoming part of political and governmental agendas. I spend time with various governments which are now ready to say, "O.K., let's come up with a development plan and indicators that go beyond economics," including Venezuela, West Germany, and the Netherlands. France and Canada are moving in this direction, and bills asking for reformulation of the GNP have been introduced in the United States. Social and quality of life indicators recognized as essential must be added. When we thus correct and expand on the GNP, we will no longer be flying blind. Many needed statistics already are available.

The real wealth of nations lies in their creative, problem-solving citizens. Even the *Economist* magazine in London has come to this conclusion, and now tracks education indicators. We also need health care statistics, including life expectancy, statistics on political participation (such as those gathered by Amnesty International), and air and water quality data (gathered by pollution control departments). Also needed is a breakdown of the GNP to show the distribution of income and wealth, the ratio of civilian to military expenditures, and the rate of energy used per unit of GNP, as well as the quantifying and incorporating of the *un*paid sectors.

We have too many economists, but at least some of them can be taught to overcome their resistance and trained to gather the needed new statistics. Dozens of jobs will open for statisticians able to go beyond the economic method to implement more systematic models. As this global transition accelerates, three "existential" zones of transition emerge—Breakdown, Bifurcation, and Breakthrough. The first is currently being experienced: destructuring, pollution, cultural confusion, wars and conflicts to straighten out our various "-isms." Whether it is Belfast or Lebanon, all around the planet people are learning to mediate each other's "-isms" by learning tolerance. We have "slow motion crises"—holes in the ozone layer, acid rain, the destruction of rain forests. We have erratic governments, unable to manage their affairs, toppling before our eyes. Many more are afraid that we have noticed their dilemmas, as reflected in incoherent media, economic destabilization, disinformation, anarchy, and totalitarian rigidity, all ultimately leading to breakdowns.

But we also can see glimmers of the "breakthrough zone" of metamorphosis, and the "slow motion good news" as many societies go beyond left and right to reformulate their ideas of sustainable development. One such example is Costa Rica where, under the leadership of President Arias and his government, the crucial debate about what constitutes true development has begun. We are recognizing that development means human development, the development of communities and of ecosystems. A very different set of ideas is coming into focus, new structures are being created, and new maps are being drawn of the new territories. New criteria for success are required to shift our attention. I spend most of my time going around the world, and in almost every country I visit I have found the idea of planetary citizenship. Because I cannot learn all the languages I would like to learn, my calling card is the poster I helped create called "Earth Vision." I find that people everywhere understand this image of global unity. When I ask to be introduced to the planetary citizens, I always receive enthusiastic responses, and am led to the most incredible people.

Yet, most of us are still experiencing the discomforts inherent in the middle zone of Bifurcation, which is the transition between Breakdown and Breakthrough. We oscillate back and forth, not knowing whether, in our own lives, it is safer to stay where we are or to jump into something new. The eternal trade-offs between adaption and adaptability are the keys here. I have sensed that many people are beginning to wonder whether their tenure is really secure or whether their program will be funded; whether their company will be merged or acquired. The rate of change is so rapid that people are saying, "I might as well look inward at my *own* values." They ask themselves "What am I doing on this planet? What is my highest purpose and my highest goal for being here? It may be just as well for me to follow my own star as to work for some institution that may be on the verge of collapse." They are learning the difference between money and wealth. Stress, after all, is evolution's tool. We are all being stressed—not to grow in the way of GNP growth, but to grow *up*.

NOTES

1. The now defunct group, Citizens for Clean Air, was founded in New York City in 1964 and successfully lobbied for an air pollution index reported on television and radio news programs.

2. Personal communication with David McClelland at a conference on economics and ecology, 1971.

3. See Hazel Henderson, *The Politics of the Solar Age*, Part 2 (New York: Doubleday /Anchor, 1981; 2d ed., Indianapolis: Knowledge Systems, Inc., 1988), pp. 155–241.

4. A. C. Pigou quoted in Guy Routh, *The Origin of Economic Ideas* (New York: Vintage Press, 1977), p. 105.

5. Hazel Henderson, *The Politics of the Solar Age*, Chapter 10, "Dissecting the Declining Productivity 'Flap,' " pp. 283–321.

6. See Hazel Henderson, "Alternative Economics," *Inquiry*, 3, no. 6 (June 1986).

7. Rene Thom, *Structural Stability and Morphogenesis* (Reading, Mass.: W. A. Benjamin, 1975).

8. See, for example, Magoroh Maruyama, "Paradigmatology and Its Applications," *CYBERNETICA*, 2 (1974).

9. Ilya Prigogine, *From Being to Becoming* (San Francisco: W. H. Freeman, 1980).

10. James Gleick, *Chaos* (New York: Viking Press, 1987).

11. Ralph Abraham, *Dynamics: The Geometry of Behavior*, Part 3, "Global Behavior" (Santa Cruz, Calif.: Arid Press, 1985).

12. Hazel Henderson, *Creating Alternative Futures: The End of Economics* (New York: G. P. Putnam's Sons, 1978), pp. 351–69.

13. See Adam Smith, *An Inquiry into the Nature and Causes of the Wealth of Nations* (Chicago: University of Chicago Press, 1976).

14. The meeting, hosted by Venezuela's International Institute for Advanced Studies (IDEA), was held in Caracas, July 31–August 3, 1989. Excerpts from my report on the meeting, "Measuring the Difference Between Money and Wealth," follow:

The Caracas meeting took a . . . comprehensive approach, calling first for a focus on internationally comparable, fundamental social indicators already available, such as infant mortality, low birth weight and malnutrition (which correlates well with other areas of concern, such as literacy), poverty and basic needs—which can alert countries to predictable social crises now often worsened by IMF (International Monetary Fund) adjustment policies. Secondly, the Caracas group urged that deficiencies in GNP be improved by reformulating statistics already available, including those on income and wealth distribution and poverty gaps; the inclusion of the informal and household sectors (i.e., the total productive hours worked, whether paid or unpaid, which is usually gathered by sociologists), now widely recognized in Latin America as a key to improving overall performance; employment figures that highlight self-employment, community and family enterprises; an energy input to GNP ratio to assess overall efficiency of the processes of extraction, production, delivery and recycling of goods and services; the ratio between military and civilian expenditures, as well as the *net* production figures after deducting social costs, some of which are available or can be estimated, and other forms of double-counting, as well as a more careful evaluation of capital stocks of infrastructure and natural resources and their depletion. At least two environmental indicators were recommended: one to measure depletion, such as hectares of land destroyed, and the other of pollution, such as in urban areas, where large populations are exposed.

SELECTED BIBLIOGRAPHY

Abraham, Ralph. *Dynamics: The Geometry of Behavior*. Santa Cruz, Calif.: Arid Press, 1985.
Gleick, James. *Chaos*. New York: Viking Press, 1987.
Henderson, Hazel. *Creating Alternative Futures: The End of Economics*. New York: G. P. Putnam's Sons, 1978.
————. *The Politics of the Solar Age: Alternatives to Economics*. New York: Doubleday/Anchor, 1981; 2d ed., Indianapolis: Knowledge Systems, Inc., 1988.
Maruyama, Magoroh. "Paradigmatology and Its Applications." *CYBERNETICA*, 2, 1974.
Prigogine, Ilya. *From Being to Becoming*. San Francisco: W. H. Freeman, 1980.
Routh, Guy. *The Origin of Economic Ideas*. New York: Vintage Press, 1977.
Smith, Adam. *An Inquiry into the Nature and Causes of the Wealth of Nations*. Chicago: University of Chicago Press, 1976.
Thom, Rene. *Structural Stability and Morphogenesis*. Reading, Mass.: W. A. Benjamin, 1975.

8 ESCAPING THE OVER-SPECIALIZATION TRAP
CREATING INCENTIVES FOR A TRANSDISCIPLINARY SYNTHESIS

Robert Costanza

WHAT IS TRANSDISCIPLINARY RESEARCH AND WHY DO WE NEED IT?

We live in a complex, rapidly changing technological society whose major problems cannot be effectively tackled using the intellectual tools of any one discipline.[1] Acid rain, global climate change, deforestation, loss of bio-diversity, and energy policy—all cry out for at least an interdisciplinary synthesis. In fact, we need to go beyond interdisciplinary to "transdisciplinary" problem solving.[2]

There is increasing coordination and cooperation involved in research and management from multidisciplinarity (several disciplines with no interaction) through interdisciplinarity (some interactions) and finally to transdisciplinarity (full interaction). Despite almost universal agreement that we need the highest possible levels of integration and cooperation to address our current problems, the last several decades have seen little movement in that direction. This chapter tries to uncover the fundamental reasons for this lack of progress and to provide insights into possible solutions.

Inter- and transdisciplinary research differs from typical disciplinary research in its basic focus and goals. Disciplinary research seeks to increase knowledge and techniques within a limited intellectual sphere while inter- and transdisciplinary research are multiskilled and problem focused. We need both; the problem is how to encourage both in proper proportions.

The problem with today's academic specialization is that it is too inflexible, and hence is inappropriate in a time of rapid and unpredictable technical and social change. It is a carryover from an earlier, more stable and predictable period. The world has changed, but the reinforcement system that maintains our rigid academic disciplines has not. Society today would be better served by more generalists, but the system continues to produce only specialists. We are caught in a trap of overspecialization.

SOCIAL TRAPS

Life is full of circumstances where apparently rational individual choices are nevertheless inconsistent with the long-term interests of either the individual or society. The decision-maker seems "trapped" by local conditions into making what ultimately turns out to be a sub-optimal decision.[3] We go through life making decisions about which path to take based largely on "road signs," the immediate reinforcements that we perceive, such as monetary incentives, social acceptance or admonishment, and physical pleasure or pain. Normally, following these road signs works well, unless they are inaccurate or misleading. Then we become trapped into following a path that is ultimately detrimental. For example, cigarette smoking is a social trap because by following the short-run road signs of the pleasure and social status associated with smoking, we embark on the road to an increased risk of premature death. Furthermore, once a road is taken, most people find it difficult to change to another.

Social scientists employ various terms for this kind of experience.[4] The "social traps" terminology developed in the field of social psychology provides the most general and experimentally based coverage of the whole class of phenomena.[5] Social traps can have several causes. Table 8.1 is a taxonomy of these causes, along with some representative traps associated with each.[6] Cigarette smoking, for example, is mainly a time-delay trap where positive and negative reinforcements are separated in time. Traps can also arise from ignorance of the relevant reinforcements; from the change of reinforcements with time (sliding reinforcer traps); from the externalization of some important reinforcements from the accounting system (externality traps); from the actions of some individuals affecting the group in adverse ways (collective traps); or from a combination of these (hybrid traps). Some specific examples follow.

An important example in recent social psychology research has been the "prisoner's dilemma" game, a famous externality trap.[7] In this game two players must each choose either to cooperate with one another or defect to authorities. If both cooperate, they both reap a moderate reward (say three units each). If both defect they both get a much smaller reward (say one unit each). If one cooperates while the other defects the cooperator gets nothing (the "sucker's payoff") while the defector gets a reward larger

Table 8.1
A Short Taxonomy of Social Traps (After 6)

Cause	Examples
Time Delay	Discounting, smoking, drug addiction in general
Ignorance	Slot machines, gambler's fallacy
Sliding Reinforcer	Pesticide overuse
Externality	Pollution, the prisoner's dilemma
Collective	Tragedy of the commons
Hybrid	

than that for mutual cooperation (say five units). Under these conditions, if the players cannot communicate with each other, the optimum strategy is to defect. Without information about the other player, one must assume the worst to avoid the sucker's payoff. The situation changes radically if the game is played several times with the same participants, however. Then each player has the record of the other's past behavior to go on, and the optimum strategy is not obvious.

When Robert Axelrod held a computer tournament pitting various submitted strategies against one another in a round robin tournament of the iterated prisoner's dilemma, he found that a simple strategy called *tit for tat* won the tournament.[8] It cooperates on the first move, then does whatever its opponent did last time. By not looking beyond the current move, one fell into the always-defect trap, missing the opportunity to reap the benefits of mutual cooperation. *Tit for tat*, only one move more farsighted than *always defect*, worked dramatically better!

There are strategies that could have won the tournament. One of these cooperates on the first move and then looks at the entire past history of the opponent's moves to generate a time-weighted expected value for the opponent's next move. In the iterated prisoner's dilemma, then, it pays to assume the best of the other player at least until you have been proven wrong, and to have a good memory.

The tragedy of the commons is another well-known social trap used to study overexploitation of renewable natural resources.[9] The classic commons trap goes something like this: There is a common property resource (say grazing land). Each individual user (rancher) sees the personal cost for utilizing an additional unit of the resource (the purchase price of one more animal) as small and constant, and much less than the expected benefit (from later selling that animal). However, the overall cost to all the users of each additional resource unit consumed (animal added) increases exponentially as the resource becomes stressed. Eventually, one additional animal (which costs its owner no more than the first) leads to the destruction of the resource (at tremendous cost to the animal's owner and the rest of the ranchers). The tragedy of the commons is a collective trap that occurs because the short-term costs and benefits of utilizing the resource apparent to the individual are inconsistent with the long-term costs and benefits to the collective society of failing to maintain the resource.

The elimination of social traps requires intervention—the modification of the reinforcement system. John Cross and Melvin Guyer list four strategies to avoid or escape such traps: education about the long-term distributed impacts; insurance; superordinate authority (i.e., legal systems, government, religion); and conversion of the trap into a trade-off (i.e., correcting the road signs).[10]

Education can be used to warn of long-term impacts not immediately obvious. Examples are the warning labels on cigarette packages and the warnings of environmentalists about future hazardous waste problems. But warnings can be ignored, particularly if the path seems otherwise enticing. Education, moreover, is time-consuming in a society as large and complex as ours, where we do not expect even professionals, much less the general public, to know the details of all the extant traps. In addition, for education to be effective in avoiding commons-type traps, such as resource depletion or pollution, *all* participants must be educated or the system breaks down.

Governments can, of course, forbid or regulate certain actions that have been deemed socially inappropriate. The problem with this approach is that in the absence of widespread education and acceptance, it must be rigidly monitored and enforced, and the strong short-term incentive for individuals to try to ignore or avoid the regulations remains. A police force and legal system are overheads of this approach, with costs increasing exponentially the more complete the level of regulation.

Appropriate behaviors instilled through religious beliefs and social customs are much less expensive ways to avoid certain social traps. On the other hand, these only work under certain conditions: the required behavior must be relatively static to allow beliefs learned early in life to remain in force later, and a relatively homogeneous community of like-minded individuals is required to be truly effective. This system works well in culturally homogeneous societies that are changing very slowly, but not in modern, heterogeneous, rapidly changing societies.

Many trap theorists believe that the most effective method for avoiding and escaping from social traps is to turn the trap into a trade-off by correcting the inaccuracies in the road signs. Take slot machines as an example. Playing slot machines is a social trap because the long-term costs and benefits are inconsistent with the perceived short-term costs and benefits.[11] People play because they expect a large short-term jackpot, while the machines are in fact programed to pay off, say, $0.80 on the dollar in the long term. People may "win" hundreds of dollars in the short run, but if they play long enough they will certainly lose $0.20 for every dollar played. To change this trap to a trade-off, one could simply reprogram the machines so that every time a dollar was put in, $0.80 would come out, making short-term reinforcements ($0.80 on the dollar) consistent with long-term reinforcements ($0.80 on the dollar). Only dedicated aficionados of spinning wheels with fruit painted on them would continue to play. In the more prosaic world of resource management, one could turn the trap into a trade-off by taxing any consumption above the optimum level for resource stability.[12] This would remove the short-term incentive to take more than the system could sustain, since cost and benefit are felt simultaneously.

LOCAL, SHORT-TERM INCENTIVES TO SPECIALIZE VS. GLOBAL, LONG-TERM NEEDS FOR INTEGRATED KNOWLEDGE

Our educational system is caught in several overlapping hybrid traps. The overspecialization trap results from the incentives built into the system that encourage specialization, obfuscation, territoriality, and problem perpetration, instead of cooperative, integrated problem solving and the development of a useful base of "knowledge" (as opposed to "information"). No grand plan or planner set this trap. It is a natural outcome of the past rules of the system, the result of not paying enough explicit attention to global, long-term educational and research needs, and more importantly, of not developing effective mechanisms for implementing these needs.

The roots of this trap can be traced to the local reinforcement system for academics: decisions about hiring, tenure and promotion. In most colleges and universities, these decisions are based mainly on the number of refereed publications *in reputable journals in one's discipline*. Teaching and public service are always mentioned as equal criteria, but are rarely given much weight. Young assistant professors are under tremendous pressure to publish, and the best way to meet this short-term demand is to find something that no one else is doing and to pick away at it a little at a time (more papers that way). The less relevant this niche the better, so that it generates a minimum of controversy that can slow publication. Once tenure is secured, professors are theoretically free to pursue larger, more relevant questions, but their training from graduate school onward so accustoms them to the specialized mode that broadening seldom occurs. In the sciences, outside funding policies for research further reinforce a lifetime of narrow specialization.

The net result of this reinforcement system is the erection of walls between disciplines and between subdisciplines, and a gradual narrowing of each discipline's research agenda. The research agenda are largely set autonomously from within the discipline, and gradually become so esoteric that only initiates in the discipline have even a rudimentary understanding of the subject matter. This also helps protect the discipline's intellectual turf.

Finally, overspecialization among professors directly affects curricula, which are becoming more and more detailed at earlier and earlier stages. This overemphasis on detail and curricular narrowness is even trickling down into high schools and out into society as a whole, which is becoming a loose aggregation of "experts" who can scarcely communicate with each other.

ESCAPING FROM THE OVERSPECIALIZATION TRAP

Escaping from the overspecialization trap requires, at minimum, changing the criteria for tenure and promotion. In the future, problem solving will become the primary function of academics, occurring through multiple activities, not just research publications. We shall need specific rewards for pursuing inter- and transdisciplinary problems. Under the current system, activities outside one's narrow specialty receive little (sometimes even negative) professional credit. Given their time constraints, young faculty *cannot afford to stray* from narrow disciplinary boundaries. We must therefore explicitly reward inter- and transdisciplinary effort in the tenure and promotion review process so young faculty *can afford to become transdisciplinary*.

There are several mutually reinforcing ways to achieve this:

1. By creating permanent colleges, departments, or programs of integrated, transdisciplinary studies within which the criteria for promotion and tenure are explicitly transdisciplinary. These departments could coexist with traditional disciplinary departments.
2. By creating programs outside the university to nurture inter- and transdisciplinary research. This would include both traditional research funding agencies as well as programs that encourage networks of researchers to come together on specific problems.

3. By creating new inter- and transdisciplinary fields of study, or "meta-disciplines."
4. By modifying the tenure and promotion criteria of existing disciplinary departments so that transdisciplinary excursions are seen as positive, rather than negative or neutral activities.

All of these courses of action need to be pursued simultaneously. Here I shall briefly describe several interdisciplinary programs and activities within and external to universities with which I have direct experience, and that seem to have been at least partially successful.

Extra-University Interdisciplinary Programs

If the disciplinary structure within the university is what is hampering interdisciplinary studies, why not start programs outside the university? The Kellogg Foundation of Battle Creek, Michigan, has run an interdisciplinary fellowship program since 1980, aimed at solving human problems. Each year, approximately fifty fellows are chosen from a broad range of disciplines. I was a fellow from 1982 to 1985. Fellows commit 25 percent of their time for three years to the program, which includes a self-directed interdisciplinary project and several week-long workshops with other fellows. This allows long-term friendships to develop within a network of interdisciplinary researchers. The program is very successful at encouraging interdisciplinary awareness and research by allowing fellows to interact at a high level with others from a broad range of disciplines.

Significant problems with the extra-university program approach are:

1. It does not change the tenure and promotion criteria at the participants' home institutions. The fellowship program takes time away from disciplinary research and the interdisciplinary activities of the fellow's program are not adequately credited.
2. Being expensive, it affords interdisciplinary experience to only a small number of fellows. The majority of university researchers are left out.

Departments of Interdisciplinary Studies

Universities have developed many explicitly interdisciplinary programs, departments, colleges, centers, and schools over the years. The Schools of Natural Resources at the University of Michigan and Ohio State University, and the Center for Quantitative Studies at the University of Washington are good examples of large-scale implementations of this idea. The Center for Environmental and Estuarine Studies (CEES) at the University of Maryland, where I am currently employed, is another. These problem-focused programs use a multiskill approach to attack complex environmental and resource issues. CEES has been very successful at performing high quality environmental research and attracting high quality researchers. Its Marine-Estuarine-Environmental Sciences (MEES) program, a university-wide interdisciplinary graduate education program, has grown from five students in 1979 to 160 in 1989, reflecting the growing desire of students to participate in broad interdisciplinary environmental programs.

Maryland also recently started a unique program in Coastal and Environmental Policy, that combines components from CEES, the Law School, the School of Public Affairs, and other components both inside and outside the university to address the full range of disciplines involved in environmental problems.

Significant problems with the "separate program" approach are:

1. Unless tenure and promotion decisions reside completely within the interdisciplinary program, faculty may still be judged only by disciplinary criteria. It is rare that tenure and promotion decisions *do* reside completely within the program and it is therefore rare that interdisciplinary programs survive within the university.

2. Because there are so few interdisciplinary programs, the academic job market still selects for disciplinary specialists when hiring. This tends to erode the interdisciplinary nature of the programs because faculty and students are constantly trying to remain in some disciplinary category so they will be tenurable or marketable.

New Interdisciplinary Fields of Study: The Meta-discipline

Another approach is to create new fields of study that are explicitly inter- and transdisciplinary. These "meta-disciplines" might eventually achieve equal stature with the traditional disciplines within the university. Three newly hatched meta-disciplines are: Ecological Economics, Landscape Ecology, and Earth System Science.

Ecological Economics is concerned with integrating the study and management of "nature's household" (ecology) and "humankind's household" (economics). No discipline today studies the web of interconnections uniting the economic subsystem to the overall ecosystem of which it is a part. Ecological Economics aims to fill this gap by becoming a meta-discipline incorporating aspects of ecology, economics, anthropology, sociology, political science, biology, and so on.[13] There is a new journal, *Ecological Economics*, which I edit, an International Society for Ecological Economics (ISEE), and a Foundation for Ecological Economics at the University of Sienna, Italy. These constitute the new meta-discipline, Ecological Economics.

Landscape Ecology is concerned with extending ecology to large spatial and temporal scales and integrating it with geography, landscape architecture and urban planning, anthropology, climatology, and so on. It has a journal titled *Landscape Ecology*, an International Society for Landscape Ecology, and several university departments of Landscape Ecology scattered around the world.

Earth System Science is an outgrowth of the recent scientific and policy interest in global climate change. It has a strong research agenda based on integrating geography, climatology, remote sensing, ecology, marine sciences, and so on. I know of no journal or society with this specific name, but several university programs are being structured around Earth System Science and I imagine journals and societies will soon follow.

These are but examples of the many meta-disciplines in existence. They often overlap, pointing to the non-exclusive character that differentiates them from traditional disciplines. By focusing on problems rather than intellectual turf they have no need for exclusivity, exhibiting instead cooperation, synergism, pluralism, and enhanced communication.

Significant problems with the meta-discipline approach are:

1. It takes many years to establish a new discipline or meta-discipline, and unless faculty can meantime find support elsewhere (i.e. in traditional disciplines) the meta-discipline may never emerge.

2. Unless specific countermeasures are taken, meta-disciplines may succumb to the same forces that affect traditional disciplines, becoming more specialized and narrow with time.

Modifying the Incentive Structures of Existing Departments

A necessary adjunct to setting up any program of transdisciplinary studies is to encourage existing departments to acknowledge the value of transdisciplinary activity by their faculty. Often given lip service, this is seldom taken to heart where it counts: in the tenure and promotion criteria. To allow both disciplinary and transdisciplinary research—and related professional activities—to co-exist in a synergistic and equally rewarded way, promotions criteria might include something like:

The criteria for tenure and promotion are excellence in problem solving and/or teaching, within a single discipline and/or in an inter- or transdisciplinary program.

There would, of course, be details on how to handle individual versus team contributions, the inherent difficulty of the problems attacked, and so forth.

This statement of criteria would allow several strategies for academic success, as shown in Table 8.2. The traditional strategy of single discipline research with little emphasis on teaching would continue to be supported, but with the emphasis on "problem solving" and not just "research as reflected in publications" as is now the case. This makes the relevance and difficulty of the problems attacked part of the criteria and discourages the "least publishable unit" syndrome. Teaching, however, would be recognized and given equal weight. One could thus remain within a single discipline and pursue any of the three teaching/research strategies shown in Table 8.2 with equal expectation of promotion.

Table 8.2
Possible Successful Strategies within Traditional Academic Departments under the New Criteria

| | Research/Teaching Strategy | | |
Disciplinary Strategy	Mainly Research	Mixed Research and Teaching	Mainly Teaching
Disciplinary	Disciplinary Researcher	Disciplinary Researcher/Teacher	Disciplinary Teacher
Mixed Disciplinary and Transdisciplinary	Mixed Researcher	Mixed Researcher/Teacher	Mixed Teacher
Transdisciplinary	Transdisciplinary Researcher	Transdisciplinary Researcher/Teacher	Transdisciplinary Teacher

Similarly, equal rewards would be given for those spending part or full time in transdisciplinary pursuits, as shown in the rest of the matrix in Table 8.2. In total there would be nine survivable strategies for faculty under the new criteria, as opposed to the single strategy (Disciplinary Researcher) available to most faculty today. It would allow faculty in traditional departments to participate in transdisciplinary programs because those activities would be given positive weight in tenure and promotion decisions.

Implementation would probably be a struggle on most campuses, since academic departments are among the most tradition-bound and territorial entities known. But on campuses with forward-thinking presidents and faculty, the struggle may succeed. Campuses that successfully implemented the new criteria would begin to reap significant benefits in the form of more research contracts, more relevant research, better teaching, better communication and coordination among faculty, and better faculty morale due to a more cooperative sense of shared purpose. Their new transdisciplinary programs and meta-disciplinary departments would attract more funding, better faculty, and most importantly, high quality students. Eventually, through a process of selection, the new criteria would become the most common.

CONCLUSIONS

We can create a new transdisciplinary intellectual Renaissance, and the Renaissance men and women to populate it, by appropriately modifying the incentive structures for faculty and students. The lever we can use to initiate this is the criteria for tenure and promotion at the university level. If we can effectively change these criteria we can open the door to problem-focused, inter- and transdisciplinary research and teaching. There is no shortage of potential new programs, but experience has shown that they will not long survive without modifying the tenure and promotion criteria to allow freer participation by all university faculty.

NOTES

Many thanks to R. Ulanowicz, B. Rothschild, and J. Bartholomew for their useful comments on earlier drafts. The Kellogg Foundation provided three years of funding to think about these topics and did not require immediate results. That, I think, is truly commendable. This paper is dedicated to the memory of the late Dr. Ian Morris, former director of the Center for Environmental and Estuarine Studies, whose vision of transdisciplinary research inspired so many.

1. Daryl E. Chubin, Alan L. Porter, Frederick A. Rossini, and Terry Connolly, eds., *Interdisciplinary Analysis and Research: Theory and Practice of Problem-Focused Research and Development* (Mt. Airy, Md.: Lomond Publications, Inc., 1986); B. Wilpert, "Meshing Interdisciplinarity with Internationality," in R. T. Barth and R. Steck, eds., *Interdisciplinary Research Groups: Their Management and Organization*, Proceedings of the First International Conference on Interdisciplinary Research Groups, Schloss, Reisenburg, FRG, 1979, pp. 168–79; Francesco di Castri, "Planning International Interdisciplinary Research," *Science and Public Policy*, 5 (1978), 254–66.

2. Erich Jantsch, "Inter- and Transdisciplinary University: A Systems Approach to Education and Innovation, *Policy Sciences*, 1 (1970), 4–18; Erich Jantsch, *Technological Planning and Social Futures* (London: Cassell Business Programs, 1972).

3. John G. Cross and Melvin J. Guyer, *Social Traps* (Ann Arbor: University of Michigan Press, 1980); John Platt, "Social Traps," *American Psychologist*, 28 (1973),

642–51; Allan I. Teger, *Too Much Invested to Quit* (New York: Pergamon, 1980); Robert Costanza, "Social Traps and Environmental Policy," *BioScience*, 37 (1987), 407–12.

4. Garrett Hardin, "The Tragedy of the Commons," *Science*, 162 (1968), 1243–8.

5. See references cited in Note 3.

6. Cross and Guyer, *Social Traps*.

7. Robert Axelrod, *The Evolution of Cooperation* (New York: Basic Books, 1984).

8. Axelrod, *The Evolution of Cooperation*.

9. Hardin, "The Tragedy of the Commons."

10. Cross and Guyer, *Social Traps*.

11. Cross and Guyer, *Social Traps*.

12. Julian J. Edney and Christopher S. Harper, "The Effects of Information in a Resource Management Problem: A Social Trap Analog," *Human Ecology*, 6 (1978), 387–95; Robert Costanza and Wesley Shrum, "The Effects of Taxation on Moderating the Conflict Escalation Process: An Experiment Using the Dollar Auction Game," *Social Science Quarterly*, 69 (1988), 416–32.

13. Robert Costanza, "What Is Ecological Economics?" *Ecological Economics*, 1 (1989), 1–7; Robert Costanza and Herman E. Daly, "Toward an Ecological Economics," *Ecological Modeling*, 38 (1987), 1–7.

SELECTED BIBLIOGRAPHY

Axelrod, Robert. *The Evolution of Cooperation*. New York: Basic Books, 1984.

Brockner, Joel, and Jeffrey Z. Rubin. *Entrapment in Escalating Conflicts: A Social Psychological Analysis*. New York: Springer-Verlag, 1985.

Chubin, Daryl E., Alan L. Porter, Frederick A. Rossini, and Terry Connolly, eds. *Interdisciplinary Analysis and Research: Theory and Practice of Problem-Focused Research and Development*. Mt. Airy, Md.: Lomond Publications, Inc., 1986.

Costanza, Robert. "What Is Ecological Economics?" *Ecological Economics* 1(1989), 1–7.

———. "Social Traps and Environmental Policy." *BioScience* 37 (1987), 407–12.

Cross, John G., and Melvin J. Guyer. *Social Traps*. Ann Arbor: University of Michigan Press, 1980.

Hardin, Garrett. "The Tragedy of the Commons." *Science* 162 (1968), 1243–48.

Jantsch, Erich. *Technological Planning and Social Futures* London: Cassell Business Programs, 1972.

Odum, Eugene P. "The Emergence of Ecology as a New Integrative Discipline." *Science* 195 (1977), 1289–93.

Teger, Allan I. *Too Much Invested to Quit*. New York: Pergamon, 1980.

9 CONSTRUCTIVE LINKING
TOWARD A MATRIX
APPROACH IN HIGHER
EDUCATION

Terrence H. White

THE CONTEMPORARY GLOBAL SCENE

In those rare moments when we are able to sit back and reflect on what is going on around us, it is easy to be overwhelmed with the sense that these are chaotic and changing times. Not only changing times, but tricky times—rapid and major technological advances; drought and famine; major health problems such as cancer and AIDS; continuing and unthinking degradation of our precious environmental resources; apparent normalizing of violence in human interactions through hijackings, terrorism, family violence, youth gangs "swarming" or "wilding," and other equally cowardly acts; continuing festering sores of wars and bitter disputes aided by the killing efficiency of modern weaponry; uncertainties in the disposal of nuclear wastes and decommissioned reactors; and the tragic living death and misery resulting from rampaging illicit drug trades.

Even to begin such a listing is difficult, and doubly discouraging, because you soon realize that it is going to be impossible to include every relevant concern. Our world—our environment—is characterized by enormous uncertainties and complexities, and is anyone forecasting that the future will be simpler and more tranquil?

Comedian Woody Allen has described our times as "a crossroads—down one road is gloom, doom, and misery; down the other is nuclear war. I hope that our leaders have the wisdom to pick the right path." Certainly these are tricky times and individuals do need to be educated well, to be in tune with their environments, with what is going on around them, as never before, if they are to be adaptive, successful, and, most importantly, survivors.

As educated citizens, we are well aware of these slippages in the quality of our lives. Some of us, although very busy with our careers and other activities, may even have become involved in fighting an issue that so irritated our sensitivities that we felt we had no choice. But for the most part, while people may not like society's drift, they seem inclined to step aside with a detached resignation and let the tide roll by them, thinking someone else will look after things. This is not a very encouraging picture and history may not be too kind in judging our resignation and avoidance of responsibility.

EDUCATION

But what about our role as educators? Universities are unique institutions in our societies. Like other educational institutions, their primary mandate is to disseminate knowledge. But it is their secondary task, generating new knowledge, that sets universities apart. How well we perform these two roles is vital to the success of our contributions to significant progress on the staggering problems now faced.

Unfortunately, some members of the world university community may not be as well suited to make their best contributions to the identification and eventual resolution of problems impinging on the overall quality of our lives. Many universities, for instance, are perennially underfunded, provide substandard learning environments for students, inadequate and often deteriorating buildings, outdated equipment, and increasingly limited library collections.

Moreover, some universities fall far short of being vibrant intellectual communities that both respect the foundations of individual disciplines and encourage scholars with diverse backgrounds to address problems from an interdisciplinary perspective. In other words, some universities are not communities of interrelating scholars, but merely collections of separate discipline fiefdoms, sharing a common real estate tract.

Commitment to Change

Due to these and other factors, there seems to be little sustained anxiety about or interest in the academy concerning what should be done to better equip our students for the realities of the world in which they will be expected to participate. I am reminded of a two-peaked baseball cap I saw—each peak pointing in different directions. Emblazoned across the front, it read, "Hey, Wait for Me, I'm the Leader." Not enough of our universities are taking the lead in these critical times to focus on the complexities of what should be the central elements in their undergraduate curricula. Instead, many are coasting along the same old paths.

How many of our universities have as an explicit educational objective the need to sensitize their students to the urgent nature of what is unfolding on planet Earth? How many are arming their graduates with not only an increased awareness of these issues, but also a sense of hope that with the appropriate values, attitudes, and tools, we can begin to significantly redirect our behaviors toward more sane, responsible, and civilized objectives? People must be charged to take a greater interest in and concern for the consequences of their actions. They must become agents for informed change and work against resignation and detachment, while more carefully weighing the consequences of environmental and value trade-offs.

Students

A useful catalyst and stimulus for examining a university's purpose and direction in these challenging times is Allan Bloom's book, *The Closing of the American Mind* ("How Higher Education Has Failed Democracy and Impoverished the Souls of Today's Students"). Although not a detailed prescription for curriculum revision, it asks many probing and searching questions essential to informed decisions about the vital redirection universities must consider.

Thus Bloom observes, "I have for more than thirty years, with the utmost interest, watched and listened to students. What they bring to their higher education, in passions, curiosities, longings, and especially previous experience, has changed; and therewith the task of educating them has changed."[1] We can all agree that students entering universities mirror what they have experienced in society and this influences their expectations about what they seek from their time at universities.

Bloom is concerned about the current shape of American society and the direction of its drift. He regrets a decline in the sense of what the United States, as a nation, stands for and the sense of who they are. The shared sense of community with standards of right and wrong seems to be elusive as we face tough questions involving values and morals in the complex issues of abortion, euthanasia, capital punishment, homosexuality, and so on.

Instead of having a social consensus as to the appropriate course to follow on these and other difficult life questions, Bloom maintains that the many nationalities, races, religions, and other pluralistic traditions of the diverse makeup of Americans are all viewed as being equally valid. In the absence of an American way, an American standard, truth is viewed as relative. The United States has become so committed to openness and democratic egalitarianism that in order not to discriminate against opposing views, all positions are to be tolerated. In Bloom's words, "What right, they ask, do I or anyone else have to say one is better than the others?"[2] As a result, truth becomes relative. Under these circumstances of openness, relativism, and efforts to avoid discrimination, prejudice, and conflict, people stop looking for truth—for what is right and wrong. They stop thinking and so the American mind seeks solace in inner solitude.

This view of the relativity of truth that young people hold as a precondition of existence in a democratic state, Bloom sees as destroying their ability to engage in the critical thought necessary to extend knowledge. He has a sympathetic ally in a Canadian Professor of English, Dominic Manganiello, who recently wrote a review of Bloom's book. Manganiello says, "The tendency of the democratic mind to accept every opinion as equally valid has led to a shallowness and intellectual mush. I once read of a Harvard professor who used to tell his students every year, 'By all means have an open mind . . . but not so open that your brains fall out.' "[3]

Universities

What about the universities and their ability to adopt a changing educational role? As the student rebellions of the sixties undermined societal institutions, universities were particularly hard hit. In Bloom's words, "The democratization of the university helped dismantle its structure and caused it to lose focus."[4] He suggests that today American universities generally lack clarity in the design of their curriculum, providing little guidance for students in shaping meaningful academic programs. Lacking coherence, little effort is made to link the various departmentalized disciplines, and scant university-wide agreement exists as to what constitutes an appropriate university education. Hence, the university that "has to stand for something,"[5] does not. In sum, "These great universities—which can split the atom, find cures for the most terrible diseases, conduct surveys of whole populations and produce massive dictionaries of lost languages—cannot generate a modest program of general education for undergraduate students. This is a parable for our times."[6] Whether one agrees with Bloom's thesis, his observations are provoking, challenging, and extremely useful as a stimulus for thinking through and assessing what universities are doing and where they should be heading.

Other Factors in Society

There is no doubt that in our increasingly complex societies, social issues are more plentiful and difficult. What hope is there for concerned citizens to be able to sort through and comprehend these issues, to become knowledgeable enough to make informed judgments as to appropriate positions—whether on gun control, AIDS, abortion, nuclear energy, or whatever? Given our increased mobility and frequent change of residence, is it any wonder that relationships may become increasingly superficial?

These two observations suggest that the social tendencies referred to by Bloom are characteristic, in varying degrees, of most modern, advanced, multicultural societies. In addition to the factors of openness, egalitarianism, tolerance, and a relativity of truth, I see others, perhaps even more important ones, at work as well. For instance, I am reminded of Alvin Toffler's point in *Future Shock*. It has been more than fifteen years since Toffler speculated about what our future would look like before the end of the century. A major message of the book has tended to get lost in the shuffle—his suggestion that as relentless change and uncertainty grinds away at people, they begin to develop signs of "future shock." Future shock refers to the stresses, confusions, and sense of resignation experienced by people exposed to too much change too quickly. It happens when we get overloaded with more change than we can comfortably handle. Future shock—too much change too quickly.[7] I suspect that something like future shock or burnout contributes to a sense of resignation, passive acceptance, powerlessness, or shallowness regarding the major issues, born of our inability to cope with change.

Another important aspect of our society that shapes young people's attitudes is consumerism. We have been experiencing a lengthy period where heavy emphasis has been placed on material measures of success, including the car one drives and whether one follows the latest fad or fashion. Conspicuous consumption and the media barrage pushing us to buy, buy, buy have affected us all, particularly successive generations of young people. For them, education takes on a utilitarian dimension—as a means to a material end, a good job that brings the kind of money needed to become a prolific consumer.

Hence, many factors make effective citizenship demanding and perplexing, presenting a challenge to universities. These factors must be addressed in deciding how to educate our students. Education is a primary catalyst in any formula for greater sanity and global responsibility, and universities have a significant leadership role to play. H. G. Wells prophetically suggested that "Human history becomes more and more a race between education and catastrophe."8

Curriculum

Given the complexities and uncertainties of life, what should be the role of universities in educating people—preparing them for what lies ahead? What elements should be included in an undergraduate curriculum?

One approach is illustrated in the story of a mother shopping for a toy for her child's birthday. She looked at one toy and could not figure out how it worked. "Isn't this a rather complicated toy for a small child?" she asked the clerk. "Madam," he replied, "that is an *educational* toy, designed by psychologists to help prepare youngsters to live in today's world. No matter how the kid puts the thing together, it's wrong."

A more useful insight comes from Giovanni Agnelli, Chairman of Fiat—the giant Italian automaker. Speaking to an international gathering of academics and dignitaries celebrating the 900th anniversary of the establishment of the University of Bologna, Agnelli suggested that the two purposes of universities—to teach and to do research—were even more important today because of the complexities we have already discussed. Universities need to provide students with a general education because, in his view,

Advanced training is needed in many more activities than before. Some people fear that a technological civilization degrades human labour. I think that fear is groundless. Handwork is certainly less common, but this state of affairs leaves more room for brainwork and makes it more necessary. The need to employ very different disciplines in a single occupation broadens the required scope of study and knowledge; a good economist has to know something about technology, and a good engineer something of economics. No one can run a business successfully unless he has extensive general knowledge, each part of which is complementary to the rest.9

I strongly endorse Agnelli's thoughts and conclusions about the university's mission as:

primarily a place where young people learn their true profession, which is being able to use their intelligence in all the unforeseeable difficulties that crop up in working life, and in the constantly changing conditions of the outside world. The university should once again be the place where even humanistic culture (now all too lightly dismissed as useless in an industrial society) can find a sense of purpose and a new role for itself.10

Bloom was not very complimentary in his view of today's students entering universities in the United States. His concerns centered, among other things, on their lack of both motivation for real learning and intellectual curiosity, and their instrumental view of education. My experience, however, is not as negative—I find today's students bring much more of a mixture of values and attitudes with them. Some, it is true, are as Bloom describes, and to them the university seems like the next stop on a bus ride through life. Their attitude is reflected in the ubiquitous question, "What is the easiest way for me to get over this hurdle?" For some students intent on entering law or medicine, for example, their sole interest and motivation in preliminary studies is to get the highest grades possible, thus guaranteeing admission to the next step in their professional training. In contrast, other students who enter the university seem challenged by a good curriculum and good teaching, and have exciting and stimulating learning experiences. What *happens* in a university can greatly affect a student's attitude and performance. Large classes and uninspired teaching turn off even the most dedicated students.

I am suggesting that in complex times and with students who are unsure of their values and goals, universities that know what to do and do it well can make an enormous difference. A friend of mine who teaches Chinese told me that the translation for the word university (*ta hsüeh*) is "great learning." Today, universities and colleges have the opportunity and the challenge to provide "great learning" for our students and our societies. Education is not just narrowly based technical training; rather, a good university education must contain a blend of life skills and job skills.

Among other things, education should contribute to personal enrichment by developing perceptive analytical and critical judgment, effective communication skills, appreciation of the arts and languages, an understanding of world history, the operation of our major institutions, the scientific method, and comparative study of major value systems. To achieve these ends, a university has to selectively construct curricular frameworks for all students, regardless of discipline or field of study. A good base of carefully prescribed general education courses and learning activities encourages development of life skills, which given a more specialized focus develop job skills.

No single combination of courses provides a perfect educational mix. Instead, the specifics of core educational elements and experiences vary widely and depend upon the particular focus and resources of each university. The debate over how to determine the central, skeletal elements of a curriculum is not easily resolved, however, as vested interests and other distractions hinder consensus. Still the debates must commence if universities are to provide the leadership needed in arresting the prevailing societal drift.

STRATEGIES FOR CHANGE

At many universities the specifics of curricula are *not* a university-wide concern. Instead, each constituent faculty, school, or college is left to determine, usually in association with its individual departments, the pattern of courses required to complete a degree in a particular major or field of specialty. Innovative curriculum designs that prepare graduates for the complexities of society we have been describing may indeed arise from such a decentralized design process. However the curriculum tends to reflect the narrower background preparation for understanding the particular discipline of the student's major. Trade-offs are made at the expense of general life skills courses.

Thus, universities must exercise *central* leadership and responsibility for the life skills portion of their curricula if there is to be an effective and creative response to the rigorous educational requirements needed today. This is likely to be achieved only when universities being their curriculum planning with the key question in curriculum reform, namely, "What qualities do we want *all* of our graduates to possess when they leave this university with their first degree?" This broader view moves the emphasis away from the narrow perspective of disciplines to a concern for the basic essentials of a university-educated person. If, for instance, it is agreed that in response to the advancing trend of McLuhan's "global village," suitably prepared university graduates require at least some familiarity with a second language, then this requirement must apply to all students, not just those in the Arts or Humanities.

Focusing a university community on the basic needs of *all* graduates involves a major commitment of time and energy. Building a consensus will be difficult and the risks of failure relatively high. But not to attempt to do so contains even greater risks as the relevance and appropriateness of a university's preparation of its graduates comes under increasing scrutiny in our turbulent times.

Once key objectives for a core curriculum have been isolated, the implementation process will vary according to the unique culture and practices of particular institutions. A high-level steering committee with representatives from various areas of the university, chaired by a senior academic administrator, might take the leadership role. Maximizing faculty involvement would build a broad base of support and sense of ownership concerning the curriculum planning principles so developed.

Speakers, papers, and workshops could provide for a thorough scan of the environment graduates are likely to encounter in the coming decades. Surveys of selected alumni and employers might provide insights into the strengths of current graduates and areas with opportunities for improvement. Information of this sort, along with information on what other universities are doing, would stimulate interest in the university community. As a result, there would be an informed context for determining desirable qualities for *all* graduates upon leaving university with their first degree. The steering committee would then coordinate appropriate exercises to generate broadly based input on specific recommendations and provide feedback on the developing consensus. An interactive process similar to the Delphi process might be used.

Although each university will derive its own particular blend of desirable characteristics for its graduates, presumably the list would include variations of the following: a high level of literacy inclusive of computer literacy, understanding of self and others, ethical sensitivity, analytical and critical thinking skills, fine arts appreciation, understanding of world history, familiarity with the scientific method, comprehension of technological change and its impacts, a second language, effective speaking skills, knowledge of the operations of major institutions, understanding the dynamics of conflict and its resolution, appreciation of comparative value systems, and at least one major subject of concentration.

Just as the societal and environmental context described earlier is bewildering and staggering in its complexity, so too are the challenges in developing an advanced education curriculum that will prepare, even in a modest way, university graduates for their future lives—the universities' equivalent of NASA's goal to put a person on the moon. By isolating these learning objectives and implementing them in a small core curriculum or in a series of student-selected options, only a few can be achieved in the course of completing an undergraduate degree. More realistically, measured progress is possible when a university makes a total commitment and develops comprehensive strategies involving all segments of the university community at all stages of a degree. Everyone has to take a responsible and active role.

For instance, to ensure a high standard of competence in written work and analytical and critical thinking, most instructors would need to assign written work requiring original and creative thought. This would need to be carefully evaluated and critiqued in terms of content, style, and clarity of thought and expression. In universities with huge lecture classes or with professors who give priority to research over teaching, the achievement of these practices would require revolution rather than evolution.

Thus, while determining the characteristics a university community desires all of its graduates to possess is a major undertaking, finding and developing appropriate means to achieve these objectives is an even greater challenge. Moreover, that task will require students to take more than a few pre-existing courses. Instead, a new set of broadly based courses cutting across many disciplines will need to be developed, applying unorthodox instructional methodology and made much more creative, engaging, and stimulating. Correspondingly, a greater sense of responsibility for the achievement of the general educational goals must be instilled in the teaching staff. A neatly delimited, modular approach that assumes general life skills are taken care of so that faculty can focus on their own disciplines or specialties, will not be effective in achieving the desired curricular objectives.

Structures and Procedures for Change

Constructive linkages between many specialties are necessary if universities are to address the desired curricular and educational aims in significant ways. To ease the ensuing difficult coordination among disciplines, universities might adopt the matrix organizational model used by the aerospace industry to coordinate the multiple resources essential to develop and build complicated high technology satellites, space shuttles, and so on.

The matrix organization brings together people and resources from diverse backgrounds and units throughout the larger organization and focuses their activity on the achievement of a specific objective or set of objectives crossing the normal boundaries of departments or other units. The organization remains operative for the duration of the project, when participants return to their "home." While the traditional and widespread use of committees may be seen as a parallel in the academic context, the matrix organization or task force seems more appropriate. Committee work is normally an extra assignment performed in addition to one's usual work duties. The depth and scale of curriculum design, implementation, and monitoring required will be substantial. They will need to be the primary focus of certain individuals for relatively long time periods, rather than simply a supplemental assignment.

A series of interdisciplinary, matrix task forces would be charged with creating new approaches in curriculum and delivery to achieve a particular general educational goal or goals. Individual team members must be carefully selected to ensure their commitment to the objective. Requirements would include a strong teaching record and sensitivity to student needs, a capacity for lateral thinking and working with others from disparate disciplines. Each member would bring unique knowledge and experience to finding creative and workable solutions for complicated problems. Of course adequate funding would be necessary to provide release time for participants and for other development costs.

The charge of these task forces would be to develop ways to implement the general educational goals. One such group might investigate how graduating students can acquire a better understanding of new technologies, technological change, and its impacts. Members might include a medical researcher, engineer, computing specialist, biologist, environmentalist, historian, sociologist, pharmacist, and philosopher. Their guiding question might be something like, "What can the university do to ensure that all of our graduating students have a reasonable understanding about the nature and interrelated impacts of technology and technological change on individuals, societies, and our physical environment?" These ends should be achieved without exclusive reliance on the classroom setting or requiring completion within a single, narrow time frame.

Responses might include a single approach, but more likely a combination of a number of initiatives will emerge, such as development of an interdisciplinary course, an annual distinguished speakers' series on technology issues, teaching materials for use by professors in various fields to suggest ways of highlighting these issues in their courses, modules for inclusion in computer-assisted learning approaches such as hypermedia, field trips to local sites, work study experiences, or student projects requiring the preparation of detailed analytical case studies.

Similar activity would occur in the matrix groups responsible for other core educational objectives. Thus universities will be mobilizing resources in a more comprehensive and sustained manner. Many universities have fallen so far behind the quickly progressing changes in our societies that major curricular reforms are now mandated, rather than curricular tinkerings.

COMPUTER-ASSISTED LEARNING

Another example of the enormity of the tasks in rethinking the curriculum comes in the major challenge of deciding what to emphasize in covering a topic. As one writer has observed:

There is a growing mountain of research. But there is increased evidence that we are being bogged down today as specialization extends. The investigator is staggered by the findings and conclusions of thousands of other workers—conclusions which he cannot find time to grasp, much less to remember, as they appear. Yet specialization becomes increasingly necessary for progress, and the effort to bridge [the gap] between disciplines is correspondingly superficial.[11]

These thoughts, penned almost forty-five years ago by Vannevar Bush, are even more apt today. How can we, under such circumstances, enable our students to sample the classical great thinkers in addition to experiencing the ongoing proliferation of research and new knowledge? In any single field of study there is such an enormity of material that a neophyte (and indeed, even a sophisticated researcher) can easily experience "knowledge shock" (a variation of Toffler's "future shock"), resulting in a sense of the impossibility of the task of learning everything; a sense of frustration that there is too much to learn with insufficient time in which to learn it, and no effective strategies to help one access, analyze, organize, and make the necessary connections among the pieces. Students may see no option to relying on their teacher and textbook to spoon-feed just the most important bits of information. The subsequent noninvolvement of students in individual explorations and their acceptance of a shallow comprehension of a discipline's basics has come to be regarded as the norm.

Anticipating such consequences, Bush suggested that, in the future, interrelated machines should be able to link vast amounts of information into a network that researchers could utilize in exploring and organizing associations and relations among apparently disparate concepts into a more coherent web of knowledge. Recent developments in computers, electronics, and software have brought this forecast closer to reality through information management systems known as "hypertext."

Very promising and exciting applications of hypertext to teaching and learning are occurring, such as Brown University's Intermedia software. One of the professors utilizing this approach explains the underlying educational philosophy as follows:

Much of the sheeplike behavior that one observes in students, particularly when they first arrive at [a] college or university, comes from their having both so little information and so little idea of what to do with the information they do have. One cannot discover or create connections between fact A and six other facts if one knows only fact A, and this lack of factual knowledge tends to make one think in a reductive manner. Just offering additional factual information, however, will not help one think critically unless one has techniques for relating those facts to each other and to everything else one knows. College liberates because it both provides us with facts and offers examples of the way we can make connections for ourselves. Intellectual freedom derives from an ability to make choices. Anything that can thus help us make information available to those who want it and also provide them with techniques to relate it to what they already know provides a model for education. The habits of mind thus encouraged apply to all kinds of activities, inside the classroom and out, and they remind one that education and thinking are active procedures. Intermedia has the capacity to speak to all these educational issues. Above all, it encourages the student to ask questions and to make choices.[12]

The Intermedia system incorporates other media into the knowledge network by making it possible to link "text, static graphics, animated graphics, video, sound, music, and so forth."[13] Intermedia and other computer-assisted learning systems help students grasp the complex inter-relationships, make connections between areas of knowledge, explore original texts, organize large volumes of factual material, better understand the context of major issues, and develop more informed critical and analytical skills. More importantly, these systems appear to provide a mechanism for combining multidiscipline approaches to common problems.

CONCLUSION

The shape and form of societies today is very complex. The fragility of our environment is a constant reminder that so many of our actions and abuses have impacts beyond our own national boundaries. The proliferation of knowledge, technology, and issues makes it very complicated and frustrating for even the most conscientious persons to remain informed. Increasingly education will come under the scrutiny of governments, business, environmentalists, and other groups questioning how well the populace is being prepared to cope with and achieve greater effectiveness in dealing with the uncertainties of responsible citizenship.

Many universities are in the vanguard with important research, shedding new light on significant problems. They are clearly demonstrating the powerful relevance of that side of their mandate. Still we must ask, how well do their educational programs help students to grapple meaningfully with vast amounts of information and how well do they prepare them to develop the critical and analytical skills required to identify and comprehend the roots of involved societal and global issues? The answers to these questions are less clear. Strong boundaries between disciplines and an almost complete reliance on ancient pedagogical techniques have combined frequently to constrain the responsiveness of curricula and educational objectives to the realities of life that post-secondary graduates will face.

It is time for a major effort by universities to examine carefully and thoroughly the question, "What qualities do we want *all* of our graduates to possess when they leave this university with their first degree?" Where the approach to this assignment is serious, the responses certainly will involve a rethinking of the curriculum. More importantly, it will require more than "quick fix" remedies. It will require creative ways of establishing constructive linkages of an enduring nature between widespread disciplines and specialties. In these difficult times universities have no choice but to seek new and creative paths to satisfy the increasingly demanding requirements for an educated populace.

NOTES

1. Allan Bloom, *The Closing of the American Mind* (New York: Simon & Schuster, 1987), p. 21.
2. Bloom, p. 26.
3. Dominic Manganiello, "The Closing of the American Mind," *The New Federation* (January/February, 1989), 5–6.
4. Bloom, p. 65.
5. Bloom, p. 337.
6. Bloom, p. 340.
7. Alvin Toffler, *Future Shock* (New York: Random House, 1970), p. 4.
8. H. G. Wells, *The Outline of History* (Toronto: Doubleday, Doran and Grundy Ltd., 1920), p. 1100.
9. Giovanni Agnelli, "Industry's Expectations of the University," Ontario Confederation of University Faculty Associations *Forum*, 6, no. 6 (November, 1988), 3.
10. Agnelli, 3.
11. Vannevar Bush, "As We May Think," *Atlantic Monthly* (July 1945), 101.
12. George P. Landow, "Hypertext in Literary Education, Criticism, and Scholarship," Institute for Research in Information and Scholarship (IRIS) (Providence, R.I.: Brown University, 1988), p. 3.
13. N. Yankelovich, G. Landow, and D. Cody, "Creating Hypermedia Materials for English Literature Students," *SIGCUE Outlook* 19 (1987), 13.

SELECTED BIBLIOGRAPHY

Agnelli, Giovanni. "Industry's Expectations of the University." Ontario Confederation of University Faculty Associations *Forum*, 6, no. 6 (November 1988), 3.
Bloom, Allan. *The Closing of the American Mind.* New York: Simon & Schuster, 1987.
Bush, Vannevar. "As We May Think." *Atlantic Monthly.* (July 1945), 101–108.
Landow, George P. "Hypertext in Literary Education, Criticism, and Scholarship." Institute for Research in Information and Scholarship (IRIS), Providence, R.I.: Brown University, 1988.
Manganiello, Dominic. "The Closing of the American Mind." *The New Federation* (January/February 1989), 5–6.
Toffler, Alvin. *Future Shock.* New York: Random House, 1970.
Wells, H. G. *The Outline of History.* Toronto: Doubleday, Doran and Grundy, Ltd., 1920.
Yankelovich, N., G. Landow, and D. Cody. "Creating Hypermedia Materials for English Literature Students." *SIGCUE Outlook*, 19 (1987). 112–25.

III The Value Content of Education

10 THE CENTRAL CURRICULAR ISSUE OF OUR AGE

Huston Smith

IDENTIFYING THE GAP

I was asked to address the fact that even so-called objective knowledge is always value-laden, but I consider that battle won. We do need regularly to remind ourselves of the point, but I do not think that the point itself remains in dispute. That we even allude to an "objective fact" is evidence that we think that it is important (and hence value-laden) at least for the purposes at hand.[1]

Instead of squandering our time on what we already know (and in present company, I feel safe in assuming, already agree on), we shall get further, I believe, if we venture into less charted and even controversial waters. Our goal is "to identify the central curricular issues of our age," and *the* central issue, I have become persuaded, relates not to values but to existence—not to what is good (though that issue enters almost immediately) but to what there is. Education is concerned with knowing, and by extension with knowing what exists importantly for human well-being. Current higher education can be excused for not seeing clearly reality's extent, for it is the human condition to be ringed round about by clouds of nescience or unknowing. What is not excusable, although it is understandable, is the way the university has locked itself into methodologies that preclude serious consideration of certain regions of reality, the most important and extensive regions, I happen to believe. The central curricular issue of our age is whether the university is grounded in an epistemology that allows for open rather than constricted vision.

THE UNIVERSITY'S ROOTS IN THE SCIENTIFIC METHOD

"The biggest failing in higher education today," Steven Muller noted when he was inaugurated as President of The Johns Hopkins University at the opening of the 1980s, "is that the modern university is rooted in the scientific method." This is a failing, he went on to say, because "the scientific method doesn't provide a value system," and this leaves us turning out "skilled barbarians."[2]

I agree with this assessment, but would add that there are things beside a value system that the scientific method cannot provide, and this further restricts the university's yield. Science cannot cover the entire range of reality, which causes the university to offer students only partial maps of what exists. The regions that are omitted are important, so the omissions are serious. Everything I say will be pointed toward suggesting what the omissions are, but let me work up to them by confirming President Muller's perception that it is indeed the scientific method that vectors the university's approach to knowledge.

That the natural sciences are committed to the scientific method goes without saying. The point concerning them is the disproportionate influence they, and therewith their method, exert on the university as a whole. Lee Yearley has a charming story of a faculty meeting at Stanford University in which a Nobel Prize winner rose to his feet to announce that "all that it takes to make a great university is four departments: mathematics, physics, biology, and. . ." Feigning confusion, he said he could not remember what the fourth department was, but when someone asked whether it might be his own—chemistry—he agreed that it was, and resumed his seat.

Let us assume that he was speaking half in jest; the fact remains that he had to be coming from a position of strength even to voice such a thought. Issuing (as it did) from on high, his remark was greeted with good-humored laughter. A counterproposal to the effect that English, foreign languages, art, and philosophy might suffice would have been dismissed as silly.

Solid facts undergird this anecdote. The natural scientists are the lords of the university because they deal with what our technological society considers most real—the material universe—in ways that have proven effective. So their budgets are larger, partly because they are self-supporting; they draw money *to* the university from industry and government. This seems appropriate, but there are shadow sides to the picture. Not having the resources to float expensive laboratories and elaborate experiments (Karl Pribram told me recently that it takes about seven years now to get a significant experiment on the brain in place) universities have become increasingly beholden, initially to private foundations but progressively to the federal government. Following the extraordinary contributions of science to World War II the National Science Foundation was created to advise the federal government on how to support science in peacetime, but governmental agencies—the Office of Naval Operations, the U.S. Public Health Service, the Space Agency and the like—have found ways to channel money to universities directly. And now (as Gerald Piel pointed out in his 1986 Presidential Address to the American Association for the Advancement of Science) "mission oriented" programs are upstaging the agencies.[3] Enough money has already been appropriated for the Strategic Defense Initiative (Star Wars) to buy the services of half the research physicists in the United States, diverting them from research they consider more important and would prefer to be working on.

That "universities are [now] regarded as contract research centers at the command of the federal government," as Piel notes, poses important questions for the future of both science and the university, but I must not let them sidetrack me. Bracketing them, and attendant issues of technology and funding, will not affect my argument, for the noetic prowess of pure science is quite enough to account for its prestige on campus. Nothing is more obvious than that the sciences possess an almost miraculously effective way of knowing, one whose precision and proofs are unrivaled anywhere else in academe. It is not surprising, therefore, to find other divisions of the university trying to adapt scientific methods to their own ends, with disastrous results. But the adaptations must first be documented, for we are normally unaware of their extent.

With respect to the social sciences, Robert Bellah (co-author of *Habits of the Heart* and former chairman of the Department of Sociology at the University of California, Berkeley) registers their domination by science so clearly that I shall quote him at length. "The assumptions underlying mainstream social science," he writes, are

positivism, reductionism, relativism, and determinism. . . . By positivism I mean . . . the assumption that the methods of natural science are the only approach to valid knowledge, and the corollary that social science differs from natural science only in maturity and that the two will become ever more alike. By reductionism I mean the tendency to explain the complex in terms of the simple and to find behind complex cultural forms biological, psychological or sociological drives, needs and instincts. By relativism I mean the assumption that matters of morality and religion, being explicable by particular constellations of psychological and sociological conditions, cannot be judged true or false . . . but simply vary with persons, cultures and societies. [Echoes of President Muller's point that science does not provide a value framework.] By determinism I mean . . . the tendency to think that human actions are explained in terms of "variables" that will account for them.[4]

Turning to individual departments within the social sciences, we find that "economics thinks of itself as a science, heavily quantitative, using mathematics and statistics as its vocabulary."[5] "English-speaking anthropology . . . continues to be passionately scientistic in its hopes and claims, and methods."[6] A distinguished political theorist reports on psychology as well as his own field when he tells us that "the temptation has been overwhelming to reconstruct the sciences of man on the [natural science] model. . . . Psychology, where an earlier vogue of behaviorism is being replaced by a boom of computer-based models, is far from the only case."[7] To round off the social sciences with another report on that division as a whole, an inquiry by *The Atlantic Monthly* concluded that "they aspire to be sciences; they have a scientific methodology."[8]

It is less easy to generalize about the humanities, but one evidence of the pull that science has exerted on them is the swing of their attention to what, within their fields, can be demonstrated objectively. In philosophy this led to Bertrand Russell's slogan that "logic is the essence of philosophy," and to replacing foreign language (as a professional requirement) with ability to follow completeness proofs for formal systems. On substantive issues, "materialism [has become] the reigning orthodoxy among philosophers of mind,"[9] but I shall leave philosophy with that and pass on to literature. Here the fear that one is not dealing with "real knowledge" unless it is verifiable has resulted in disproportionate attention being given to when texts were written, by whom, and under what circumstances, to the neglect of what the texts say, and even greater neglect of whether what they say is true. Lynne Cheney did not make this point explicitly in her 1988 report to Congress on the National Endowment for the Humanities, but I hear it implied in her assertion that "most colleges have yet to think through the way in which the humanistic tradition relates to the rest of human knowledge."

The growing attention that is being given to hermeneutics shows that the problem is being addressed, but there is a dark side to the hermeneutic surge. Because subtle, advanced knowing is not rule-governed (there are no rules that deliver Nobel Prizes, for we invariably know more than we know how we know it), obsession with method diverts us from content. It is difficult to suppress the suspicion that the current stampede toward hermeneutics is motivated by insecurity, a lack of confidence that the humanities have a referent that shares with the physical universe of the natural scientists an equal footing in the world's deep structure. If one is not sure that the object of one's inquiry importantly exists, attention turns to brooding over what one should be doing and how one should be doing it. With sidelong references to the suffering masses, I feel compelled to add, for Lynne Cheney's NEH report cites the politicizing of the humanities as another of its current diversionary tactics: "The key questions are thought to be about gender, race and class."

I am not saying that interpretive method (hermeneutics), much less politics, are unimportant. My concern is that the disproportionate and, yes, diversionary attention they are receiving in the humanities today is a consequence of humanists having lost confidence in the object of their study and its standing in the ultimate nature of things. For "poets write of the soul, of intellectual beauty, of the living spirit of the world," Kathleen Raine points out,

but what does such work communicate to readers who do not believe in the soul, in the spirit of life, or in anything that can be (unless the physically desirable) called "the beautiful"? What can be saved in an age peopled by the human primate of the scientist is only the quantifiable; the mechanics of construction, in whatever art. And the engineering element in the making of a poem is negligible in comparison with the spaceship. So what meaning remains, in materialistic terms, to the word "poet," or the essence (poetry) and quality (the poetic) of works of art?[10]

THE LIMITS OF SCIENCE

I have devoted almost half this chapter to documenting President Muller's observation that the university is rooted in the scientific method because I do not think we are aware of the extent to which scientific approaches to knowledge color everything the university does. I turn now to what is wrong with this rootage. The failing derives from what science cannot get its hands on, and what, in consequence, gets omitted from the curricula of universities that are vectored by the scientific enterprise.

President Muller initiated this step in my argument by noting that science does not provide a value framework, but to pursue his lead I must first say what science is, for to see where it ends requires seeing its extent. As its limits are what interest us here, I shall be brief in characterizing its extent—what science actually is—and import a diagram from my *Forgotten Truth*,[11] to help save words.

No knowledge deserves to be called scientific unless it is objective in the sense of being intersubjectively confirmable. It is more obviously scientific, however, if it enables us to predict; to predict eclipses, for example. We take another step down its road when we learn how to control

Figure 10.1
The Centripetal Aspects of Scientific Knowledge

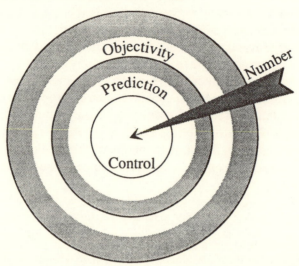

Objectivity, or intersubjective confirmability, characterizes all science. Its ability to predict increases its value to us. And finally, the ability to control variables increases our ability to penetrate Nature's structure. Number, the language of mathematics, permeates all aspects of science.

the variables in experiments, for that enables us to penetrate deeper into Nature's structure; quantum mechanics is the prize example. Finally, scientific knowledge comes fully into its own when it is couched mathematically in computations and equations, for number is the language of science.[12]

This brief characterization of science will have to suffice here. I want to get on with its limitations and will begin by drawing on my discussion of this point too in *Forgotten Truth*.

1. *Values*. Here President Muller's point must be elaborated somewhat. Science can deal with descriptive and instrumental values, but not with normative and intrinsic ones. It can tell us what people do like, but not what they should like. Opinion polls and market research are sciences, but there will never be a science of the *summum bonum*. Similarly, science can tell us that if we prize longevity over immediate somatic gratification, we should stop smoking (an instrumental value), but between longevity and somatic gratification as intrinsic values, it cannot adjudicate.

2. *Purposes*. Science includes teleonomy, but teleology cannot enter its picture. Teleonomy relates to the purposive character of biological organisms (which biology tries to account for nonteleologically), whereas

teleology introduces purpose into the final or ultimate explanations for the way things are. Science regards teleology as anthropomorphic, and anthropomorphic explanations are the opposite of scientific ones. In the words of Jacques Monod, "the cornerstone of scientific method is . . . the *systematic* denial that 'true' knowledge can be got at by interpreting phenomena in terms of final causes—that is to say of 'purpose.' "13

3. *Global and existential meanings*. Science is meaningful throughout, but there are two kinds of meaning it cannot touch. One of these is global meanings—what is the meaning of life, or the meaning of it all? The other is existential meanings, the kind that is involved when we ask if something is meaning-*ful*. Depressed persons sometimes find themselves in a condition where nothing seems meaningful.

4. *Quality*. Quality eludes the quantitative measuring grid that science must impose on events if they are to become precise data. Certain qualities (such as tones or colors) are connected with quantifiable substrates (light or sound waves of varying lengths), but qualities themselves are unmeasurable. Being subjectively experienced, they cannot be laid on the table for public examination. Being simple—not composed of parts—they cannot be dissected even introspectively.

To these four flat sides of science, which were covered in *Forgotten Truth* (pp. 14–16) and *Beyond the Post-Modern Mind* (pp. 84–86), I want now to add two more. I place them in a separate category because they introduce radical elements into my argument, radical being defined here (with Noam Chomsky) as pertaining to what lies outside the realm of acceptable discourse.

5. *Immateriality*. Science cannot deal with what is immaterial and invisible. If there is anything which (because it possesses no physical component) does not impact our sense organs, or even their most sensitive extensions via the instruments of science, science cannot connect with it.

6. *Our Superiors*. If there is anything that is greater than we are—I do not mean greater in size like the sun, or in brute power like a hurricane, but genuinely superior to us in exceeding us by every criterion of worth we know (such as intelligence and compassion) and perhaps some we know not—if, to repeat, things of this sort exist (angels and God are obvious examples, but platonic forms as Plotinus understood them would qualify as well), science can afford no knowledge of them. No such beings have turned up in the textbooks of science, and we can see why. Their very nature exempts them from controlled experiments—any we could ever devise. The commonsense way to argue this is to note that we can only control what is inferior to us. This is basically true, but we can be more precise by pointing out that controlled experiments can be devised only

when we are aware of all the relevant variables, a condition that could never pertain in the case of our superiors. For, being more intelligent than we are, they would inhabit an ampler cognitive domain. To try to fit them into the perimeters of our understanding would be tantamount to dogs trying to determine whether mathematics exists by sniff tests. It is important to recognize that nothing in this reasoning tells us whether beings superior to ourselves exist. It does demonstrate, though, I think, that *if* they exist, science will never disclose that fact.

As I say, these last two considerations are radical in academic discussions because our Western outlook, particularly in the university, has come to be so dominated by the scientific worldview that it sounds almost heretical now to raise the question of whether things that do not turn up in science's viewfinder—for present purposes, things that are immaterial on the one hand, and superior to us on the other—exist. Yet ironically, 90 percent of the "matter" in the universe is now judged to be invisible; it registers on no scientific instrument, and scientists call it "matter" only because of the attraction it exerts on the matter we are familiar with. Or again: because at the micro-level power is inversely related to size,[14] it could be reasonably posited—though no more than that—that infinite power would possess no size whatsoever. Closer to home, no one has ever seen consciousness, or even life. We see organisms that exhibit these attributes, and because we have been scientistically brought up to believe that matter is what is real, we tend to assume that they are emergent properties that depend, epiphenomenally, on distinctive arrangements in their molecular substrates. But there is no evidence that this is the case; the conclusion derives solely from the working premises of science and the metaphysics those premises enthrone. The possibility (universally accepted until the working premises of science challenged it) that consciousness can exist without a physical substrate fits phenomenal observations equally well. And neither the humanities nor the social sciences (if the latter are not to sacrifice the "social" in their title to a "science" imported from lesser domains) will recover their full potential until their objects —which include life (as shared with plants), consciousness (as shared with other animals), and self-awareness (as the distinctive human attribute)—are accorded autonomous ontological status. This means, *epistemologically*, that they must be understood in their own right, as having their own properties and principles which instruments tailored to lesser things cannot probe, and, *ontologically*, that they do not depend on the physical bodies that periodically become their hosts.

That paragraph sought to open the door to the possibility of reinstating the immaterial (and hence the invisible) into our maps of reality. One seeks to do the same for beings or things that are superior to us. Again, prior to the rise of modern science, it was assumed that human life was situated midway on the great chain of being, between things inferior to it on the one hand (the lesser animals, plants, and inanimate objects) and, on the other hand, beings (angels, gods, God and the Godhead) that were its superiors. But because science reveals only the lower part of the register —as earlier argued, only our inferiors can be fitted into its controlled experiments—we have come to assume that we and our inferiors are all that the objective world contains. It is we who crown creation; there is nothing it contains that in intrinsic value exceeds ourselves.

The greatest works in the humanities were written, painted, or composed by people who thought otherwise. The humanities will not recover their former stature until we see—or at least seriously entertain the prospect— that they were right.

RETURNING ADVENTURE TO THE UNIVERSITY

To reduce my argument to bare bones and in so doing recapitulate: motivations (what we want) engender epistemologies (ways to find out how to get to what we want), which in turn generate worldviews (conceptions of what exists, as disclosed by the epistemologies that get us to the things we want). Finally, worldviews create anthropologies, using that word loosely to refer to the feel of life as it is lived within the worldviews that our motivations and epistemologies create.

Accepting President Muller's dictum that the university is rooted in science—how could it not be, when the university seeks truth and our age considers science to be truth's best revealer?—I have sought to show how this skews the entire university curriculum in ways that are limiting because they exclude or underrate regions of reality that science cannot register. If this is true, hard work lies ahead to see how, department by department, course by course, these neglected regions, or at least serious allowance for their possibility, might be readmitted to the curriculum. Lacking space to pursue that difficult, largely uncharted area here, I can only point to "Excluded Knowledge" and "Flakes of Fire, Handfuls of Light: The Humanities as Uncontrolled Experiment"as my own modest essays on the task.[15] Figure 10.2 suggests the direction in which those essays proceed.

Taking this diagram's right-hand column seriously will require hard work, but to suggest that it holds high rewards, I shall conclude with what a student appended to his final examination in a course I taught last fall at Villanova University:

Figure 10.2
The University Curriculum As It Is and As It Might Be

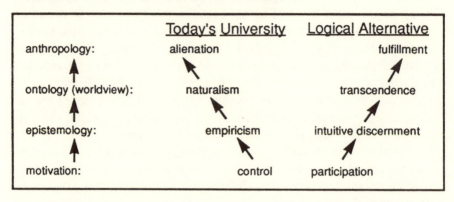

Our motivations determine our epistemology, which in turn fashions our worldview, from which emerge our feelings about life, our "anthropology." Current, science-based curricula lead ultimately to our sense of alienation; a logical alternative, starting from different motivating values, leads instead to fulfillment. ("Naturalism" is used to mean the view (a) that nothing that lacks a material component exists, and (b) that in what does exist, the physical component has the final say.)

Well, that's about it. I'd like to say, though, that this class has been absolutely incredible. I learned a lot, but I also had fun. You took something usually relegated to conversations at 4 a.m. with a friend over a steaming pizza and dove headfirst into it, and in the process taught us how to swim through life a bit. Thanks for teaching us. It wasn't a class—it was an adventure.[16]

NOTES

I am indebted to Kendra Smith for editorial assistance in converting my original talk into readable prose.

1. Anyone who wishes to pursue the issue beyond this elemental starting point will find it handled succinctly on pages 75–76 of James Marsh's *Post-Cartesian Meditations* (Fordham University Press, 1989).
2. *U.S. News and World Report*, November 10, 1980.
3. *Science*, September 5, 1986.
4. *National Institute of Campus Ministries Journal*, VI:3 (Summer 1981), p. 10.
5. Adam Smith, *New York Times Book Review*, 18 September 1977, 10.
6. Robert Ackerman, "J. G. Frazer Revisited," *American Scholar* (Spring 1978), 232.
7. Charles Taylor, "Interpretation and the Sciences of Man," in Fred Dallmayr and Thomas McCarthy, eds., *Understanding and Human Inquiry* (South Bend, Indiana: University of Notre Dame Press, 1977), p. 124.

8. Alston Chase, "Skipping through College: Reflections on the Decline of Liberal Arts Education," *The Atlantic Monthly*, September 1978, 38.

9. Daniel Dennett, "Review of *The Self and Its Brain* by Karl Popper and John Eccles," *Journal of Philosophy*, 76:2 (February 1979), 97.

10. Kathleen Raine, "Premises and Poetry," *Sophia Perennis*, 3:2 (Autumn, 1977), 58–60. I have altered the punctuation and several words to smooth the reading in this abridgment of three pages in the original text.

11. Huston Smith, *Forgotten Truth* (New York: Harper and Row, 1976), p. 9.

12. This characterization of science oversimplifies things somewhat, but I believe it captures its central thrust. I defend my characterization and fill in some needed qualifications on pages 86–89 of my *Beyond the Post-Modern Mind*, 2d ed. (Wheaton, Ill.: Quest Book, 1989).

13. Jacques Monod, *Chance and Necessity* (New York: Random House, 1972), p. 21.

14. "The amount of energy associated with light corpuscles increases *as the size is reduced.* . . . The energy necessary to create a proton is contained in a light pulse only about 10^{-13} centimeter in diameter. And the energy of a million protons would be contained in a light pulse a million times smaller" (Arthur Young, *Which Way Out?* Berkeley: Robert Briggs Associates, 1980), p. 2.

15. Included in Smith, *Beyond the Post-Modern Mind*. See also my essay, "Another World to Live In, or How I Teach the Introductory Course," in Mark Juergensmeyer, ed., *Teaching the Introductory Course in Religious Studies: A Sourcebook* (Atlanta, Georgia: Scholars Press, 1990).

16. Brian P. Knestout, student.

SELECTED BIBLIOGRAPHY

Ackerman, Robert. "J. G. Frazer Revisited." *American Scholar* Spring 1978, 232.

Chase, Alston. "Skipping through College: Reflections on the Decline of Liberal Arts Education." *The Atlantic Monthly* (September 1978).

Dennett, Daniel. "Review of *The Self and Its Brain* by Karl Popper and John Eccles." *Journal of Philosophy*, 76:2 (February 1979).

Monod, Jacques. *Chance and Necessity*. New York: Random House, 1972.

Smith, Huston. "Another World to Live In, or How I Teach the Introductory Course." In Mark Juergensmeyer, ed., *Teaching the Introductory Course in Religious Studies: A Sourcebook*. Atlanta, Georgia: Scholars Press, 1990.

———. *Beyond the Post-Modern Mind*, 2d ed. Wheaton, Ill.: Quest Book, 1989.

———. *Forgotten Truth*. New York: Harper and Row, 1976.

Taylor, Charles. "Interpretation and the Sciences of Man." In Fred Dallmayr and Thomas McCarthy, eds., *Understanding and Human Inquiry*. South Bend, Indiana: University of Notre Dame Press, 1977.

Young, Arthur. *Which Way Out?* Berkeley: Robert Briggs Associates, 1980.

11 TOWARD A CREATIVE EAST-WEST DIALOGUE IN MORAL EDUCATION AND VALUE ORIENTATION

Charles Wei-hsun Fu

THE ADVANTAGES OF CROSS-CULTURAL STUDIES

To rethink the curriculum, especially on the college level, we must avail ourselves of all possible resources, cross-cultural as well as interdisciplinary. These resources must include perspectives beyond the cultural assumptions and scientific-technological mindset of modern Western societies, which in part have contributed to our present problems in moral education and value orientation. I would like to propose certain elements in Eastasian tradition—specifically the traditions of Confucianism, Buddhism, and Taoism—which indicate ways the moral shortcomings of our educational system may be filled.[1] My intent is not to find fault with Western approaches, but to offer complementary and supplementary visions with respect to moral education and overall value orientation—potential means by which we can indeed venture to guide our students into the next century.

By focusing on cross-cultural and interdisciplinary elements, we shall be able to help our students widen their scope of vision regarding humanity, morality, religion, philosophy, psychotherapy, and the nature and direction of the sciences. The cross-cultural task has been considerably aided by the meeting of East and West experienced since the end of World War II. Paradoxically, the military confrontation of that war, followed by subsequent conflicts in Korea and Vietnam, led to an increasing interest in and sensitivity to Eastasian thought and culture on the part of the Americans involved, due to their exposure to widely divergent lifestyles and values. The net result was a broadening and deepening of the American vision. A related development was the influx of Eastasian immigrants, enriching the mosaic of ethnic diversity in American society.

Education, especially at the university level, can benefit greatly from these intercultural cross-fertilizations. To illustrate these potential benefits, I will focus on two of the most important topics, moral education and its overall expansion into value orientation. These two areas can serve as exemplary ways in which we can improve our curriculum on a cross-cultural basis.

In terms of interdisciplinary college education, there is a growing awareness of the need for proper integration of the sciences, philosophy, and religious studies. A comparative study of the contrasts between Eastasian and Western approaches has much to offer here. Having never undergone the paradigm shift to pro-analytic, compartmentalized thinking spearheaded by Rene Descartes and other seminal figures of modern Western scientific and philosophical thought, Asian educational tradition has not been placed under the necessity of interdisciplinary reintegration. Philosophical and religious Taoism, for example, deals with what by Western standards represents a diversity of topics—philosophy, religion, medicine, psychology, physical and psychotherapies, artistic creativity, and so on, all constituting an integrated whole. As we strive to bring our own disciplines back to a creative rapport with one another, we would do well to consider the inviolate integrity of Eastasian models harking back to a pre-analytic and holistic past.

I will first present my own model of five pairs of ethical concepts comparing the assets of East with West on matters of ethics and morality. Generally speaking, these pairings contrast Western and Eastasian (specifically Confucian) modes of ethical thinking and moral behavior. Applying this model, I shall then examine the assets and liabilities of the respective approaches, with an emphasis on the pedagogical importance of introducing certain of the Eastasian moral/educational ideas into our existing curriculum.

Next, I shall present my own alternative model of moral education in a broader sense, a tenfold dimensional analysis of value orientation in human existence. The application of the model demonstrates how cross-cultural studies can lead to an interdisciplinary integration of the best of Western and Eastasian sources. I offer no definitive solution to the modern moral and pedagogical malaise, only some modest suggestions as to how we may learn from each other through an ongoing process of critical self-reflection and creative dialogue.

THE FIVEFOLD MODEL IN RELATION TO MORAL EDUCATION

The usefulness of Eastasian traditions for educational enrichment became apparent to me through my work in the ongoing task of reconstructing Confucian ethics and morality.[2] My proposal consists of five pairs of ethical concepts, sharply contrasting Eastasian (Confucian) and Western approaches to ethical thinking, moral behavior, and personal cultivation relative to education.[3] These pairs are:

1. family-oriented micro-morality *versus* society-oriented macro-morality;
2. person-to-person human-kindness (*jen*) *versus* impersonal justice;
3. personal cultivation through name-rectification and individual responsibility *versus* accountability through rules;
4. motive-based morality in terms of *liang-chih* (innate knowledge of the good) *versus* consequence-based morality of social utility;
5. *maxima moralia* (the Confucian way of inner sagehood) *versus minima moralia* (legalistic observance of law and order).

The first component of each pair represents the moral idealism of Confucianism and the second, Western moral realism. These pairs are not necessarily contradictory, but may be seen as two sets of varying emphases regarding ethical culture and human conduct. This leaves open the hope that our critical study of them may yield a mutually balancing integration. The first pair is the most crucial, setting the basic parameters that are elaborated in the remaining four correlates. Taken together they represent a shifting Gestalt consisting of the foreground of the family set against the background of society at large. Let us consider each pair in turn to uncover the grounding principles of the two systems.

In the first pairing, the parameters of family-oriented micro-morality and society-oriented macro-morality reflect the scope and starting point of ethics for each approach. Micro-morality assumes that values can be naturally extended from the family to the broader society; hence, it may be represented by a series of ever-larger concentric circles, the innermost circle being the individual, next the nuclear family and intimate friends, the clan, the community, the state, and finally the world. The family provides the basic paradigm for proper human relationships, such that the ruler-subject relationship is patterned on that of parent and child. Moral values exist on a continuum across each of these layers, consistent from one level to the next. As set forth in the *Great Learning*, Confucian thinking takes moral education as the means by which inner sagehood is developed. This in turn becomes the basis for the ultimate perfection of the sociopolitical ideal of outer kingship, in contrast to the modern Western sense of political morality which tends to distinguish between public figures and their private lives.[4] Consequently, the gradual perfection of the human individual is an ethical and cultivational prerequisite for, and guarantor of, the eventual perfection of human society as a whole.

The modern Western ethical point of view, however, presents a far different picture. It posits a gap between family and social values, leading to separate but "equal" values that must be safeguarded. In this sense, the American melting pot is not a crucible negating differences, but rather a mosaic able to accommodate a rich diversity of cultural heritages. In this context, the Confucian moral continuum constitutes an infringement of individual privacy, as mandated in the Western separation of church and state, and runs the risk of sinking into an oppressive moral authoritarianism. This fundamental difference in approach clearly reflects the difference in the assumed beginning point of morality and the respective ways of dealing with moral education, as will be illustrated through the remaining pairs.

The second pairing is a concretization of family-based and society-based moralities. It manifests the essential nature of micro- and macro-morality rooted respectively in the Confucian virtue of *jen* or human-kindness and in an impersonal justice, specifying a uniform code of conduct toward all. The first posits a personalized approach to other human beings and a sensitivity to specific situations, using the model of interfamily relationships, while the latter rests on an impersonal set of interactions with the world at large. The first founds morality on the perfection of human personality, the second relies upon a code of "laws not men." The moral liability of the modern Western perspective is highlighted in Shakespeare's *Merchant of Venice*, as Portia seeks to have the demands of justice tempered by mercy (IV,i) in order to prevent Antonio's "lawful" mutilation by Shylock. The potential flaw of micro-morality comes in the misuse of power when wielded by less than moral personalities. Thus, the practice of nepotism is well-described in the old Chinese proverb that says, "when a person becomes a government official, all of his chickens and dogs [that is, his relatives] ascend to Heaven."

The difference between these approaches can be illustrated in terms of how strangers are dealt with in the respective cultural contexts, and more specifically in a business context. Chinese students coming to America are impressed by the formal veneer of politeness that characterizes business interactions, reflected in the "thank you" the buyer routinely expects from the seller. In traditional family-oriented Chinese society such niceties are unknown. Courtesy is reserved for a more intimate context. The final sign of acceptance within the Chinese inner circle of intimacy comes when one receives the honorary status of "brother" or "sister." Accordingly, for the traditional Chinese businessperson negotiations make little headway until ties of intimacy first have been established. This puzzles their Western counterparts, who put their faith in the written contract, with its recourse to legal sanctions, rather than in personal relationships and the spoken word.

The same difference occurs in forms of friendship. To the newly arrived Chinese student, the ease with which Americans acquire "friends" is astounding, signaled by the instant intimacy of referring to mere acquaintances on a first name basis. This betrays an abiding superficiality in those relationships to the Chinese, who make a clear-cut distinction between one's small circle of friends and others. Friends enjoy a deep-seated intimacy that spans one's entire life. True friendship is not a matter of readily disposable quantities, but rather of enduring quality.

Japan represents a middle ground between Chinese and Western sociomoral sensibilities. Western influence has allowed the Japanese to deal with strangers, such as customers, by applying Confucian *li* (norms of propriety) as formalized ritual, while maintaining the special intimacy of family-centered relationships. They have adeptly steered a middle course between micro- and macro-morality through a creative synthesis of the two extremes. Nowhere is this more evident than in Japanese business practices, most especially in the skillful adaptation of the American Quality Control method to the Japanese management system (which in turn has become a new model for many American companies).

At the Toyota Company, for example, workers are encouraged to think of the company as an extended family, while the decision-makers practice participatory management. The company thus becomes an extended family for its workers, whose personal development is carefully nurtured. Management takes an active interest in the families of the workers by organizing weekend activities, providing educational opportunities for their children, guaranteeing lifetime employment, and so on.[5] In this way, the ethical gap between the personal sphere of family and the public sphere of society is bridged, a spirit of familial cooperation replacing business competition.

The Japanese strike a balance between the micro- and macro-emphases noted in the initial pair, while attempting to bridge the gap between the second pair of personalized human-kindness and impersonal justice. Here we have a concrete role model for both Eastasians and Westerners to emulate as we seek to integrate the positive aspects of both value orientations. This is not to suggest that Japan has been totally successful.

Significant moral difficulties remain to be surmounted, as evidenced in recent scandals related to the Japanese cabinet. The worst aspects of both systems can emerge when the bridging process breaks down—breeding nepotism on the one hand and the grossest form of utilitarianism on the other.

Our third pair of moral concepts highlights a sharp contrast in perceived moral motivations. The Confucian Rectification of Names (*cheng-ming*) doctrine,[6] along with *li*, constitutes the essential moral code cutting across micro- and macro-morality by extending across the continuum from private family relationships to public political relationships. Moral sense is built into one's social rank, carrying with it an inherent responsibility defined by the parameters of that rank and hierarchical position. The private individual is responsible for setting a public moral example, living up to the expectations of one's respective family and social roles.

Contrastingly, modern Western rule-oriented ethics stresses individual accountability to "objective" and "universal" standards of conduct. Rather than relying on the criteria of personal performance of social roles, rules bring in their wake demands for proof of having fulfilled the letter of the law. In the West, the Rectification of Names seems to amount only to having the right person in the right place, but such an interpretation in fact arises from the narrow standpoint of appropriateness, of utilitarian functionality, disregarding the inner nature of the person (which is so central to Confucianism).

This last point is illustrated in the fourth pairing of ethical concepts. From Mencius to Wang Yang-ming, Confucianism continues to stress *liang-chih* or the inherent sense of moral goodness which, they believe, is shared by all human beings as the ultimate criterion for distinguishing moral right from wrong. This assumption is predicated on the Mencian understanding of human nature as originally (potentially) good. Hence, it tends to see ethics and human morality primarily in terms of motives or intentions—a typically intuitionistic or introspective approach. In contrast, the modern Western view shifts the ethical emphasis to utilitarian consequences, thereby relying upon external criteria as the basis for judging moral behavior—the results of an action as opposed to its originating intentions. However, motive and consequences are inextricably intertwined in the tasks of moral judgment and action. Neither can exist in isolation from the other. The difference arises in terms of which is given priority over the other. The relegation of moral values to the private realm, culminating in a near-obsession with the inviolability of personal privacy, means that motives frequently are discounted in the modern Western approach. On the other hand, the history of Confucianism documents an ever greater stress on the purity of motive, all too often neglecting objective knowledge of the moral situation and its practical consequences.

Finally, the fifth pairing exposes the fundamental difference between Confucian moral idealism and modern Western realism. *Maxima moralia* assumes that each and every human individual is potentially capable of becoming, and morally is obligated to become, a perfected person, a *chün-tzu* (the Confucian type of a moral personality) or even a moral sage, through consistent daily practice. Contrariwise, the *minima moralia* of modern Western realistic ethics emphasizes a legalistically grounded adherence to a moral code supportive of social law and order, a lowest common denominator of morality. Although each approach is ethically consistent within the limits of its own assumptions, they have vastly different concepts of and expectations concerning human nature and human behavior, as well as divergent views of human potentials and limitations as moral agents.

While Confucianism assumes human nature is originally good, the modern Western view focuses on the darker side of human nature. Consequently, vastly different political theories emerge. So it is that Thomas Hobbes, in the *Leviathan*, emphasizes the role of fear, greed, and self-aggrandizement in human behavior as the war of each against all, while Mencius evokes the image of an ecological disaster, Bull Mountain, to suggest that though it may be corrupted, human nature can revitalize its inherent goodness.[7] The key to these diverse interpretations is found in the varying views of the "state of nature"—a value-laden realm inherited from a moral Heaven in Confucianism as opposed to the West's value-neutral field of conflict, governed by the law of "survival of the fittest."

The concrete consequences of these assumptions can be seen in the respective understandings of the meaning of ethics and morality. Consider the ubiquitous case of lifeboat ethics, a typical example of how Western moral realism sees ethics and morality in a secular context as a competitive challenge to individual needs and desires. Confucianism is totally innocent of such considerations, traditionally adhering to the moral agent's *liang-chih* and an age hierarchy as the criterion of moral judgment. The notion of individual striving is totally alien to and unthinkable for the Confucian. In its place we find a well-defined hierarchy of values.

Political reality in the respective countries reflects these moral theories. In traditional China and other Eastasian nations, such as Korea and Japan, Confucianism as a moral religion frequently was used as a unifying political ideology. Its monolithic structure contrasts sharply with the sociopolitical and cultural pluralism characteristic of modern Europe, itself a reflection of historical conditions (as well as a force in shaping that history). That very pluralism, however, has been paid for at the price of conflict and a continual search for the reinstatement of law and order.

THE APPLICATION OF THE MODEL TO MORAL EDUCATION

Surveying these divergent trends in moral thinking, we are led to the recognition that no human system of ethics or morality can lay claim to universal applicability, to the exclusion of all other expressions. Hence, we need to engage in mutual learning in order to absorb and integrate the available insights, serving as correctives to the limitations inherent in any one system. My intention is to demonstrate how, in rethinking the curriculum with regard to moral education, we can accomplish these ends.

Our emphasis has been on Eastasian contributions as a counterbalance to existing presumptions in the West. Of particular note here are the resources for the development of individual moral discipline and the recognition of a continuing need for self-vigilance. Some examples from the Confucian canon will illustrate these points. The *Chung Yung* (Chapter 33), one of the Confucian Four Books, contains a revealing quotation from the *Classic of Odes* (ode 256): "Though the ceiling looks down upon you, be free from shame even in the recesses of your own house."8 In short, morality or our moral conscientiousness (self-loyalty; *chung*) pervades even our most private moments, as a continuous and consistent undercurrent.

Similarly, we have the anecdote of a man who was approached with a bribe, under the pretense that it would be known only to the two parties involved. He, however, as a true Confucian, protested that four parties would in fact be privy to the moral violation—the one who offered the bribe, the one who accepted the bribe, as well as Heaven and Earth. Once again we see the internalization of communal standards, which cannot be escaped by recourse to egoism or utilitarian individualism.

Finally, we can cite the case of the mother of the Confucian philosopher Mencius, a widow lauded in historical records for her extreme devotion to her son's moral development. As part of this concern she undertook the hardships of changing their residence, known as the "three moves," in order to provide her child with the best possible role models and environment. Mother and son started out living in the vicinity of a cemetery (where he followed the actions of grave-diggers), then a marketplace (where he was influenced by greedy merchants), and finally settled in next to a school (where he observed teachers). This illustrates the need to guard oneself, or one's child, against corruptions of moral conscientiousness and conduct in concrete terms.

It may be argued that deep within Judeo-Christian moral traditions, parallels to the Confucian position exist which offset the dissonance in modern Western moral trends. Yet an essential difference remains, traceable to the underpinning of Judeo-Christian thought—the covenant with God. This contractual relationship with the divine frames the legalistic thinking that still suffuses the West. Modern Western morality thus can be seen as an expansion of this core concept. The same legalistic root is found in Greek tradition, where Socrates refuses to escape his obviously erroneous death sentence due to his higher commitment to the Laws. Likewise the *Pax Romana* was made possible by adherence to a "universal" legal code.

By contrast, Confucian morality does not presuppose membership in a given religious or political group. Rather, it is a matter of human necessity, a moral responsibility that belongs to us *qua* human beings. (A similar notion is found in Viktor E. Frankl's discussion of our individual task to find meaning in our lives.[9]) More specifically, the Confucian moral task is one of educating and cultivating oneself and providing a moral model for others. The Confucian emphasis on life as a moral task, as well as moral self-cultivation, must be seriously considered as we rethink the curriculum to incorporate moral education. We now come to an alternative and integrative moral model that is both cross-cultural and interdisciplinary in its sources and its scope.

AN ALTERNATIVE MODEL—THE TEN DIMENSIONS OF VALUE ORIENTATION IN LIFE

Four levels of human behavior may be posited—immoral, amoral, moral, and transmoral. Confucians understand life as a moral task; the Buddhist, Taoist, and Western religious perspectives assume morality alone is insufficient for the ultimate enlightenment or salvation of humankind. With this understanding beyond Confucian moral idealism, or Confucianism as a *moral* religion, we can begin to place moral education in the broader context of the human search for the ultimate meaning of life, as a matter of value orientation.

To facilitate the integration of Western and Eastasian approaches to value orientation, I have constructed a multidimensional model that extends Frankl's logotherapeutic model of dimensional ontology. According to Frankl there are three dimensions (as opposed to levels) of human nature—the biological, the psychological, and the noological or spiritual.

My model elaborates on the last of these dimensions, Frankl's final, transcendent dimension focused on the will to meaning rather than more circumscribed wills to pleasure and power.[10]

On the basis of this simplified model, ten dimensions emerge:

1. biological or physical
2. psychological or affective
3. political/social
4. cultural/historical
5. intellectual
6. aesthetic/experiential
7. moral/ethical
8. existential
9. soteriological
10. ontological/cosmological

The list reflects a hierarchical order in value orientation, the higher levels bearing an ever more uniquely human significance than the lower ones.

APPLYING THE ALTERNATIVE MODEL

An integration of cross-cultural elements can be of great service for rethinking the curriculum. It supplies the many deficiencies apparent in existing educational programs. I will briefly sketch this potential with respect to each of the ten dimensions mentioned.

The first two dimensions, the biological and psychological, have been retained relatively intact from Frankl's original model, expressing the most basic body and mind aspects of human life. In terms of present-day education, they are covered by such disciplines as sports, physical and psychological therapy, medicine, and ecology. These may be much enhanced by the Chinese arts of T'ai Ch'i, the Taoist/Zen approach to psychiatry and psychotherapy (such as Japanese Morita therapy), and traditional Chinese medicine—all of which have begun to exert an influence in the West.

The cultural/historical dimension, whereby students are stimulated to broaden their perspective on life, is already being addressed in some programs of curriculum reform . At my home institution, Temple University, for example, a two semester course entitled "The Intellectual Heritage" is required for all undergraduate students. This course introduces seminal texts and ideas from Western, African, and Asian traditional intellectual histories and cultures. Through classic works such as the *Tao Te Ching*, the *Koran*, and the *Analects*, the heritage of all humankind, students are able to enlarge their intellectual and historical vision, while becoming sensitized to the values of their own, often unexplored, roots.

In terms of the intellectual dimension, the Western scientific community has sensed the contemporary potential of Eastasian philosophy and religion, as witnessed in the writings of Fritjof Capra, Bruce Holbrook, and Gary Zukav.[11] Unlike Western religions, which tend to rely upon a transcendent source of revealed truth as the basis of their doctrines, Eastasian perspectives take Nature as the fundamental criterion of reality. Holistic and multidimensional in outlook, they stand in need of no divine creator to delineate the limits of the universe, and so pose no restrictions on the scientific search for knowledge, but indeed support just such a search.

The aesthetic/experiential dimension can benefit greatly from the artistic creativity so central to Taoist and Zen thought, as well as to Japanese Shinto. Landscape painting, calligraphy, the Noh play, and music are among the ways in which aesthetic experience can heighten spirituality. D. T. Suzuki has documented the flourishing of this dimension in Japan in his *Zen and Japanese Culture*, which includes discussions of such art forms as swordsmanship (*kendo*), haiku, and the tea ceremony (*cha-no-yu*). Discipline, intuition, and artistic creativity are among the qualities that Suzuki sees evoked by these various Zen pursuits, as influenced by the philosophy of Taoism.[12]

As for the moral/ethical dimension, we have explored above ways in which our value orientations can be enriched by integrating complementary elements of micro- and macromorality. In particular, Confucian micromorality's emphasis on the cultivation of the individual on the path to moral perfection, when wedded with macromorality's legalistic emphasis on objective knowledge, may well produce clearly defined standards of social perfection. Similar contributions can be anticipated from Taoism, Buddhism, and Zen, each of which proposes a path of personal cultivation for moral and transmoral enlightenment.

The existential dimension brings us into the realm of Frankl's noological or spiritual values. At present, the West stands as heir to the existential ponderings of people like Jean-Paul Sartre, who himself inherited the Kierkegaardian legacy of existential choice as the primal human concern. What is lacking, however, is any recognition of the creative transformation of moral and transmoral personality, of the cultivational evolution of individual decision-making capacities. Western existentialism is infected by the same rigidity inherent in its nemesis, Immanuel Kant, both being predicated on a false dilemma of to will or not to will the good. This perception excludes the possibility of gradually *learning* how to will, as a matter of personal cultivation and transformation. Despite denunciations of Kant and his ilk as self-deluded seekers of universal and eternal truth (Kierkegaard's "truth is subjectivity" being the existential rallying cry), Western existentialists in general mimic Kant's assumption that the faculty of judgment is static and incapable of expansion through experience.

How different is the view of the Confucians, who stress the ongoing existential task of moral training. Thus, we are instructed to remain ever-vigilant over our own conduct; even when alone at midnight, the ceiling looks down upon us. Confucius is himself an exemplary model in this regard, detailing for us the evolution of his own moral judgment from the ages of 15 through 70.[13]

The soteriological dimension, the human seeking after salvation or enlightenment, involves the quality and meaning of life within a cosmic context. To this end, Eastasian thought can provide a transtheological option that does not require the advocacy of or allegiance to any given doctrine. Given the repression that all too often accompanies religious hegemony (such as in Iran, or even the "religion" of communism as practiced by certain leaders in China) this option should be most welcomed. More specifically, the Taoist/Zen way of ultimate enlightenment through creative transformation integrates the insights of Eastasian religion and psychotherapy for the end of higher spirituality, what Chuang Tzu refers to as "the true person"—an extension of post-Freudian attempts to draw upon Eastasian resources. In the process religion itself is being redefined.

An important element here is the emerging field of "thanatological psychiatry/psychotherapy." Elisabeth Kubler-Ross, one of its pioneers in the West, often has criticized the medical establishment for restricting the role of physicians to prolonging life at all costs. Her own focus has shifted from the quantity of life to its underlying quality. Patients are prepared to courageously accept the ultimate inevitability of death as a means of maximizing their remaining life experience, while clearing up any "unfinished business" that would hinder a peaceful end.

The final dimension, the ontological/cosmological, constitutes a metaphysical search for reality. As Kant says, the human being is a metaphysical being; as long as we ask metaphysical questions about ultimate reality and truth, this dimension continues to occupy the highest place among all the ten dimensions in our list of value orientations. In the West we find it reflected in Aristotelian onto-theological approaches. The best examples to be found in Eastasian tradition would include the open-ended, trans-metaphysical approaches of the Taoist philosopher Chuang Tzu, Mahayana Buddhism, and Zen. Each of these avoids circumscribing reality to fit limited human conceptions, thereby inviting more sublime visions and values to suggest themselves.

To illustrate the pedagogical application of the model proposed above, I will briefly mention an undergraduate course designed for the Department of Religion at Temple University in 1974, entitled "Buddhism, Psychoanalysis, and Existential Analysis." Due to its cross-cultural and interdisciplinary nature, the course has been enormously successful in attracting students from such diverse departments as sociology, psychology, criminal justice, journalism, and philosophy.

The course incorporates five different approaches representing important Eastern and Western methodologies: Freudian psychoanalysis, Sartrean existentialism, Frankl's Logotherapy, traditional Buddhism, and Zen. Each of these then is examined in terms of five interdisciplinary topics:

1. an analysis of the internal [mental, spiritual, and existential] problems of humanity;

2. the theoretical model of human nature and the mind constructed to resolve these problems;

3. the scientific, philosophical, and theological debates over the perennial question of free will versus determinism;

4. the meeting and mergence of East and West in psychiatry and psychotherapy with respect to human religiosity or higher spirituality;

5. a modern, creative redefinition and understanding of "religion," as a means of countering the formidable challenges posed by antireligionists, such as Bertrand Russell, Jean-Paul Sartre, Sigmund Freud, and Karl Marx.

My deep conviction concerning the need for changes in our curriculum arises from my own intercultural and interdisciplinary experiences. Although my educational and cultural background is Eastasian, my original professional training was in Western philosophy. Subsequently I taught at several departments of philosophy, and for the last eighteen years have been associated with the department of religion. In order to guide our students into the next century, it is imperative that we design more and more courses capable of stimulating students in cross-cultural and interdisciplinary terms in our ever-shrinking global village. The course mentioned here is only one such possibility illustrating my pedagogical point. That task must be shared by us all as concerned and responsible educators.

NOTES

1. The use of the term "Eastasian" here is intended to designate the countries and cultures of China (inclusive of Taiwan and the People's Republic of China), Korea, Japan, Hong Kong, and Singapore, all of which have been deeply influenced by Confucian ethics and morality, as well as Taoism and Mahayana Buddhism. I do not wish to minimize the importance of the Indian subcontinent, about which I claim no expertise, but rather to provide a more manageable focus for our discussion.

2. See my paper "*Ju-chia lun-li-(hsüeh) te hsien-tai-hua ch' ung-chien k' e-t' i*" ("On the Task of Constructive Modernization of Confucian Ethics and Morality"), presented at the International Conference on Confucianism and the Modern World, Taipei, November 13-18, 1987. It was subsequently published in *The International Symposium on Confucianism and the Modern World Proceedings* (Taipei, 1988), pp. 1213–24, as well as appearing in *Universitas* (Philosophy and Culture) *Monthly*, January, 1988.

3. See my paper, "*Ju-chia ssu-hsiang te shih-tai k' e-t' i chi ch' i chie-chüe hsien-suo*" ("On the Present-day Problems of Confucian Thought and the Key to Their Resolution"), in Yang Chün-shih and Tu Nien-chung, eds., *Ju-chia lun-li yü ching-chi fa-chan* (*Confucian Ethics and Economic Development*) (Taipei: Yüch'en Cultural Enterprise, Inc., 1987), pp. 1–43. Previously it was published in the *Chih-shih Fen-Tzu* (*Chinese Intellectuals*) *Quarterly* 2, no. 4 (New York, 1986), 4–14.

4. The concepts of inner sagehood and outer kingliness pervade Confucian philosophy, serving to indicate the means by which individual mortality is naturally extended to socio-political morality, with the sovereign serving as role model for ministers and subjects.

5. See Tsutomu Yuge, *TQC wa hito o tsukuru* (*TQC Creates Human Personality*) (Tokyo: Nikkagiren Publishing Company, 1982).

6. The Confucian doctrine of the Rectification of Names refers to the demand that each social rank realize the moral essence inherent in the name of that role. Thus, the Confucian saying "the sovereign [fulfills the role of] a sovereign, and the minister of a minister, the father of a father, the child of a child" (*Analects*, XII, xi). According to this doctrine, it is particularly incumbent upon the political leader to set a moral example for the subjects; to quote the words of Confucius, "To govern is to rectify [one's own name]. If you [Chi-k'ang Tzu] set an example by rectifying yourself, who dare not [emulate you] in rectifying himself?" (*Analects*, XII, xvii).

7. See *Mencius*, 6A.8.

8. Wing-tsit Chan, trans., *A Source Book in Chinese Philosophy* (Princeton, N.J.: Princeton University Press, 1963), p. 113.

9. Viktor E. Frankl, *Man's Search for Meaning: An Introduction to Logotherapy*, trans., Ilse Lasch (New York: Simon and Schuster, 1962), p. 104.

10. Frankl occasionally adds the "theological" dimension to these three, as a means of dealing with the supra- or ultimate meaning of life.

11. See Fritjof Capra, *The Tao of Physics: An Exploration of the Parallels Between Modern Physics and Eastern Mysticism* (Berkeley: Shambhala, 1975), and *The Turning Point: Science, Society, and the Rising Culture* (New York: Bantam Books, 1982); Bruce Holbrook, *The Stone Monkey: An Alternative, Chinese-Scientific Reality* (New York: William Morrow and Company, Inc., 1981); and Gary Zukav, *The Dancing Wu Li Masters: An Overview of the New Physics* (New York: Bantam Books, 1979).

12. Daisetz T. Suzuki, *Zen and Japanese Culture* (Princeton, N.J.: Princeton University Press, 1973); "General Remarks on Japanese Art Culture," pp. 21–37.

13. "At the age of fifteen, my mind was set on learning; at thirty, I established myself; at forty, I was free from perplexity; at fifty, I [began to] know the Mandate of Heaven; at sixty, my ears became [so] smooth [that I was able to listen receptively and was never offended]; at seventy, I [was finally able to] follow what my heart/mind desired without overstepping the bounds of what is right." *Analects* II, iv. My translation.

SELECTED BIBLIOGRAPHY

Capra, Fritjof. *The Tao of Physics: An Exploration of the Parallels Between Modern Physics and Eastern Mysticism.* Berkeley: Shambhala, 1975.

———. *The Turning Point: Science, Society, and the Rising Culture.* New York: Bantam Books, 1982.

Chan, Wing-tsit, trans. *A Source Book in Chinese Philosophy.* Princeton, New Jersey: Princeton University Press, 1963.

Confucius, *Analects.*

Frankl, Viktor E. *Man's Search for Meaning: An Introduction to Logotherapy,* trans. Ilse Lasch. New York: Simon and Schuster, 1962.

Fu, Charles Wei-hsun. *"Ju-chia lun-li-(hsüe) te hsien-tai-hua ch'ung-chien k'e-t'i"* ("On the Task of Constructive Modernization of Confucian Ethics and Morality"), *The International Symposium on Confucianism and the Modern World Proceedings.* Taipei, 1988; *Universitas* (Philosophy and Culture) *Monthly,* January, 1988.

———. *"Ju-chia ssu-hsiang te shih-tai k'e-t'i chi ch'i chie-chüe hsien-suo"* ("On the Present-day Problems of Confucian Thought and the Key to Their Resolution"), in Yang Chün-shih and Tu Nien-chung, eds., *Ju-chia lun-li yü ching-chi fa-chan (Confucian Ethics and Economic Development).* Taipei: Yüch'en Cultural Enterprise, Inc., 1987; *Chih-shih Fen-Tzu (Chinese Intellectuals) Quarterly* (New York, 1986), vol. 2, no. 4, 4–14.

Holbrook, Bruce. *The Stone Monkey: An Alternative, Chinese-Scientific Reality.* New York: William Morrow and Company, Inc., 1981.

Mencius, *Mencius.*

Suzuki, Daisetz T. *Zen and Japanese Culture.* Princeton, N.J.: Princeton University Press, 1973.

Yuge, Tsutomu. *TQC wa hito o tsukuru (TQC Creates Human Personality).* Tokyo: Nikkagiren Publishing Company, 1982.

Zukav, Gary. *The Dancing Wu Li Masters: An Overview of the New Physics.* New York: Bantam Books, 1979.

12 ASKING THE RIGHT QUESTIONS

EDUCATION AS DIALOGUE ON SOCIAL VALUES

Frances Moore Lappé

ASKING THE RIGHT QUESTIONS

I confess that I often enjoy agitating educators in my audiences when I announce, with many students present, that I started learning when I dropped out of school. I grew up in the 1950s in Texas where football was king and girls were supposed to look pretty and never admit that they had ever read a book. I went through college trying to trick my professors into not discovering that I was really the dumb, southern female that I knew I was.

So it was not until I dropped out of graduate school some years later that my education began. I discovered that I had my own questions—questions so pressing that I could not determine the direction of my life without pursuing them. I started reading, auditing courses, and spending endless hours in the library. What began to take shape were not answers, but an approach to learning that has been my life ever since.

I call it "following my nose." By this I mean that I never know exactly where I am headed; instead I let one question form the next, and then the next, and so on. My own experience has taught me that the essence of education is figuring out what the questions are. Let me give you an example.

A Case Study: World Hunger

In the late 1960s, the world food problem hit the international marquee. Paul Ehrlich's *Population Bomb* exploded. Books like *Famine 1975!* hit the stands. This was the general line of thinking they elicited:

Hunger exists.—Why?—Not enough food relative to people.—The answer? (a) produce more food (via the Green Revolution technology) or (b) cut some people off (Garrett Hardin's "Lifeboat Ethic").

But because I was not in a setting where this line of thinking was presented to me, ready-made, my own train of thought emerged, and went as follows:

Hunger exists.—Why?—People don't have food to eat.—Why?—Hungry people don't have power to secure either the food that exists or the resources that could produce food.—Why?—Because economic and political rules, customs, and institutions, backed by armed force, exclude them.—Why?—Because of belief systems that justify these human-made arrangements.—The answer? Change the economic and political rules that deny people power over life's essentials. Begin by challenging the belief systems that justify the human-made rules and institutions that distribute power so unevenly.

I use world hunger as an example not only because it has been my life's focus, but because at first blush the problem appears pretty straightforward: If people are hungry, just produce more food and get it into their mouths. I learned, however, that asking the wrong question, in this case, the narrow "how do you produce more food?" can actually end up exacerbating the problem. In *Food First: Beyond the Myth of Scarcity* and *World Hunger: Twelve Myths*, Joseph Collins and I document how this happens.[1] The new technology of production gives the already well-placed an incentive to expand their landholdings at the expense of poor peasant families. Landlessness increases, rural wages fall, and millions remain too poor to purchase the fruits of the new technology. So more food can actually mean *more* hunger. Today, Southeast Asia, where the Green Revolution technology has been most fully embraced, is home to more hungry people than any other part of the world.

After focusing for almost two decades on the tragedy of needless hunger, I have learned that to address any of the grave social and environmental challenges before us we must understand that how we ask the questions is the most important part of finding solutions. This means that we must have the confidence to keep asking why and why again. *Why* is there hunger? Not enough food. No, there is enough. *Why* is it not in the hands of the hungry? They lack resources with which to grow or buy it. *Why*? and so on. For me, the essence of the educational enterprise is to foster such honest probing, to continue asking into adult life those "why's" that once drove our parents nearly crazy! Never be satisfied with simple, pat answers.

DISCOVERING "THE QUESTIONS" IN DIALOGUE

If learning to ask the right questions is central to education, how do we teach and learn it? My one-word answer is *dialogue*. By this I do not mean anything mysterious. In my view, all genuine education is a type of dialogue—a dialogue within oneself, between oneself and the world, and between oneself and those whose wisdom one respects and hopes to acquire.

Dialogue—an environment we can create when we converse, write, or teach—has certain freeing characteristics:

1. it probes and does not assume, ever ready to ask why and why again;
2. it welcomes challenges to the prevailing framing of core questions;
3. it searches for underlying assumptions and values, encouraging participants to examine critically those that shape their own and others' views.

Furthermore, dialogue suggests three assumptions and possibilities of its own that I believe are important.

Dialogue Is an Open-ended Process, Not a Rigid Blueprint

The goal of dialogue is to facilitate, for all participants, the building of working hypotheses, continually tested through experience and interchange. The very method of dialogue carries an all-important message: Social change is an unending creative process, not an end point or ultimate state. Dialogue—by its very practice demonstrating that basic questions remain open—communicates to all involved that there is work to be done! The most important questions have not been settled for us once and for all. We have to figure things out; it is up to us. Dialogue is thus fundamentally democratic.

Dialogue Means Risk-taking

A second feature of the dialogic environment is risk. Dialogue suggests willingness to ask directly the biggest, most basic questions, to not skirt them for fear of sounding naive. In 1971, when *Diet for a Small Planet* was first released, I was terrified. What I was saying—that the world produces enough food and that more production itself would not solve the hunger problem—was so obvious, I figured *I* must be wrong. Otherwise, why were others not saying it?

I soon learned why. Many were not able to ask the fundamental, seemingly naive questions because they had been schooled by formal education and by their roles in institutions of power to narrow their vision, to specialize. Specialization can mean narrowing our questions to those that we can be sure to get right (How do I devise a more powerful pesticide?) and to avoid those where answers are less clear (How do I address the gross imbalance of power that leaves millions without land on which to use such new [and dubious] technologies to begin with?).

Asking the biggest questions also means willingness to make mistakes. (One is sure to!) But through dialogue one corrects mistakes, adjusts hypotheses, and moves forward. Real education, then, means learning to take this kind of risk—of being willing to be wrong.

Dialogue Teaches Judgment

Dialogue is the only way to develop judgment—discriminating reason. During a recent speaking trip to a small college in Ohio, I was struck by the distress of the very dedicated and "awake" biology professor who had invited me. It seemed that in the previous weeks his guest lecturers had been representatives of industrial agriculture—a Dow Chemical representative defending the necessity of heavy pesticide use in farming and a professor from the "bigger-is-better" school of agricultural economics. "How do I know whom to believe?" he asked me. "There's so much contradictory information. I don't know who is right."

What this young professor was really asking was: How does one develop judgment? How do we learn to sift out from the mass of information in today's learning environment what is important, useful, and true? How do we discriminate? My answer is that judgment forms only as we actively probe our underlying values. Useful information, we discover, is that which contributes to building the world we want to create, which in turn depends upon our values. But this requires that we know what our values are, that we can in fact envision a better future. Here I am reminded of the recommendation of Russian political philosopher, Peter Kropotkin, to students of the last century: "Think about the kind of world you want to live and work in. What do you need to build that world? Demand that your teachers teach you that."

But what kind of world *do* we want to live in? In other words, what *are* our values?

EDUCATION AS A DIALOGUE ABOUT VALUES

As *Washington Post* columnist Colman McCarthy reminded me a few weeks ago, "The trouble with all good ideas is that they soon degenerate into hard work." He is right, of course. But why should we take on this hard work of probing our assumptions? Because it simply is not possible to dislodge the diagnosis of the problems facing us from their many false premises without directly addressing the value assumptions underlying them.

Returning to the issue of hunger once more, recall that the prevailing view is that hunger results from a simple equation that has gotten out of balance: too many mouths on one side of the scale, and too little production on the other. But in the real world this diagnosis falls apart: An increase on the production side does not necessarily lessen hunger. The problem is that in its mechanistic supply-and-demand model, the conventional diagnosis leaves out *human relationships* based on human values. The equation-out-of-balance diagnosis is embedded in the prevailing mechanistic, Newtonian worldview in which human beings are reduced to calculating atoms. In a nutshell it goes something like this: Human beings are isolated egos. Self-protection and greed provide the momentum driving these separate atoms, while the market and private property are the laws of motion guiding their movement. And the natural world is a resource pool that the social atoms mine in their competitive struggle.[2]

Now there is, in this particular view of ourselves, a great deal that, on reflection, is clearly wrong. Yet the framework of social and economic theory based on it is so ingrained and sacrosanct that we are unable to conceive of the alternative ways of thinking needed to meet the unprecedented challenges ahead. However dysfunctional, these deeply embedded assumptions about our nature are very hard to perceive.

How do we examine something as amorphous and subconsciously rooted as our "worldview"? We have to analyze it. What are its parts? They are what I call our public or social *values*—the mental and emotional glue of our common life. Our public values are the assumptions and aspirations about what will "work"—what creates a healthy society. In our society these values include such lofty concepts as freedom, democracy, and fairness. They motivate and legitimize many of the social arrangements we take for granted. Only when we probe the meaning of these underlying values can we begin critically to reflect on our deepest beliefs and assumptions.

I turn now to my personal vision of how the educational process can be designed to carry out this analytic process. Because I reject the fairly prevalent notion that we are obliged to act, socially and economically, according to certain fixed laws of human behavior, my proposed educational method embodies the presumption of human agency, which is best discovered through a dialogic method. Thus, I wrote my latest book,

Rediscovering America's Values, as a dialogue, suggesting our human capacity actively to participate in creating new ways of thinking and being.

Rediscovering America's Values is a conversation about freedom, democracy, and fairness. One voice represents the prevailing perspective I just summarized, where freedom is equated with individual autonomy and where the political process itself is automatically suspect. The best we can hope for, it argues, is a society governed by laws of the marketplace and sanctified private property, allowing individuals to pursue their private ends.

The other voice in the dialogue (mine) represents an alternative grounded in the view that human behavior is socially constituted. We are who we are because of the matrix of relationships within which we live. In it, laws of the market and private property become mere tools of conscious human design, to be used in the service of whatever human aspirations we most value.

The method of dialogue thus suggests that the values about which we converse—freedom, democracy, fairness—neither emerge from nor are guaranteed by the fact that certain institutions exist. They are not equivalent to, for example, elected government, multiple parties, or the free market. Dialogue suggests that it is up to us first to define and then to actualize our public values. We cannot assume that simply because certain institutions are in place, our values will be guaranteed!

Dialogue further suggests that there are often quite divergent, and in some cases contradictory, definitions of public values, called by the same names, and that these differences must be brought to light and hammered out if we are to evolve, and not dissolve, as a society. Briefly, let me hint at some of those challenging differences in regard to "freedom" and "democracy."

Freedom

In late twentieth-century America, one definition of freedom has come to dominate. If we indeed are isolated egos and our stance toward one another is defensive, then private property is a good weapon of defense. The more we have, the freer we are, and the less we have to listen to or depend on others. Freedom easily becomes defined as *unrestricted* accumulation. Ronald Reagan put it well in 1983 when he proclaimed: "What I want to see above all else is that this country remain a country where someone can always get rich."

So by 1989, a Wall Street wizard such as Michael Milken, known for inventing "junkbonds" for leveraged buy-outs, makes $1000 a minute, and the gap between rich and poor is a widening chasm. In 1950 a chief executive officer made 41 times as much as the factory worker. That is no small gap. But by 1988 that gap had more than doubled, to 93 times![3]

In contrast to this view of freedom as individual, unlimited accumulation, a much longer tradition holds that freedom means the possibility for human growth. For many people—and in most religious traditions—freedom is not an end in itself. Rather, its purpose is the development of the uniquely human and individually unique potentialities of each person, be they intellectual, physical, artistic, or spiritual. Freedom of expression, religion, and participation, and more basically freedom from physical assault (both direct and through deprivation of life's necessities) are prerequisites to such development. Freedom so understood is not a finite, zero-sum quantity. My artistic development need not detract from yours. Your intellectual advances need not reduce my ability to develop my own intellectual powers. Assurances of my protection from physical assault, including my right to subsistence, need not prevent you from enjoying equal protection. (Sufficient resources already exist *to secure basic economic rights for everyone*, as our Institute has documented in *Food First* and *World Hunger: Twelve Myths*, among other works.)

Not only is freedom so defined not a zero-sum equation based on scarcity, it is a case in which the sum truly is greater than its parts. For not only does your freedom to develop your unique gifts not limit my expression, but my development often *depends upon* your freedom. How, for example can one achieve one's full potential of physical health unless others with talents in science and medicine are free to cultivate those talents? In this view, as the freedom of the poor is thwarted by poverty and hunger, so is the freedom of those who are well-fed. The failure of our society to protect economic rights means that all of its members are deprived of the intellectual breakthroughs, spiritual insights, musical gifts, and athletic achievements of those whose development has been blocked by poverty and hunger. Freedom understood only as the right to unlimited accumulation of productive property is indeed finite and divisible, but freedom to develop our unique capacities is infinite and indivisible.

Finally we should emphasize that these very different definitions of freedom—freedom for unlimited accumulation and freedom for unfettered human development—are incompatible. They cannot both flourish.

Democracy

Democracy: What is it? Is it an institution? Elections, political parties? In many societies where both these institutions exist, the vast majority of citizens live in misery, without even their most minimal needs being met. I think of the Philippines or many of the countries in Central America. In our prevailing worldview, we have conflated supposedly "democratic institutions" with democracy itself. From an alternative perspective, democracy is *not* particular institutions, but a set of working principles that create *a way of life*.

The central principle of democracy is accountability—the linking of rights with responsibility. Those empowered to make final decisions are responsible to all who must live with these decisions. Accountability means, of course, the sharing of power. Without the sharing of power to include all citizens, decision-makers remain unaccountable, and democracy is betrayed. While an equal sharing may be beyond human reach, in my definition of democracy no one is denied all power.

With this definition, we perceive the meaning of hunger in a new way. Since eating and feeding one's offspring come first for all living creatures, wherever people go chronically hungry amidst adequate food resources, have they not been robbed of power? If so, the very existence of hunger— here in the United States, or in Central America, or in India—belies democracy.

Here, then, in capsule form are two very different conceptions of values that Americans say they prize: "freedom" and "democracy." My point is twofold. First, our core public values do not automatically exist in the institutions of our society; they must be actively created and nurtured. Second, it follows that what is required is nothing less than a concept of citizens as definers and guardians of their shared social values and as active agents of change—talking, thinking, creating history. Herein lies the challenge to educators—for we face a major obstacle.

EDUCATION FOR CITIZENSHIP

Today citizenship is passive. Youths do not perceive themselves as actors with efficacy in the world. Certainly they do not see the political process as a vehicle through which to express their anger, concerns, and values. In a 1988 poll conducted by Peter D. Hart and Associates, young people said that they do not see a connection between their concerns about, for example, "homeless people walking the street" or "kids selling drugs," and government policies—either as causes or solutions. The young people do "not see political participation as a way to address the problems," Hart noted. The poll's findings included a notably passive concept of citizenship: Being a good citizen means that you "don't do anything wrong," or "hurt anybody else."

Citizenship. Today the very word seems to connote dull duty, not a life-enhancing aspect of daily living. But what, after all, *is* the difference between democratic, life-serving societies and authoritarian/totalitarian life-thwarting ones if not that of citizenship—of the assumption that in a democracy ordinary people are responsible for shaping their own future?

What distinguishes democratic from authoritarian society is the assumption that participation in political life—or public life—expresses and develops an essential dimension of our humanity: the need to be actors in a public world with purpose and power. Political life, as I am using it here, includes all our interactions with those beyond family and friendship circles to create and shape institutions of work, government, education, religion, health care, transportation, and recreation that make human society possible and life-enhancing.

Schooling in the Political Arts

So here is the challenge to educators. Despite the prevailing, passive understanding of citizenship, the reality is this: The very scale and complexity of today's problems mean that they can only be resolved within a social process of growing citizen knowledge and responsibility. This means first admitting our failure to educate knowledgeable and responsible citizens. For example, only one-quarter of adults can name the two senators from their own state, and one-third of Americans polled fear writing their representative to express an unpopular view. (Since the McCarthy era, the percentage of Americans who believe that they cannot freely express their views has doubled to 20 percent.)[4]

Next we must ask: What is the appropriate response? The 1980s produced dozens of major studies diagnosing America's educational problems and recommending solutions. Yet, many of the recommendations bring to mind the approach I referred to earlier as the conventional wisdom regarding world hunger. Applied to education, it targets the "factors of production": more hours in the classroom, higher salaries and/or standards for teachers, open enrollment in schools, and so on.

What educational reform typically does *not* address is the role of education in the challenge facing society and the planet as a whole: *How do we educate for citizenship*? That is, how do human beings come to feel empowered to change—and heal—our world? For me, that is *the* question. How do young people come to see a connection between their lives, what they learn, and the larger world that seems to be collapsing around them?

To be a citizen, I am convinced, is a learned art. We are not born effective actors in political life. We must learn the appropriate skills, including the abilities to:

understand and exercise power relationally rather than one-directionally;

listen actively;

express anger, compassion, and other emotions constructively;

reflect continually on experience as a guide to action;

exercise imagination in appreciating the self-interests of others;

accept ambiguity and tragedy as among the givens of the human condition.

Such are the arts that make democracy possible, and many of them can be learned in the classroom. It is my contention that what we do in the classroom to educate for citizenship cuts right to the core of our planet's survival. So, how do we do it? How do we educate for active engagement in addressing the problems before us?

First, the classroom environment must embody the reality of personal empowerment. I have stressed the importance of dialogue, guided to encourage the continuous asking of "why's." Now let me go further. In dialogue, it is not just the issues that we learn to discuss, or the structures of government we memorize, or the values that we explore. We can also learn concepts and exercise practices essential to democracy. I will mention two: relational power and self-interest.

Relational Power

In the prevailing worldview, power is one-directional. It is the ability to influence: the cue-ball sinks the 8-ball in the corner pocket. That is power! Once we perceive the human essence as social, however, such a unidirectional notion of power becomes unthinkable. Categories of actor and acted-upon are no longer distinct. Every interaction changes all parties involved. From these insights it follows that none of us is ever completely powerless, completely unable to change others or ourselves.

Today's prevailing image of power, however, encourages those viewed as powerless to see themselves as helpless victims. It divides us into power-holders and victims. It is static. Relational power, on the other hand, is dynamic. It opens possibilities.

How do individuals come to perceive and reflect on the implications of relational power? In all our writing, teaching, and organizational work, we educators—and society as a whole—can create settings in which individuals come to experience power as grounded in learning and self-knowledge. In such settings power is no longer "zero-sum" and one-way—it expands for all. In so doing, education shifts the emphasis of coursework from passive learning to a sequence of learning–acting–reflecting.

A personal experience brought some of these themes home to me recently. In his senior year in a large public high school, my son Anthony took a course last year called "Politics and Power." The teacher constituted two classes as a mock Congress—one the House, the other, the Senate. My son was elected Senate majority leader—Robert Byrd. The students had to write legislation, hold hearings, mark up bills, lobby each other, and vote. They learned how Congress works by *being* a congress themselves.

The effect on my son amazed me. He had always been interested in "the issues," and picked up a lot of information and political viewpoints from our family discussions, but his interest had been passive. Suddenly, that changed. He was on the telephone most nights planning strategies with fellow Democrats or trying to persuade Republicans on everything from the death penalty, to Contra aid, to nuclear power. In many of these exchanges, he had to probe his own value assumptions more deeply. To be persuasive he discovered that he had to understand why others believed the way they did and directly address their concerns. Because the course required that he take a stand and know why, what were before somebody else's issues became his. I noticed that on college applications where he had put architecture as a possible major field he began to add political science. Anthony began to perceive power not just as something out there over him, but something that he could participate in as he learned the demanding skills required.

Another example struck me this spring: a report of a social studies class in a New Jersey high school. The class was studying Thomas Paine and one student decided to write a paper in the spirit of Paine's pamphlets. Her moving case for how polystyrene trays in the school cafeteria were contributing to environmental damage convinced her fellow students to take action. Her ideas ended up not only getting rid of polystyrene in her school cafeteria but in all the township schools. Her teacher told the *New York Times*: "[T]his is what teaching is really about. It's getting involved in things in society. There's a sense of hope in these youngsters."[5]

Classrooms thus must become an environment for rethinking power—learning that no one is completely powerless, that we need skills to wield power effectively, that power is not a dirty word but essential to act on our values.

Self-interest

In today's prevailing worldview, self-interest and selfishness are indistinguishable—simply that which serves the private gain of the individual. But self-interest is a much richer concept. Self-interest is one's arena of meaning: all the things that matter—one's family, friends, religious faith, work commitments, security, health and so on. It is one's identity. So understood, self-interest is impossible to further except in relationships, both public and private; selfishness then quickly becomes the enemy of self-interest. Thus the classroom should be an environment that abjures selfish competition and nurtures and develops true self-interest through an understanding of its relationship with others' self-interest—the very basis of cooperation and constructive political engagement. To exercise such relational power and experience a deepened understanding of self-interest requires specific skills, such as listening, critical thinking, and reflection, which can all be learned in the classroom.

So I am suggesting that education must be understood as schooling in the arts of political life, hardly a novel idea. It is an idea to which we must return. As the American philosopher and educator John Dewey put it:

The keynote of democracy as a way of life may be expressed, it seems to me, as the necessity for the participation of every mature human being in formation of the values that regulate the living of men together. . . .

The school cannot be a preparation for social life excepting as it reproduces, within itself, the typical conditions of social life.[6]

Today, surely, our very survival depends upon such an understanding of education.

CONCLUDING REFLECTIONS

Planetary crisis calls upon us to rethink all our major institutions, but perhaps education above all. At a time when our inherited worldview, on which our educational system is based, is dysfunctional, is incapable of offering solutions, we are forced back to the drawing board. The role of educators is transformed. The curriculum is no longer a set of answers, but a series of questions. Teaching perforce becomes a dialogue, not simply about the answers but about what are the questions we must be asking in order to see a future.

Seeing education as an ongoing dialogue about core social values makes it possible to probe underlying assumptions, allowing us to examine an inherited worldview. We gain confidence in asking the biggest questions,

questions for which there are no easy rights and wrongs. By doing this, we learn that answers are not all there for us simply to absorb. And this means the realization that it is up to us! There are no broadly informed experts up there, taking care of business for us. We must hone the tools we need to wield effective power; we must learn the arts of political life.

In so doing, we create an active concept of citizenship as meaningful power to shape one's life and society according to one's deepest values. Our understanding of power and self-interest begins to change. Education then becomes a force for the profound democratic awakening needed if we are to meet the challenges of the twenty-first century.

NOTES

1. Frances Moore Lappé and Joseph Collins. *Food First: Beyond the Myth of Scarcity* (New York: Ballantine Books, 1977) and *World Hunger: Twelve Myths* (San Francisco: Food First Books and Grove Press, 1986).

2. For a more detailed summary of this view, with historical references, see the introduction to Frances Moore Lappé, *Beyond America's Values* (New York: Ballantine Books, 1989).

3. Roy A. Schotland, "Rich Get Even Richer," letter to the editor, *New York Times*, May 14, 1989, p. E22; it is based on research by the AFL-CIO.

4. *San Francisco Chronicle*, September 12, 1987, p. 5; citing a study by James Gibson, a political scientist from the University of Houston.

5. George James, "A Revolutionary Idea: Schools' Plastics Ban," *The New York Times*, April 28, 1989, p. A16.

6. A. H. Johnson, ed., *The Wit and Wisdom of John Dewey* (1949), pp. 90, 103.

SELECTED BIBLIOGRAPHY

Barber, Benjamin. *Strong Democracy: Participatory Politics for a New Age*. Berkeley and Los Angeles: University of California Press, 1984.

Boyte, Harry C. *CommonWealth: A Return to Citizen Politics*. New York: Free Press, 1989.

Lappé, Frances Moore. *Rediscovering America's Values*. New York: Ballantine Books, 1989.

Walsh, Debbie, and Richard W. Paul. *The Goal of Critical Thinking from Educational Ideal to Educational Reality*. New York: American Federation of Teachers Educational Issues Department, 1988.

IV Alternative Visions Not Currently Taught

13 THE NEED FOR GLOBAL EDUCATION

Robert W. Malone

THE MAGNITUDE OF THE PROBLEM

Human dignity demands the promotion of health. To be healthy is to be whole, to be whole is to be unfragmented, to be unfragmented is to be unified in body and spirit, and to be unified is to speak in one voice. But today we speak in many tongues; we are fragmented in politics, economics, and spirit; we have no leader; and, as a species, we have no dignity.

Perhaps this is to be expected. Humanity, after all, is only in its infancy. Our history would occupy less than a minute if we counted the time from the origin of the Earth to the present as one year. Given what we do know of our beginnings in the evolution of complex biological systems, it seems that something of a miracle has happened. Whether it be by the emergence of awareness from inert matter or by the emergence of matter from a morphogenetic consciousness, the development of our understanding over the millennia—through our creative activity in the sciences, the arts, and in commerce with one another—has led to a tiny, but crucial, recognition of the inherent nobility, worth, and divinity of awareness itself. But, as Christopher Hitchens has said, we stand "in the prehistory of the human race, where no tribalism can be better than another, and where humanism and internationalism, so much derided and betrayed, need an unsentimental and decisive restatement."[1] We are at a crossroads where we either promote poise, self-respect, and a reverence for one another and our place in the cosmos, or suffer terribly and die.

Some of the best minds in this century have intimated there is no hope. Arthur Koestler, for one, suggested that we are doomed because of Nature's evolutionary error in putting a cerebrum on top of an uncooperative lizard brain.[2] Koestler argued that our tendency to aggression is innate; what once served as a tool for survival is too powerful to be stopped. If he is right, then our global fragmentation may be only the projective reflection of our individual inner biological functioning and there may be nothing we can do about it except wait for the end.

However, I contend that Koestler's despair was due to a lack of imagination. For, despite our history of violence, there do exist many examples of cooperative and creative societies supporting mutual well-being. My hometown, St. Catharines, within certain bounds, is one of them, and, on a larger scale, the emergence of Europe as a single entity may be another. That we can imagine a cooperative and mutually supportive global society is sufficient for its possibility. But, as Gro Brundtland has stated, threats to the security, well-being, and very survival of our planet make the development of global unity necessary now.[3]

Given our options, what should we do? One thing is certain—we cannot depend upon anyone else to save us. As the Tibetan Buddhist, Tarthang Tulku, has said, "Ultimately there is no way to escape taking responsibility for ourselves."[4] Taking responsibility means we must teach and promote our well-being through action. It requires healthy, that is unfragmented, education. It requires that we not separate *theoria* (our understanding of our condition) from *praxis* (our activities), and that we continually question whether our behavior is promoting our well-being or is contributing toward our demise.

Education today, however, is not healthy. Fragmented into disparate disciplines with no species-ethical grounding, it neither disseminates the global facts of our condition, nor promotes appropriate action. When the basics of our global condition are ongoing warfare, a disregard for the well-being of our children, and a contempt for the ecosystem that sustains us, then something is drastically wrong with both our *theoria* and our *praxis*. We have failed to make connections.

True, since the publication of *Our Common Future* two years ago, with its call for *immediate* action to insure our survival, there have been hundreds of meetings of experts, a plethora of conferences, and a heightened public awareness that our future is less than certain. But we have yet to act with any conviction. We know, on some level, that today's most important problems are global in nature. We know that their presence threatens our well-being. On the horizon of our consciousness we, the general public, are becoming vaguely uneasy in our awareness of the emerging details.

We are now aware that the world's population is increasing exponentially, while our agricultural output has been steadily declining since 1984; aware that within thirty years only four large tracts of wilderness will be left on the planet; aware that although the current functioning of Gaia is dependent upon the current multiplicity of flora and fauna, species extinction is taking place at the rate of two per hour; aware that major shipments of toxic wastes are being disposed of in the seas and in Third World countries at the rate of one every five minutes throughout the year; aware that in New Zealand a recent study confirmed that skin cancer has increased while agricultural production has declined as a result of ozone thinning; aware that the seas will be rising; aware that our children's lives will likely be drastically different from our own.[5]

How different? No one knows for sure. Politicians, fearing the alienation of their constituents, urge further studies, arguing that present models are not precise enough to justify action. But we do have models, and we are using them. Indeed, Isaac Newton's vision of Nature permeates the most intimate aspects of our lives. The questions we should all be asking are whether such models are appropriate, and whose ends they serve. Given the seriousness of our condition, it is idiotic that we are not developing better mathematical models of our global situation.[6] That so little funding is available for their development is indicative of the sorry state of our current short-term oriented consciousness. Furthermore it is appalling that global modeling is far behind the development of models for business growth—models that falsely assume that in the next thirty years, overall, the world will be somewhat the same as it is now, and that, by the miracle of sustained development, our future will be assured. We also know, however, that we need not wait for mathematical certitude to understand the extent and gravity of our difficulties, to feel and to act.

Long ago, around the sixth century A.D., Easter Island, lying peacefully in the Pacific about 2,300 miles from South America, was a paradise of lush foliage, and the home of an advanced people. Today what remains is bleak arid rock, gargantuan statues, tablets of hieroglyphic script, and bones as a testimony to a civilization's failure and eventual death.[7] The studies of Heyerdahl and Cousteau suggest that some 200 people originally arrived from Marquesas or South America, and grew to about 20,000. But by 1722 wars had decreased the population to 3,000, and in 1774 Cook discovered but 600 inhabitants, of which only 30 were women. We know what happened, for they left records. With overpopulation, they stripped their resources. In the ensuing battle for survival they rigidified a class structure led by priests who were assumed to know what was best. But even the priests were unable to avoid an eventual bloodbath as those who lacked firewood and food banded together to unwittingly destroy the last bastions of that civilization.

Today, although our material wealth in some parts of the world is beyond what could have been envisioned by the Easter Islanders, our overall situation is not much different from theirs just prior to their demise. We know, without sophisticated mathematical models, that our behavior is now leading us in the same direction, toward a probable end not in the distant future but possibly within our children's lifetimes.

So why are so many of us going about our usual business? Is it because we have an innate tendency to avoid coming to terms with imminent catastrophe?

DEFINING THE GLOBAL CURRICULUM

The "Global Education" mentioned in my title might be understood as the universal education of humankind—a worthy goal. But we first have to ask: what will we teach? Shall we attempt to teach the facts of our condition as if they lay before us waiting to be read from some Baconian book of Nature? This is absurd. There are too many facts to be taught, yet they are insufficient. We need instead to exercise our intelligence to grasp and teach what is best—namely the promotion of our well-being—whatever shibboleths must fall by the wayside, no matter how painful.

Global education demands an understanding of the underlying ethical attitudes of our activities. Who will question those attitudes if we, as academics, do not? For example, is our educational system so insane that we accept and thereby promote the mad ravings of those who believe that the proliferation of instruments of violence is good for us, and the only way to peace?

Some of the unhappy facts of our condition are being disseminated through the media, but in spite of this we still suffer from serious misunderstandings about the nature of global problems. While we have all been told that there are environmental, economic, and political crises—the greenhouse effect, species extinction, the hole in the ozone layer, the Third World debt, the instability of political institutions—and have been informed that there are some causative agents such as carbon dioxide emissions, deforestation, poverty, and a dearth of the appropriate sustainable development, we clearly do not comprehend. We misunderstand precisely because an insistence on the facts alone constitutes that little bit of knowledge that is a dangerous thing.

A fact-oriented perspective dangerously and falsely assumes that massive financial support will effect a cure. It presupposes that identifiable components of our global problems have linear connections with individual causes, and that the removal of *the* cause is sufficient for the solution.

This view is predicated on the false belief that our global problems, although serious, are merely the *sum* of a set of familiar problems, and only demand more of the same familiar expert attention to effect a resolution. It assumes that if our Earth has problems, these can be solved by experts. We take our car to Midas for a muffler repair, or to a body shop for a dent. But where will we take the Earth?

THE NEED FOR SYSTEMIC SOLUTIONS

Our global problems are not a simple sum but are systemic, and there are no experts to whom they can be taken. A system can be defined as a functional whole not reducible to the sum of its parts. Systems surround us. Each one of us is a biological system.[8] An automobile is a system. Our computers are systems. Understanding a system means knowing how each component contributes to the *functioning* of the higher organization. Curing a systems problem means knowing how the system operates in its entirety and what contributes to its maintenance. Good doctors and mechanics are small systems experts. What good doctor would prescribe salve for an itch that represents a symptom of the body's inability to function well without adequate vitamin A? What good mechanic would merely replace a battery when a faulty voltage regulator has burned out the starter and the alternator?

To solve global problems we need *world*-systems experts able to coordinate and synthesize the expertise of agronomists, demographers, ecologists, and so forth. To proceed otherwise assumes that the Earth is made up of separate parts, unconnected with one another and independent of the functioning of the whole. But we know better. J. E. Lovelock, in *Gaia*, makes an eloquent and convincing case for the systemic nature of our planet, and the perilousness of continuing with a fragmented approach to isolated aspects of the Global Problematique.[9]

Among the complexly interacting global problems facing us are widespread pollution of air, soil, and water; climate changes; depletion of resources through deforestation, desertification, mining, and species extinctions; population growth, accompanied by hunger, disease, and poverty; social and economic instability, coupled with urban decay, unemployment, fiscal uncertainty, and psychological alienation; and continuing political discontent exhibited in authoritarianism, oppression, arms buildups, and local wars. These are not separable. A change in any one of them has a corresponding ripple effect upon the rest.

Population growth, for example, is both a cause and a result of social instability, and leads on the one hand to increased resource depletion and pollution, and on the other to disease and political unrest. Likewise, arms races are both a consequence and a cause of sociopolitical unrest owing to resources deflected into armaments that might better be invested in health, education, research, and economic infrastructure.

We are beginning to understand that we are making an egregious error if we look only at single factors.[10] Such reductionist approaches are useless. There is no cornerstone, no one place to start. The origin of our condition is not disarmament, deforestation, distrust, or any other single variable. It is our failure to address a whole whose nature cannot be reduced linearly to Aristotelian first cause components. We know that we need to think globally, that to solve global problems we need world systems analysis. But how many universities have this subject as part of the curriculum? Which courses are students required to take that address the systemic nature of our condition? Right now, we have virtually no programs that even attempt to teach this.

What we need are individuals trained to address problems from a systems perspective, making connections that cut across narrow special-izations. As an example, consider an orchestra playing a symphony. Imagine that orchestra without a conductor, so that each player has his or her own music and only an inkling of what the others are playing from moment to moment, unaware that other musicians may be taking cues from his or her playing. Some musicians might be playing Beethoven and others Wagner. The resulting cacophonous music would be blamed on the others. "The conservative bass player has not enough oomph." "The liberal violins are playing too loudly." "The militaristic percussion has taken over." Today's economists, politicians, and businessmen remind me of these musicians. No wonder we are hearing so much talk of leadership, excel-lence, teamwork, management, and organization, and are obsessed with the need for these skills!

Another example is found in the medical profession. Imagine that there were only kidney experts; heart specialists; podiatrists; and eye, ear, nose, and throat specialists, but no general practitioners with the overall under-standing of how these specialties fit together. Do you feel a general malaise—boils, acne, multiple colds, the flu—because your basic immune system is not working properly? Take some salve for your boils, wash your face more thoroughly, take two aspirins and go to bed! It is the same way with the world. How long will we treat only the isolated symptoms of our global malaise?

World systems is not a traditional area of study in universities or elsewhere. Lamentably, the closest thing to it is the excellent, if wretchedly underfunded, quantitative modeling of political-military dynamics, where political decisions, economics, population growth and movement, geographic boundaries, and agricultural and industrial production are some of the multivariables given consideration in attempts to uncover and predict the factors that lead to war.[11]

Nor do the media contribute to a wider understanding of the issues involved, for their presentations of global problems continue to promote piecemeal solutions. Sadly, neither do the film and rock stars who support such worthy goals as saving rain forests. Deforestation, like all of the other problems in the complex, has underlying causes that must be *system*-ically addressed. We cannot merely reforest, although Norman Meyers, a senior fellow with the World Wildlife Fund, estimates that cost (approximately $120 billion) as far less than the cost of the dams and sea walls that will be necessary to protect coastal regions of the United States from rising sea levels due to the greenhouse effect.[12] Meyers's work is superb. The World Wildlife Foundation's contributions to our understanding of the necessity of preserving the multiplicity of flora and fauna on our planet cannot be overstated. But we cannot merely reforest.

Once we see the systems nature of global problems, this simple approach amounts to little more than rearranging the deck chairs on the Titanic. Should we not ask whose ends any single proposal serves— whether humankind and the Earth, or a privileged elite? Are we so stupid as to believe we can get away with that kind of simplistic thinking? Despite writings popularized over the last ten years, an overriding tendency toward reductionist solutions persists. Reductionists assume that the edifice of our difficulties can be dismantled by analyzing it down to its simplest atomic constituents. We have come a long way since Laplace believed that all of reality could be reduced to motion amongst particles, yet reductionism is alive and well.

The Western *Zeitgeist* is dominated by the drive toward *success*, measured by *position* (wealth and social status), and *momentum* (of business acumen). Hence the Newtonian particles of Laplace could be replaced by the constructs of "individuals," under the influence of "market forces." In this metaphysical phase space of buying and selling, market forces become the constituent of reality upon which everything turns. Those who unwittingly adopt this perspective believe "common sense" decrees that the problem is purely an economic one. For example, in a column in the business section of Canada's national newspaper, Terence Corcoran recently wrote:

Environmental Consciousness Is Not Enough

The Brundtland Commission report, issued in April 1987, proposed an approach to global environmental and economic problems called 'Sustained development.' [*sic!*] Because the report explicitly acknowledges that growth is essential to economic prosperity and a cleaner environment, some Canadian business leaders appear to feel comfortable with the idea . . . .

But in buying into the Brundtland approach to environmental economics—a deeply muddled, bureaucratic, interventionist approach—Canadian business executives may have bought into an inhospitable idea system that in the long run will do nothing but cause political and economic damage.[13]

The next day Corcoran added insult to injury with: "BRUNDTLAND MESSAGE LACKS ECONOMIC BASE." In a cliché-ridden attack on Brundtland, he stated:

Occasional references to market forces give the report a patina of acceptability to western industry . . . but for the most part reading it is like riding a fast moving treadmill through the towering bromides of U.N. egalitarianism and third world economic planning.

Note his emphasis on interventionism. Intervene in what? Market forces? Do market forces arise *ex nihilo*—sacrosanct, unbiasedly serving our well-being as natural and ethically neutral as apple pie? Political and economic damage? There will certainly be enough of that if we do not change our way of thinking and acting, as if free enterprise were itself the cornerstone of right thinking and right action! I am deeply disturbed about a "common sense," reductionist worldview that places market forces above concern for our global and species well-being.

At a meeting in Geneva Switzerland in May 1989, I discussed global problems at length with electronic information experts, representatives of United Nations groups, and nongovernment organizations, East and West. In our conversations, the head information officer for the International Organization of Journalists in Prague and I talked extensively about political bias, and he noted the need for a common language of discourse.[14]

Now despite their differences in ideological approaches, one might assume that scientists have a common language and are working toward value-neutral solutions in the best interests of both East and West. However, it is precisely the ideological approaches that scientists and the rest of us adopt that are a part of the problem. Until we understand that the "unbiased" reporting of "facts" in "common-sense" terms is but a product of our ideological and mythological categories, our doors of perception cannot be cleared to allow for the new insights we so desperately need.

In the West the dominant myth is that our system of political organization and the free-market release of business energy can solve anything.

The marketplace, without intervention, is the great equalizer, creating the best of all possible worlds. Corcoran's call for nonintervention in the marketplace is ironic, for if there were ever a system devised by humankind that intervenes in the ongoing processes of life on our planet, it is the marketplace, with its attempts to woo us into a sense of well-being through the ownership of commodities. What we need instead is the cultivation of the understanding that we are part of a very large *system* which we are only beginning to comprehend, much less only beginning to take joy in. Furthermore, everything I have said about the ideology of a free-market economy could be said about those economies that are centrally controlled, many of which are failing fast.

To teach global problems, we must teach that, ontologically—in terms of their being—they must be understood beyond our "common-sense" presuppositions. For our problems, at heart, are not economic—at least in the business sense. Let us move beyond "common sense" analysis to some reflections about the wisdom embedded in language. We might know, for example, *a priori*, that our *economy* cannot take precedence over *ecology*. "Eco" has its root in "oikos," meaning "house." "Nomos" refers to law, and government. Economics, then, can be understood as the way we govern and manage our house. "Logos" means principle—the word, as "in the beginning was the word." Ecology is thus the study of natural principles—the principles and natural laws through which the house unfolds and works—the laws which the house, independent of our governing, obeys. Shall we manage in accordance with natural law—*logos*? Or shall we have the *hubris* to suppose that we exist outside of the natural principles that regulate, imposing our own laws of management based on "market principles"?

We live in interesting times, facing the most challenging problem of human history. Can a solution be bought? Is it possible that we can impose on Nature a monetary force that is greater than her own? An important fact we should all teach is that "Mother Nature cannot be bought—She has too much integrity!"

The forces that may now bring catastrophic upheaval to our species are not those that money or political will alone can buy. We know from some of the work of people present here today, that Nature, once set in motion, cannot be stopped—there comes a point of no return, where the dissolution and reorganization of the totality is certain. Because of this, we cannot depend on market forces to be the appropriate determinants of that necessary social change that will contribute toward our well-being. Market forces, by their very nature, are not sufficiently swift. In the case of global problems, these forces depend upon the majority of citizens feeling directly threatened before they are willing to buy into a solution—a solution we may not have time to manufacture.

THE MORAL IMPERATIVE OF POLITICAL ACTION IN ACADEMIA

During our first conference "Sanity, Science and Global Responsibility" at Brock University, a former Federal Minister of the Environment of Canada told me:

It may be possible to pull together academics behind a global vision, but what is most important is that there not be merely talk—there must be action—minimally the mobilization of will on the part of the population to support the recommendations for sustainable development found in the Brundtland report. That means we must work toward support of change now—the kinds of change none of us are going to be comfortable with. We are all slow to act. We tend to behave only in response to crises. The crisis which is certain to occur soon is still distant in most people's minds. I am afraid that by the time people become personally aware of the seriousness of our difficulties, it will be too late. Some of my constituents are now saying that they are sick of hearing of the environment. Can academics become sufficiently politically active to effect the change in attitudes which are necessary?[15]

Can academics teach political activism? We must. For example, we must be willing to speak up against the abominable dissemination of nonsense that appears everyday in our newspapers.

On the most fundamental of ethical grounds, what are we, who have the responsibility to speak the ethical truth concerning our common humanity, to make of Corcoran's expression, "towering bromides of U.N. egalitarianism"? Is it acceptable to us that the economically well-off, in response to a globally worsening economic condition, are forming a circle of wagons against the four-fifths of our fellow beings who are suffering? Do we find here, once again, a call for entrenchment by the twentieth century's equivalent of the priests on Easter Island? Don't we know better?

Egalitarianism means equal political, economic, and legal rights for all. If we do not have the ethical sensitivity to be egalitarians, then we are morally bankrupt, because egalitarianism is the ethical core. Without the ideal of egalitarianism, we can relax in our wealth and let the rest of the world go to hell. If we do not have egalitarianism as the *theoria* out of which our *praxis* emerges, then we have forgotten our political origins. "We hold these truths to be self-evident, that all men [*sic*] are created equal." This is orthodoxy—right belief. We need now, as the Roman Catholic priest Matthew Fox has argued, orthopraxis—right action. Responsible *activism*. Can it be taught in the interstices of the facts of our disciplines? We must never suppose that merely because of our economic grace (where by the exigencies of history, we are richer even than Louis XIV, who, after all, did not even have flush toilets), that those economic considerations give us any rights or privileges beyond those of the dispossessed. Can we teach this value as a part of global education? Will we?

Let me remind you that many world leaders are calling for fundamental change at all levels. At a recent meeting in Moscow, Soviet General Secretary Gorbachev called for the world's intelligentsia (that means us) to "stimulate research into the most burning problems of international life and cooperate in creating projects on the global problems of humanity, including its newest and most pernicious illnesses."[16] The International Foundation for the Survival and Development of Humanity was formed at that meeting, supported by representatives of the Carnegie, MacArthur, and Rockefeller Foundations.[17] Is there hope? Is a new vision emerging?

CONCLUSION

To sum up, global problems are not merely a sum that has piled up because of inattention, and cannot be solved by reducing them to their simplest constituents. Global problems are systemic. Since the early Greeks we have distinguished between ontology and epistemology. The former refers to what is, the latter to our understanding of it. What is, is one. What we teach is fragmented. We teach what we understand, and our universities reflect an outmoded understanding. I refer again to the compartmentalization of faculties that originated with the compartmentalization of human faculties theorists of the eighteenth and nineteenth centuries, who still influence us.

We have seen that the ontological order—that is, the facts concerning our condition—does not correspond to our manner of approach in order to promote our well-being. Shall I put it in academic terms? We are in need of study that is epistemically isomorphic to the ontological nature of the problems which beset us, and which addresses the systemic nature of our being! Although I am sympathetic toward integrated and interdisciplinary studies as a way of approaching our problems, we do not need another hybrid, arising merely from cross-pollination. We do not need more biochemistry, bioethics, business ethics, philosophical psychology. Those courses may be useful, but they are not enough.

What we do need is nothing less than an erotic and synthesizing remarriage of the Arts and Sciences as part of a systems core curriculum for every student, grounded in an ethic of respect for our species' well-being. We need to understand, teach, and overcome the abominable inertia, separating our vague theoretical awareness from the activities now demanded. We need Human and Global Studies, based on, but transcending, the traditional disciplines—studies that directly and holistically address the concerns facing us. Teaching of this kind demands a willingness to promote our well-being first, unfettered by artificial limits. It is not difficult. We need only teach students to ask: "Are current decision-making processes contributing toward the common good? And if not, why not? What can I personally *do* to ensure that my children will not merely survive, but experience joy"?

This demands teachers who comprehend that understanding without action is empty, who understand that with regard to the issues now paramount for our survival, the emperor of our current institutional core curricula has no clothes. This demands teachers willing to work toward change in the current world order, willing to work dialogically and practically on behalf of human and global responsibility. It demands activists. Is anyone out there listening?

NOTES

1. Christopher Hitchens, *Prepared for the Worst, Selected Essays and Minority Reports* (London: Chatto and Windus, 1988), p. 357.

2. Arthur Koestler, "A Glance Through the Keyhole," *Janus, A Summing Up* (New York: Vintage Books, 1978), p. 274.

3. The World Commission on Environment and Development, *Our Common Future* (Oxford University Press, 1987), p. 343. [This report is often referred to as the Brundtland Report: eds.]

4. Tarthang Tulku, *Gesture of Balance* (Berkeley: Dharma Publishing, 1982), p. 25.

5. David Suzuki, "Biosphere Dwarfs Other Issues," *Toronto Globe and Mail*, June 10, 1989, p. D4.

6. Idiotic, from the Greek *Idiotis*, meaning a private person—someone who has no awareness beyond his or her own presumed individuality. There are too many idiots today, and they all need educating.

7. See Jacques Cousteau, "Easter Island," *The Cousteau Almanac* (Norfolk: The Cousteau Society), 1981.

8. This means we are not reducible to any one of our heart, liver, muscle, or circulatory *systems*, or, in spite of contemporary popular academic philosophical absurdity to the contrary, our brain.

9. See J. E. Lovelock, *Gaia, A New Look at Life on Earth* (Oxford: Oxford University Press, 1989).

10. [This point is also made in the following paper by Johan Galtung: eds.]

11. For example, see the many good studies arising out of the Correlates of War Project at the University of Michigan, headed by J. David Singer. This work, based on empirical data, needs continued support as part of a systems analysis of our global situation. Richard Chadwick at the University of Hawaii has contributed to both modeling Military Dynamics, and Environmental and Global modeling. Don MacRae's work with

the Australian Resources and Environmental Assessment Project (AREA) was an extension of the global model created by the Systems Analysis Research Unit (SARU) of the United Kingdom Departments of Environment and Transport. Information on the AREA model may be obtained from Don MacRea, Research and Information Branch, Department of Arts, Heritage and Environment, G.P.O. Box 1252, Canberra, A.C.T. 2601, Australia. Information on exactly why this sort of research is not being funded more extensively today may be more difficult to obtain.

12. See Norman Meyers, "First Word," *OMNI*, vol. 11, no. 8 (May 1989), 8.

13. Terence Corcoran, "Brundtland Message Lacks Economic Base," *The Toronto Globe and Mail*, June 14, 1989, p. B2.

14. Director of Department of Information Resources, International Organization of Journalists, Washingtonova 17, 110 00 Praha 1, Czechoslovakia.

15. St. Catharines, Ontario, July 1988.

16. Moscow, February 16, 1987.

17. Further information on this foundation, which supports international research projects, may be obtained by writing to: *The International Foundation for the Survival and Development of Humanity*, 109 11th Street, S.E., Washington, D.C. 20003.

SELECTED BIBLIOGRAPHY

Bohm, David. *Science, Order and Creativity*. Toronto: Bantam Books, 1987.

Brundtland, Gro Harlem. *Our Common Future*. Oxford: Oxford University Press, 1987.

Corcoran, Terence. "Brundtland Message Lacks Economic Base." *The Toronto Globe and Mail*, June 14, 1989.

Cousteau, Jacques. "Easter Island," *The Cousteau Almanac*. Norfolk: The Cousteau Society, 1981.

Hitchens, Christopher. *Prepared for the Worst, Selected Essays and Minority Reports*. London: Chatto and Windus, 1988.

Koestler, Arthur. "A Glance Through the Keyhole," *Janus, A Summing Up*. New York: Vintage Books, 1978.

Lovelock, J. E. *Gaia, A New Look at Life on Earth*. Oxford: Oxford University Press, 1979.

Meyers, Norman. "First Word," *OMNI*, vol. 11, no. 8 (May 1989), 8.

Suzuki, David. "Biosphere Dwarfs Other Issues," *Toronto Globe and Mail*, June 10, 1989, p. D4.

Tulku, Tarthang. *Gesture of Balance*. Berkeley: Dharma Publishing, 1982.

Wald, George. *The New Yorker*, March 22, 1969, 29–31.

14 FORGOTTEN FUNDAMENTALS OF STEADY GROWTH

Albert A. Bartlett

INTRODUCING THE EXPONENTIAL FUNCTION

As a scientist, I happen to believe that the greatest shortcoming of the human race is our inability to understand the exponential function. The "exponential function" is the mathematical statement we write down to describe the size of anything that is growing steadily. If something is growing at 5 percent per year, the exponential function would show how large that growing quantity becomes, year after year. We are talking about a situation where the time required for the quantity to increase by a fixed fraction is a constant. So for 5 percent per year, the 5 percent is a fixed fraction and the year is a fixed length of time. That is what we want to talk about: ordinary, steady growth.

If it takes a fixed length of time to grow by 5 percent, it follows that it takes a longer fixed length of time to grow by 100 percent (to double). This longer time is called the *doubling time*, T_2, and it is easy to calculate. You just take the number 70, divide it by the percent growth per unit time, P, and that gives you the doubling time.

$$T_2 = \frac{70}{P}$$

For our example of 5 percent growth per year, we divide 5 into 70 and find that the growing quantity will double in size every 14 years. (The number 70 is roughly 100 times the natural logarithm of two, but just remember 70.)

I wish all people would make this mental calculation whenever they see a percent growth rate of *anything* in a news story. For example, on seeing a story that said things had been growing at 6.3 percent per year for several recent years, few of us would bat an eyelash. But when we see a headline that says the consumer price index has doubled in eleven years, we say, "My heavens, what is happening?" The answer is, 6.3 percent growth per year. When expressed as a percent, nobody really understands what it means, but when expressed in terms of doubling, then people begin to understand.

THE POWER OF POWERS OF TWO

Steady growth today is central to the entire operation of our economy. Let us look at some features of steady growth. If something is growing steadily, after one doubling time it is twice its initial size; after two doubling times, it is four times that size. Then it goes to 8, 16, 32, 64, 128, 256, 512—and in just ten doubling times it is 1024 times its initial size! If we graph that on ordinary graph paper, the graph will go right through the ceiling.

Here is an example of the enormous numbers we get with just a modest number of doublings. Legend has it that the game of chess was invented by a mathematician who worked for a king. The king wanted to reward the mathematician, who said, "My needs are modest. If you will just place one grain of wheat on the first square of this chess board, on the next square double the one to make two, on the third square double the two to make four—and just keep doubling until you have doubled for every square, then that will be an adequate payment." No doubt the king thought, "What a foolish man. I was ready to give him a real reward; all he asked for was just a few grains of wheat."

Let us see what is actually involved. We note in Table 14.1 that there are eight grains on the fourth square, which is three twos multiplied together (2^3), or one two less than the number of the square. That follows in each case, so on the last square the number of grains is 63 twos multiplied together (2^{63}). Now see how the total grows. With one grain on the first square, the total on the board is one; add two grains, that makes a total of three. Now add four grains for a total of seven. Seven is one grain less than eight (2^3); 15 is a grain less than 2^4. That continues, so when we are done, the total number of grains is one grain less than 2^{64}.

Now just how much wheat is that? A few sacks? A warehouse full? The answer is, it is roughly 500 times the 1976 worldwide harvest of wheat! That could be more wheat than humans have harvested in the whole history

Table 14.1
Filling the Squares on the Chessboard

square number	grains on square	total grains thus far
1	1	1
2	2	3
3	4	7
4	8	15
5	16	31
6	32	63
7	64	127
64	2^{63}	$2^{64} - 1$

of the Earth! And how did we get such a big number? Simple. We started with just one grain and let it grow steadily until it had doubled a mere 63 times!

Something else very important to note is that the growth during any doubling time is *greater than the total of all preceding growth*. So when eight grains are put on the fourth square, they are more than the total of seven already there. When 32 grains are put on the sixth square, the 32 is larger than the total of 31 already there. Every time a growing quantity doubles, it takes more than *all* that went before.

Let us now apply this to the energy crisis. A 1975 advertisement asked, "Could America run out of electricity? America depends on electricity. Our need for electricity actually doubles every ten or twelve years."[1] That is an accurate reflection of a very long history of steady growth in the electric industry in this country—growth at a rate of around 7 percent per year, which gives us a doubling every ten years. Given that long history, people expected such growth to go on forever. Fortunately, it stopped.

But suppose it had continued. Then, as on the chessboard, in the ten-year doubling time following that advertisement, the amount of electrical energy used in this country would have been greater than the total of *all* of the electrical energy ever used in the entire preceding history of the United States. Now who would think that anything as completely acceptable as 7 percent growth per year could give such an incredible consequence, that in ten years we would use more than the total of all that had been used in all our history? That is exactly what President Carter was referring to in his April 10, 1977, speech on energy, when he said: "And in each of these decades [the 1950s and 1960s], more oil was consumed than in all of man's previous history." Now we can understand such a stunning statement. The President was stating the simple consequence of the arithmetic of 7 percent growth each year in world oil consumption, and that *was* the historic growth rate up until the 1970s.

Another interesting consequence of this arithmetic exists. Anything that grows at a steady percent for 70 years, roughly one human lifetime, increases by a factor that is very easy to calculate. For example, at 4 percent growth per year for 70 years, the factor is found by multiplying four twos together (2^4); it is a factor of 16. At 5 percent growth per year for 70 years, it is 2^5 (32), and so on.

A few years ago one of the newspapers in my hometown of Boulder, Colorado, quizzed our City Council about the ideal growth rate of Boulder's population in the coming years. They gave answers ranging from a low of 1 percent per year (the same as the current U.S. growth rate), to the highest, which was 5 percent per year. I felt compelled to write them and ask, "Did you *know* that 5 percent per year over just one lifetime means Boulder's population would increase by a factor of 32 (2^5)? Whereas today we have one overloaded sewage treatment plant, in 70 years we would need 32 overloaded sewage treatment plants." How many of us realize that anything as completely all-American as 5 percent growth per year could give such an incredible consequence in such a modest period of time? Boulder's City Council people had no idea of this.

Some years ago, in a class for nonscience students on the problems of science and society, I taught them to use semilogarithmic graph paper, which is printed in such a way that each of the equal intervals along the vertical axis represents an increase by a factor of ten. On this kind of paper, a straight line represents steady growth. One can use this procedure to talk about a lot of things, such as inflation. I said to the students, "You have roughly 60 years life expectancy ahead of you. Let us see what some common things will cost if we have 60 years of 7 percent annual inflation. Well, they found that a 55-cent gallon of gasoline will cost $35.20; $2.50 for a movie will be $160; the $15 sack of groceries (that my mother used to buy for $1.25) will be $960; a $100 suit of clothes, $6,400; a $4,000 car will cost a quarter of a million dollars; and a $35,000 home will cost almost three million dollars.

Then I gave the students data from a Blue Cross/Blue Shield health insurance advertisement with figures showing the cost escalation of gall-bladder surgery since 1950, when it cost $361. On their semilogarithmic plot of the data, the students found that the first four points fell on a straight line with a slope indicating inflation of about 6 percent per year. The fourth, fifth, and sixth points were on a steeper line of nearly 10 percent per year.

By extrapolating that line out to the year 2000 they found that gall-bladder surgery then might cost $25,000!

About three years ago, the world population reportedly reached five billion, growing at the rate of 1.7 percent per year. Now one might suppose that 1.7 percent is so small, nothing bad could happen at that growth rate. Yet the doubling time is only 41 years! Before young people in college today are my age, the world population will likely reach 10 billion! If you want to grasp what that means, think of food. World food production must be increased at least twofold over its 1982 level in order adequately to feed the 8 billion people expected to be living hardly 30 years from now, and this goal must be achieved without adding appreciably to the amount of land now under cultivation.[2]

If this seemingly modest 1.7 percent growth per year were to continue unchanged, there would be one person per square meter on the dry land surface of the Earth in just 600 years, and the mass of people would equal the mass of the Earth in just 1800 years. We *know* those last two figures could not happen. Hence, *zero population growth will occur*, whether we debate it or not, or whether we like it or not. Today's high birthrate *will* drop, and today's low deathrate *will* rise, until they have the same numerical value.

What are the options available to us? A list of things we should encourage if we want to *raise* the rate of growth in world population and make the problem *worse* includes such sacred things as motherhood, medicine, public health, and sanitation. Most of these are devoted to the humane goals of lowering the death rate, and that is very important to me if it is my death they are lowering. But anything that simply lowers the death rate makes the problem worse. Also on this list are peace, law-and-order, and scientific agriculture; they all help *increase* the population. The 55-mile-an-hour speed limit has saved thousands of lives; that makes the population problem worse. Clean air makes it worse. And I have to put education here because thus far there is little to indicate that education is doing very much about reducing ignorance of the problem.

Now what should we encourage if we want to *lower* the rate of growth of the world population and so help solve the problem? There are contraception, abortion, small families, disease, war, murder, famine, accident. Smoking clearly raises the death rate, so that helps solve the problem.

Since zero population growth *is* going to happen, it is obvious that we do not *have* to do anything. Nature, one way or another, is going to raise the death rate. Alternatively, we can seek some way of actively reducing births or raising deaths. Who is in favor of promoting disease? War? Murder? Famine? Everything that we regard as good makes the problem worse; everything we regard as bad helps solve the problem. Here is a dilemma if ever there was one!

Where do we start? Let us begin locally. Take the city of Boulder. For several decades following 1940, Boulder's population was growing at 5.8 percent per year, doubling every twelve years. I ask people what major U.S. city would we prefer Boulder to be like in just 70 years from the 1970 census? Boulder could be as big as Boston if we just grew 3.25 percent per year. Now if we thought Detroit was a better model, we have to shoot for 4.5 percent. If, however, Boulder were to continue to grow at its post-1940 rate of 5.8 percent, after one lifetime it would be larger than Chicago. But you could not put Chicago in the Boulder Valley. Therefore it is obvious: *Boulder's population growth is going to stop.* The only question is will we stop it while there is still some open space, or will we wait until it is wall-to-wall people and we are all choking to death?

EXPONENTIAL GROWTH IN A FINITE ENVIRONMENT

Let us examine the characteristics of steady growth in a finite environment. Bacteria grow by doubling; one bacterium divides to become two, the two divide to become four, the four become eight, sixteen and so on. Suppose we had bacteria that double in number this way every minute. Suppose we put one of these bacteria in an empty bottle at 11:00 in the morning and then observe that the bottle is full at 12:00 noon. This is a case of ordinary steady growth; it has a doubling time of one minute and it is in the finite environment of one bottle. Now let us ask three questions (see Table 14.2):

1.   At what time is the bottle half-full? That is easy: 11:59, one minute before twelve, because they double in number every minute.

2.   If you were an average bacterium in the bottle, at what time would you first realize that you were running out of space? Let us look at the last minutes in the bottle. At 12 noon, it is full; one minute before, it is half full; two minutes before it is a quarter full, then an eighth, a sixteenth. At five minutes before 12, when the bottle is only 3 percent full and is 97 percent open space, just yearning for development, how many would realize that there was a problem? Now in our on-going controversy over Boulder, someone wrote to the newspaper and said "Look, there is no problem with population growth because we have 15 times as much open space as has already been developed." But what time is it in Boulder Valley when the open space is 15 times the open space we have already used? The answer is, it is four minutes before 12.

Table 14.2
Growth of Bacteria in a Finite Environment

A. The last minutes in the bottle

11:54 a.m.	1/64 full (1.5%)	63/64 empty
11:55 a.m.	1/32 full (3%)	31/32 empty
11:56 a.m.	1/16 full (6%)	15/16 empty
11:57 a.m.	1/8 full (12%)	7/8 empty
11:58 a.m.	1/4 full (25%)	3/4 empty
11:59 a.m.	1/2 full (50%)	1/2 empty
12 noon	bottle is full	no empty space

B. The effect of the discovery of <u>three</u> new bottles!

12:01 p.m.	two bottles are full; two are empty
12:02 p.m.	all four bottles are full; no empty space

Suppose at two minutes before 12, some of the bacteria realize they are running out of space and they launch a great search for new bottles. They search offshore, and on the outer continental shelf, in the overthrust belt, and in the Arctic, and they find three new bottles. That is a colossal discovery. The discovery is three times the total resource they ever knew about before. They now have four bottles; before the discovery they had only one. Surely this will make them self-sufficient in space, will it not? This tells us what the third question is:

3. How long can the growth continue as a result of this magnificent discovery? Look at the score. At 12 noon, one bottle is filled, there are three to go; at 12:01, two bottles are filled, there are two to go; at 12:02, all four are filled, and that is the end of the line!

We do not need any more arithmetic than this to evaluate the absolutely contradictory statements of "experts" who tell us in one breath we can go on increasing our rates of consumption of fossil fuels and in the next breath say, "But don't worry, we will always be able to make the discoveries of new resources we need to meet the requirements of that growth." In contrast, a few years ago our Energy Secretary observed that in the energy crisis "we have a classic case of exponential growth against a finite source."[3]

EXPONENTIAL EXPIRATION TIME OF FINITE RESOURCES

Let us look at some of these finite resources. For a period of almost 100 years, we have had growth in global oil production of around 7 percent per year, and so it is logical to ask, "How much longer could that 7 percent growth continue?" We can answer this as follows: In the year 1973, world oil production was 20 billion barrels. The total production, added up over all of history—including that 20—was 300 billion barrels and the remaining reserve was 1700 billion. Those are the data. If we assume the 7 percent historic growth rate had continued in the years since 1973, then by 1981 the total usage in all of history would have been 500 billion barrels, and the reserves would have declined to 1500 billion. At that point the remaining reserves would be three times the total of all that have been used before. It seems an enormous reserve. But what time is it when the remaining reserve is three times the total of all you have used before? The answer: it is two minutes before 12. At 7 percent growth per year, the doubling time is ten years, so in the decade 1981 to 1991, another 500 billion barrels will have been used, making a total of 1000 billion consumed and 1000 billion left. That is equal in quantity to all the oil consumed in nearly 140 years of the oil industry on this Earth—seemingly a colossal reserve! But what time is it when the remaining reserve is equal to everything you have used in all of history? The answer is, it is one minute before 12. Another decade of continued 7 percent growth, from 1991 to 2001, would finish using up the oil reserves of the Earth.

Although a combination of oil price increases and the subsequent global recession temporarily slowed growth in oil consumption, there is renewed pressure for economic "growth" and "development" to get back on the old growth curves of energy use. It is widely believed in Congress that if you throw enough money at holes in the ground, oil is *sure* to come up. No doubt new oil will be discovered; there may even be major discoveries. But if we return to 7 percent annual growth in consumption, we will need in just one more decade to discover as much oil in the United States as was pumped out in all of the past. The probability of such a find is vanishingly small, and all it would do is continue the historic growth rate ten extra years.

How should we think about this? Let us look at something very close to all of us—United States agriculture. It is the most energy-intensive in the world. From farm to ultimate consumer, all of its activities account for about 15 percent of total U.S. energy consumption. That gives us a very nice definition: Modern agriculture is the use of land to convert petroleum into food. And we can see the end of the petroleum.

A few years ago, the American Electric Power Company ran advertisements reassuring us not to worry too much about oil supplies because we are sitting on half of the world's known supply of coal, enough for over 500 years. Now where did that 500-year figure come from? It may have originated in a 1973 report to the Committee on Interior and Insular Affairs of the United States Senate, where we find this sentence: "At current levels of output and recovery these [American coal] reserves can be expected to last more than 500 years."[4] This is one of the most dangerous statements in the literature, because it is true. But it is not the truth, per se, that makes it dangerous. The danger lies in the fact that people take the sentence apart; they just say "Coal will last 500 years," and forget the caveat with which the sentence started: "At current levels"! The entire sentence is true if, and only if, we maintain *zero growth* of coal production.

Let us look at some hard figures. When Congress asked the U.S. Geological Survey for estimates of the size of U.S. coal reserves in 1972, it got two numbers: 1486 billion tons and 390 billion tons. The first one is larger by almost a factor of four, and includes deep coal that is very difficult to extract. In 1970, we extracted half a billion tons of coal. President Gerald Ford set goals for 1980 of 1.3 billion tons, and for 1985 of 2.1 billion tons. These numbers amount to a growth rate of 11 percent per year in U.S. coal production (see Figure 14.1). How long could American coal—or any other resource—last if we had steady growth in the rate of consumption until the last bit of it was used?

Here is the equation for the exponential expiration time (EET). It takes first-year college calculus to derive it, so it cannot be very difficult.

$$\text{EET} = \frac{1}{k} \cdot \ln\left\{\frac{k\,R}{r_0} + 1\right\}$$

r_0 = current rate of consumption
k = fractional growth per year (.07 for 7 percent growth)
R = total size of the remaining resource

This equation is probably the best-kept scientific secret of the century. The reason is shown in Table 14.3. If you use that equation to calculate the life-expectancy of the low or high estimates of U.S. coal reserves for different steady rates of growth, you find if the growth rate is zero, the low estimate will last 780 years, the large one will last almost 3,000 years. Now those are both over 500 years, so that the report to the Congress was indeed

Figure 14.1
History of United States Coal Production

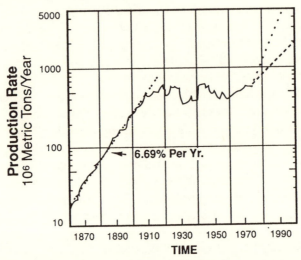

Plotted on a semilogarithmic scale, the graph shows continuous (straight-line) annual growth in coal production of 6.69 percent per year from the end of the Civil War until 1910. If this growth rate had continued undiminished, the small estimate of the size of U.S. coal reserves would have been consumed by about 1967 and the larger estimate of these reserves by about 1990!

With the introduction of oil and natural gas as fuels, however, coal production remained steady between 1910 and the end of the 1970s, when production began to increase in response to the oil crisis. President Gerald Ford urged an increase of production of 11 percent per year, which would extrapolate into the 1990s along the upper, dotted line, and U.S. coal would last between 44 and 57 years. President Jimmy Carter recommended a goal of around 5 percent growth per year, shown by the lower, dashed line, which if sustained would last between 74 and 100 years (see text).

(Figure is redrawn from Figure 4 of A. A. Bartlett, "Forgotten Fundamentals of the Energy Crisis," *American Journal of Physics*, 46 (September 1978), p. 881, with permission.)

correct. But look what we get when we plug in steady growth. We recently had goals of achieving growth up to around 10 percent per year. If that could be sustained until the coal was gone, coal in this country would last between 44 and 57 years from now. That is within the life expectancy of children now in school. More recently, under President Carter, we had goals of around 5 percent growth per year. If that could be sustained until coal was gone, coal would last between 74 and 100 years from now; that is within the life expectancy of children born today.

WHAT ARE WE BEING TOLD?

These are simple facts. Let us now compare them with what we hear and read. The director of the Energy Division of the Oak Ridge National Laboratory tells us how expensive it is to import oil. We must have big

Table 14.3
Lifetime in Years of United States Coal

Annual Rate of Growth in Coal Production	High Estimate (in years)	Low Estimate (in years)
zero	2872	680
1%	339	205
2%	203	134
3%	149	102
4%	119	83
5%	99	71
6%	86	62
7%	76	55
8%	68	50
9%	62	46
10%	57	42
11%	52	39
12%	49	37
13%	46	35

The lifetime (Exponential Expiration Time) in years of U.S. coal reserves, both the high and low estimates of the U.S. Geological Survey, are shown for several rates of growth of production from the 1972 level of 0.5×10^9 metric tons per year.

increases—*rapid growth*—in our use of coal reserves. Under these conditions, he estimates these reserves are so large they could last a minimum of 300 years, probably a maximum of a thousand years.[5] We have just seen the facts; now we see what an "expert" tells us. What can we conclude?

On a CBS special on energy, the reporter said that by the lowest estimate we have enough coal for 200 years, by the highest, for more than 12,000 years.[6] We have just seen the facts, and now we see what a journalist tells us after "careful study." And what can we conclude?

In the *Journal of Chemical Education*, on the page for high school chemistry teachers, an article written by the staff of the journal says that our proven coal reserves are enormous. They give us their figure, 120 billion tons, and then state: "These could satisfy present U.S. energy needs for nearly a thousand years."[7] Let us do the long division. Take the coal they say is there, divide by what was then the current rate of coal production (0.6 billion tons per year), and we get 200 years. But note that they did not say "current rate of U.S. coal production"; they said "present U.S. energy needs." Coal today supplies about one-fifth—20 percent—of the energy we use. So if we want to calculate how long this quantity of coal could satisfy U.S. energy needs, we have to divide the coal reserves by a further factor of five, giving us *40 years*. They *said* nearly 1,000 years!

Newsweek magazine in a cover story on energy said that at present rates of consumption we have enough coal for about 650 years.[8] That is a good estimate. But the whole point of the story was that we have to have rapid growth in our domestic consumption of coal. It is pretty obvious, is it not, if we have rapid growth, coal reserves will not last as long as with zero growth? They never mentioned this. I wrote them, pointing out this serious and misleading omission. I got back a polite form letter that had nothing to do with what I had tried to point out.

Time magazine observed that "Certainly the coal is there. Beneath the pitheads of Appalachia and the Ohio Valley, and under the sprawling strip mines of the West lie coal seams rich enough to meet the country's power needs for centuries, no matter how much energy consumption may grow."[9]

So I leave you with the fundamental caveat: *Do not believe any prediction of the life expectancy of a nonrenewable resource until you have confirmed the prediction by repeating the calculation.* The more optimistic the prediction, the greater is the probability that it is based on faulty arithmetic, or on no arithmetic at all. I hope I have made a reasonable case for my opening statement that I feel that the greatest shortcoming of the human race is our inability to understand the exponential function. If our programs of interdisciplinary education are to succeed, then they must surely include generous discussions of the applications of arithmetic such as this to our everyday lives.

NOTES

A more complete text of the subject matter of this paper can be found in the *American Journal of Physics*, 46 (September, 1978), 876–88. Videotapes of a one-hour talk by Professor Bartlett also are available from the Media Center, University of Colorado, Boulder, CO 80309-0379; or call (303) 492–7341.

    1. Advertisement by General Electric Company, *Newsweek*, July 21, 1975.

    2. Carol L. Rogers, "CHEMRAWN II Calls for Twofold Increases in World Food Production," *Science*, October 7, 1983 (vol. 222), 43.

    3. "Conferences: Opening the Debate," *Time*, April 25, 1977, p. 27–32. Quote of Energy Secretary James R. Schlesinger, p. 27.

    4. "Factors Affecting the Use of Coal in Present and Future Energy Markets," a background paper prepared by the Congressional Research Service for the Committee on Interior and Insular Affairs of the United States Senate pursuant to Senate Resolution

45, a National Fuels and Energy Policy Study, Serial Number 93-9 992-44) (Washington, D.C.: U.S. Government Printing Office, 1973), pp. 41, 42, 15.

5. Associated Press story, "Energy Head Stresses Coal Reserves," *Boulder Daily Camera*, July 5, 1975.

6. CBS television program, aired August 31, 1977.

7. Journal of Chemical Education Staff, "Chem 1, Supplement: Energy Review," *Journal of Chemical Education* (April, 1978), 263–64. Data are on p. 263.

8. Special report by Bob Conrad, "A Program for the '80s," *Newsweek*, July 16, 1979, 22–33. Misleading statements on coal reserves are on pp. 23, 24, 31.

9. "Energy: Coal's Clouded Post-Strike Future," *Time*, April 17, 1978, 74–75.

SELECTED BIBLIOGRAPHY

Bartlett, Albert A. "Forgotten Fundamentals of the Energy Crisis." *American Journal of Physics*, 46 (September 1978), 876–888.

Hubbert, M. King. *A National Fuels and Energy Policy Study, Serial 93-40 (92-75) Part 1* Washington, D.C.: U.S. Government Printing Office, 1973.

Romer, Robert H. *Energy—An Introduction to Physics*. San Francisco: W.H. Freeman, 1976.

15 VISIONING A PEACEFUL WORLD

Johan Galtung

PEACE, POWER AND THE STATE

I start with two basic assumptions. First, *any peaceful world order has to take into account all four types of power: military, economic, cultural, and political.* One cannot build peace on only one or two of them. Any power type can be transformed, even softened—but not disregarded. Power is with us forever. Second, *states, even nation-states, will be around for a long time.* There is something stabilizing in territorial contiguity and temporal continuity, combined with some degree of cultural sharing. In addition there is the simple fact that nation-states *do* provide; the state often is *l' etat-providence.*

The world may be anarchic and risky as a multistate system, but states often provide internal security, alleviate misery, guarantee a minimum of freedom, and equip people with at least one source of identity: the nation-state itself. Although war as an institution is an increasing failure, the nation-state is not, however related the two may be. The nation-state is simply too successful, and will be around for the foreseeable future.

Hence the argument here is not to dismantle nation-states, but to modify their aggressiveness. *The short-term problem is not how to abolish states but how to weaken them, soften them, and then weave them together by interlinking them in an equitable manner*, so that it becomes structurally difficult for them to engage in war or warlike processes. The question is how to convert this general formula into concrete peace in the inter-state system.

Table 15.1 incorporates much of the thinking in this important arena. *A peaceful world presupposes regulation of power so as to obtain peace.* War is power abuse. The study of power coincides with the study of

Table 15.1
Visioning a Peaceful World: How to Weave States Together, Softening Them, Interlocking Them

POWER

	Negative Peace	Positive Peace
M	<u>Military nonaggression</u>	<u>World peacekeeping forces</u>
I	non-flow, non-intervention	nonviolent intervention
L	non-stock of offensive arms	stationed as buffers in crisis areas
I		stationed as hostages
T	defensive, non-provocative defense	cooperation in defensive defense
A	transarmament	World Transarmament Association
R	disarmament	World Disarmament Association
Y	abolition of war as an institution	World War Abolition Association
E	<u>Economic nonaggression</u>	<u>World economy</u>
C	Nature, human, social, world production	Nature, human, social world production
O	for basic needs	for basic needs
N	distribution to most needy	distribution to most needy
O	SELF-RELIANCE I	SELF-RELIANCE II
M	nationally	equitable exchange
I	locally: use local factors	symbiosis, mutual benefit
C	internalizing externalities	sharing externalities equally

C
U
L
T
U
R
A
L

Cultural nonaggression
dialogues of civilizations
not backed by military and economic power

Criticize, internally and externally
--universalism + singularism
--Chosen People ideas
--absolute cultural relativism

P
O
L
I
T
I
C
A
L

Internalize national interests
broaden democracy
national and local elections:
party/candidate and issue votes
nuclear-free municipalities
nuclear-free professions, with
Hippocratic peace oaths
decentralization of foreign policy
--to local government
--to people's diplomacy

World consciousness
world statistics, world images
conceptualization and foreign policy as
world domestic politics

Positive views of humanity:
--multicentric space
--relaxed, oscillating time
--more holistic dialectic
--partnership with Nature
--Equality, Justice--inclusive
--minimizing metaphysics

World institutions for world interests
broaden democracy
Chamber of Governmental Organizations
Chamber of People's Organizations
world elections
world referenda
world service
--environment
--development

politics, and the focus here is on politics for peace. "Peace" comes in two major varieties, **negative peace** and **positive peace**. Assuming the key political actors to be nation-states, negative peace can be obtained by softening them, restraining their power, reducing their aggressiveness, and positive peace by linking them together in harmonious, cooperative relations through the cement provided by intergovernmental and interpeople organizations. With four types of power, that gives us the eight cells in the matrix of Table 15.1.

There is no linear order in the table; none of the eight cells is more important than any other. There is no single point where one should start, proceeding from one to the other, until a peaceful world has been obtained. On the contrary, there is a certain, albeit crazy, interconnectedness among the world's problems, so that any progress will have to occur in all eight cells at the same time. Thus, incremental changes in all eight cells are better than a single-minded push in one of them. A holistic approach rather than a reductionist approach is called for. The West, for instance, focuses more on detailed efficiency than on overall efficacy. Military budgets are tested for cost-effectiveness, not whether security is really obtained. Peace movements that focus only on disarmament share that mentality. Single-issue movements and policies are as incompatible with the politics of peace as with the politics of health.

Ideally, examination of the table should proceed in a similar holistic manner, but constraints on how we communicate ideas preclude it, and so I shall zig-zag through the table, starting in the "negative" military corner.

THE MILITARY POWER DIMENSION

The abolition of war appears at the bottom of the top left hand cell. I shall say only this about it: What is in the rest of the table is supposed to provide the context within which wars, not states, might simply wither away. Random wars will remain, just as random slavery still exists, but they will not be globally institutionalized, legitimized, even internalized evils.

Defensive Defense

In a peaceful world deterrence would be based on the capacity to defend oneself, not on an offensive capacity to retaliate, indistinguishable—for all practical purposes—from the capacity to launch an attack. The consequences of the latter are very clear: Offensive capability targeted *on* the adversary tends to stimulate offensive capabilities *in* the adversary, in other words an offensive arms race; and an arms race tends sooner or later to lead to war. It is often argued that if neither party wants war, the possession of offensive capabilities does not lead to war. But this ignores both preemptive wars launched to prevent the other side from launching aggressive war, and displaced, "surrogate" wars in less dangerous theaters.

When defensive defense is discussed, an important problem is the vague borderline between offensive and defensive weapons. For example, some systems designed as "defensive" may easily be converted into highly offensive systems. The angle of anti-aircraft guns mounted on ships can be lowered to strafe the coasts of rebellious islands. There is always a gray zone between the clearly defensive and the clearly offensive, never a sharp line. But that problem is minor relative to the one the "defense experts" of our age have utterly failed to solve: namely, how to distinguish between retaliatory weapon systems and weapon systems that can be used for attack. Here the overlap is enormous, since so many systems obviously can be used for both purposes. Moreover, for deterrence to be "credible" a certain recklessness is indispensable. Although designed to make the adversary believe the weapon system is one of retaliation (second strike), it in fact is one of aggression (first strike). This is a key and persistent problem in U.S.-Soviet relations. Thus, although the problem of the gray boundary between offensive and defensive weapons is always present, its burden is enormously greater for those attempting to justify "retaliatory" defense.

There are three components in defensive defense: *short-range conventional military defense, paramilitary defense*, and *nonmilitary defense*. Ideally, all would engage the populace generally and would operate within the national territory, in order not to provoke an adversary.

A key problem of defensive defense is that it can be turned against the state/government *or* against the people by the state/government. For the latter reason, it should be organized more as a broadly based people's defense than as a state/government-based defense. Switzerland is a good example of a state with an effective decentralized defensive capability that has avoided anarchism. If a state treats its citizens well they do not use their military and nonmilitary power against it, and that is a reasonable basis for a good social contract. Today this condition is to a large extent fulfilled for the adult male population of Switzerland, but the Swiss defensive army has on occasion been used against Swiss citizens (as in the 1930s).

A second problem defensive defense poses for the nation-state is that it cannot be used to protect economic and political interests abroad. The answer is simple: If those interests have to be "protected" militarily, there must be something wrong with them. "National interests" located abroad are an anachronism, an example of residual imperialism.

Nonviolent Defense

Ultimately, deterrence based on threats of violence breaks down; perennial fear is not peace, not even negative peace. How does nonviolence fit into the four power dimensions? The answer is simple: Nonviolence has to be based on a strength different from that of destructive force, since both the use and the threat of the use of force are ruled out in nonviolent struggles. Strength has to be based on invulnerability rather than destructive capability; from *being* strong, rather than *having* destructive strength. How?

One counter to military power is **fearlessness**. Force moves people only when mediated by fear. Correspondingly, for economic power, exchange only moves people when mediated by desire, or worse, by economic dependency. **Disinterest** and a minimum of **self-sufficiency** are the obvious answers to that problem. Similarly, for cultural power, only the insecure person is moved by external values. The obvious answer here is **cultural identity** and **integrity**. Finally, for political power, the nonviolent person will refuse to participate in the illegitimate use of power, thus emptying such institutions of their strength through noncooperation and civil disobedience. The answer lies in **autonomy**, in "doing one's own politics." Strengthened by faith in their own values, disinterested in what the adversary has to offer because of economic self-sufficiency, and armed with fearlessness, nonviolent persons become invincible, like Gandhi in India, the Buddhist monks in Saigon, and the nonviolent masses separating military factions in Manila.

The power of nonviolence may today be insufficient to stave off an attack, so it should be seen as a growing component in a people's defensive defense, its growth rate depending on the maturity of the population and a host of other circumstances. Yet nonmilitary defense is indispensable to defensive defense; any government that leaves the population defenseless when military resistance fails is simply irresponsible. Aggressors must know there will still be resistance; they may occupy but not rule, and certainly not govern.

Basic to the whole notion of **transarmament** from offensive to defensive capability is gradual unilateralism. The need for a "balance of power" recedes since defensive arms are not pitted against each other. Latecomers to this change in military posture may find themselves like the last countries practicing slavery: international pariahs.

There are also rewards to those who enter the circle of transarmed states. One is sharply decreased military costs; another, less destruction in case of a holocaust. A member of a military alliance who wants to transarm, however, may experience sanctions from fellows who see their own position being weakened. Pressures from such alliance members may become tremendous in the near future. This may lead either to the breakup of alliances, or to new, nonprovocative postures for the alliances, in which case they might be worth keeping. The problem is not the alliances, but their military doctrine. If an alliance does not change its doctrine, a country should leave; if a government does not change its doctrine, its people should withdraw their mandate.

World Peacekeeping

If transarmament is something a nation can do to "soften" itself, what would be the cooperative counterpart, since we also need to interlink nation-states? One answer is **world peacekeeping**. Despite enormous obstacles, humankind has gained considerable experience here under the auspices of the United Nations. The destructive capabilities of such operations should never exceed those of a transarmed nation-state; they should never be offensive, but rely essentially on hand weapons. This already is the doctrine for United Nations peacekeeping forces, showing that the military and politicians *can* draw the line between offensive and defensive when they want to.

An important function of world peacekeeping forces is as a physical buffer zone located between two contending parties, on the land of both. This zone, literally a dense human wall of peacekeeping forces, becomes a major impediment for anyone contemplating a surprise attack, thus encouraging the politics of transarmament. Nearby neutral nations could help by refusing to allow transit of war materials, and could back that up by inviting in world peacekeeping inspectors.

Buffer zones, however, are easily leapfrogged by aircraft and sometimes by naval forces. Any potential aggressor should therefore face not only land-based buffer zones, but also land-based hostages, from all kinds of nations, possibly even from his own. The aggressor's target is no longer simply *a* nation-state, but multinational, ambiguous, problematic. Furthermore, whether stationed as buffers or hostages, world peacekeeping forces need not be wastefully inactive. They could do useful jobs as parts of a **world service** for a better environment, and for social and economic development. Long-term war zones are often in need of both and there is a long tradition for military forces, national or international, to be used constructively.

World Transarmament

If a country has extensive experience in making itself indigestible to an adversary, its security will not decrease if it shares doctrine, strategy, even some tactics, with others. There may be hiding places or certain surprises in store for an intruding adversary that the country might like to keep secret, but these are details. One could thus imagine a **World Transarmament Association** of nations, not necessarily contiguous, who would enter this new post-war stage in human history together, exchanging and sharing ideas and experiences. Membership would be open to any nation-state whose transarming credentials are approved by the group. This would be a major step away from joining an alliance, and a step beyond joining a group of nonaligned countries with no clear defensive military doctrine. However, if a whole alliance could transarm (as the Warsaw Treaty Organization now seems to be contemplating), so much the better.

Please note: None of what has been said presupposes a world military authority associated with a world government. What is needed is potentially provided by the United Nations, perhaps more as it was first envisaged, with its Military Committee, than as it has developed. It *does* presuppose a political will to action, but that will probably occur sooner or later because its time has come. Too long has the world been trapped in the false dichotomy of arms races or disarmament, altogether overlooking the transarmament option.

Transarmed nations already exist, based on defensive defense and nonalignment, such as Switzerland, Austria, Yugoslavia, Sweden, and Finland. International peacekeeping forces already exist. There is considerable political will and experience in the field. Some permanent members of the United Nations Security Council may have a dim view of either initiative. World peacekeeping forces might be resented by the superpowers because they would have greater moral legitimacy than the superpowers who like to see themselves as peacekeepers, in need of nobody to watch them. In fact, world peacekeeping forces might awaken the superpowers to that strange, intangible reality to which Kant and others have referred: the moral law inside us and the cosmos above us. In but a generation or two, national military service may seem strange, illegitimate; **World Service** would be the natural thing. Even today, conscientious objectors to military service all over the world demand the option of alternative forms of service, a demand resisted by authorities since national military service would often be the last choice.

A World Transarmament Association might ultimately lead to disarmament and war abolition via an intermediate world with only defensive armies. But our first priority must be the reduction of offensive capability, such as long-range nuclear missiles, aircraft carriers, submarines, and tanks, which are basic sources of fear and arms races. Disarmament is a complex process and to discuss it as if withdrawal of defensive nuclear landmines and of long-range nuclear missiles should count the same is intellectually flawed. But one can proceed simultaneously with both offensive and defensive reduction. Some countries might even follow Costa Rica's bold lead and abolish the military altogether, or at least have a referendum on the issue like Switzerland in November 1989.

THE ECONOMIC POWER DIMENSION

Similar reasoning holds when thinking about economic power. Economic activity, too, has to respect the same kinds of boundaries and constraints. There is something basically wrong when economic activity produces ecological imbalances, fails to satisfy the basic needs of a substantial portion of humankind, leads to less rather than more democracy and development around the world, to dependency rather than autonomy, and to war rather than peace. The task of economic activity must be to satisfy reasonable human needs in ways compatible both with Nature and with the values of democracy, development, and peace.

We need concrete proposals for economic nonaggression and for building a sustainable world economy, but they must be consistent with these guidelines: Priority must be given to meeting the basic human needs of *all* people and to ensuring ecological sustainability, but in such a way as to enhance social development and world peace. Clearly, modern economic theory will have to be rewritten if economists wish to play a role in a peaceful world of nonaggression and cooperation. Today's economic system cannot be a model for the future.

Self-Reliance may be one approach here. It divides into two parts, domestic and international: First, try to produce whatever is needed from national or even local production factors (resources, labor, capital, research and administration) (**Self-Reliance I**). Second, when domestic production possibilities have been realized, proceed on the basis of exchange (trade), but on an equitable, mutual-benefit basis (**Self-Reliance II**). Neither axiom presupposes a particular kind of economy; both apply equally to socialist, capitalist, and many other economies.

By producing for one's own consumption, locally or nationally (Self-Reliance I), externalities—positive as well as negative—tend to be internalized by sending local signals that increase positive and reduce negative impacts. People do not normally put toxic wastes in their own backyard. When it comes to trade (Self-Reliance II), the rule would be this: Organize exchanges so that positive externalities still outweigh the negative, then share both positive and negative externalities equally. This perspective is missing from modern economic theory and practice.

A peaceful world economy, however, would not only require *restructuring of trade relations*, but also *reconsideration of priorities for production and distribution.* In a clumsy way this already happens with catastrophe assistance. But today's global overproduction of grain is barely enough to cope with a serious catastrophe, such as two sequential summers like 1988. Current efforts are mere stopgap measures.

Next we must institutionalize local and national self-reliance and equitable trade, thus decreasing the frequency of catastrophes. When these occur—as occasionally they still will—we will need formal means of intervening without, however, recreating today's dependency relationships.

THE CULTURAL POWER DIMENSION

Cultural power is more intractable than military and economic power, being more deeply internalized. Our basic question is: What do we mean by cultural nonaggression? I think there are three answers, all of them important.

First, we need cultural communication, but *not* cultural aggression associated with military and/or economic power (see Table 15.1, top of third left hand box). Although missionaries and other cultural salespersons no longer arrive along with gun boats, recent events in Afghanistan and Nicaragua show that the pattern of force to impose ideologies is not totally dead. Today's cultural missionaries frequently arrive bearing a variety of economic bribes.

Second, some cultures are inherently aggressive, conceiving themselves or their religion as not only fit for *all* people (**universalist**), but as the *only* suitable culture or religion (**singularist**). Now a claim to universality combined with tolerance is innocuous, simply asking that everybody around the world take that culture into account. The same applies to singularism combined with particularism, meaning that this is the only truth *for us.* Everyone is free to entertain such cultural fantasies. They may even stimulate cultural growth and dialogue. The problem comes when *the* truth is proclaimed for the *whole* world. Here, Islam and Christianity are the major religious examples; liberalism-capitalism and Marxism-socialism the major secular examples.

Third is the inherent aggressiveness of those holding the religious fantasy of being a Chosen People, with not only the right, but the duty to rule the world, or parts of it. In recent decades both the United States and the Soviet Union have come dangerously close to being countries chosen, by God or by History, for some special mission on Earth; and other peoples with potentially similar, albeit territorially more limited, tendencies are the Jews, the Boers and the Japanese.

Cultural Self-Criticism

Is there some way of exorcising such deeply held but culturally narrow and inherently aggressive fantasies? In individuals, such fantasies are labeled as megalomania; in the cases of Nazi Germany and South Africa, as racial supremacy. Given outsiders' natural aversions to such fantasies, paranoia often follows. Cures short of confrontation are hard to imagine.

The ultimate correctives are dialogue, tolerance, and mutual respect—in short, cultural relativism. But this is no invitation to *absolute* cultural relativism. Not all cultures, nor all civilizations, are equally good or equally bad. Those that are inherently aggressive in one or all of the ways mentioned, even though they present the world with glittering achievements, nevertheless possess a dark streak. Such cultures, who "legitimize" their military and/or economic aggressions by imagining themselves beyond ordinary human and national failings, pose enormous threats to world peace. Thus, the expression "relative cultural relativism" might be more appropriate. Tackling the roots of cultural aggression is difficult, however. A people may change military hardware and doctrine; they may even change economic doctrine. But to change their culture is to change themselves, to engage in the deepest forms of self-criticism. In general, this will be harder for the Occident than the Orient, but in the Orient it will certainly affect Japan. Sooner or later it has to be done if we are to live together on this small planet.

World Consciousness

But these are only negative pursuits. What is the corresponding positive pursuit, beyond helping each other in a searching, critical dialogue where no culture/religion is seen as entirely sacrosanct; beyond asking, in a spirit of sincerity, "What is it in my culture (military posture, economic practice, cultural arrogance) that offends you most?" and expecting the same question in return? In brief, it is to build **world consciousness**, even a world culture, a world civilization, not instead of local, national, and regional consciousness but in addition to them, just as a world economy does not presuppose doing away with local and national economies.

A first and simple step—that is already being done—is to *create images of the world as a whole*. Train people in global thinking, in talking of the world as a whole. Social scientists need to do what geophysicists and others have done: see the Earth as one system; use global concepts such as Humans and Biosphere; totally disregard national borders, as in the International Geophysical Year.

There is a consistent tendency among social scientists to represent global data in terms of the 159 member states of the United Nations, as if the point were to draw attention to their differences. This reinforces both the idea that the state is *the* unit of development, and the idea that development is the process whereby less developed countries catch up with more developed countries. The idea of "catching up" is a bad one for reasons too numerous to be discussed here (is it feasible? is it desirable?), and should be discarded as hierarchical and one-dimensional.

Now representing global data on a state by state basis is useful for some purposes and should not be abandoned. But it is also highly useful to present data in global terms: world numbers of very rich and very poor, of very educated and very uneducated, on how many live in what kind of habitat (cities, towns, slums, villages, and so on), on how many are in the various professions. Data thus presented make us think in a different way. So do statistics about raw materials and energy and other factors used up during economic production when contrasted with statistics about the goods and services actually produced. Only in this way can we get a better image of how wisely or unwisely we dispose of world resources.

Under this heading of world consciousness there is a colossal need to develop **positive views of humanity**, of ourselves. We need more posters showing us as a globally united family. The potential for a peaceful world is there; many already sense that the potential can indeed be realized. Age, gender, race, nation, class, citizenship in a country, membership in an organization or association do divide, but not necessarily in a destructive manner, for diversity permits higher levels of maturity in the human family. We have to see ourselves as capable of great achievements with greater still to come, at the expense of no one and to the benefit of all.

World Cosmology

A world consciousness probably requires the underpinning of **a general world cosmology**, meaning a minimum sharing of assumptions about the world in general and humankind in particular. The basic watchwords here are *minimum* and *sufficient*; we do not want a world ideology with no tolerance of variation, yet what *is* shared must be sufficient to generate a sense of oneness.

First, we must share a view of **world space** as multicentric, with many centers scattered over the world, each one a center of concern rather than control. Unicentric images of the world, seeing the world as controllable and controlled from one or perhaps two command posts only, should be intensely rejected. The new centers should be modest not only in the number of people focused around them but also in how much power they command. These peaks in world space should be low, the troughs (the peripheries) shallow. Hence, Western cosmologies—whether Christian or Muslim, liberal or Marxist—can only contribute to a peaceful world in their softer versions, freed from universalism/singularism and Chosen People complexes.

Second, we need a shared view of **social time** other than that of unidirectional change. The sense that there are natural undulations throughout human history, transformative waves of ups and downs, is a more mature conception. Here certain Eastern notions of time can better serve us than can Western time with its sense of linear "progress" toward an apocalyptic end of history. The latter engenders reckless behaviors in times of stress, when instead human beings need more stoic approaches.

Third, we need a reasonably shared image of the different ways knowledge can be constructed, of diverse **ways of knowing**. The epistemological atomism of Western tradition has to be tempered with the epistemological holism of other traditions. Partial knowledge arising from deductive theories must be tempered by dialectical approaches that help uncover the inherent contradictions in everything. Somehow we have to perceive totalities, instead of merely partial, highly selected realities. Although Western science claims *universality*, it bears the unmistakable *singularist* stamp of the Western civilizational vision. More importantly, we must avoid thinking in terms of watertight dichotomies: "Western" *versus* "Eastern" thought. The Occident has produced enormously useful conceptual visions, to be tempered with those of Oriental and other cultures. Neither is complete, nor even together do they exhaust all epistemological possibilities.

Fourth, we must share an image of the **person-Nature relationship** as a partnership. There is growing world consciousness here. We know there is a limit to how much we can destroy our planet, that we have to preserve and conserve. We must move away from the dominance approach of an exploitative Western civilization, curtailing its excesses and modifying its economic doctrines based on dominion over Nature, not partnership with it.

Fifth, we need a shared image of **person-person relations**. Humankind, environment, development, peace—all are indivisible. Everyone is not only born free, but also entitled to live and die without flagrant inequality. Freedom and equality may intrinsically be difficult to attain simultaneously, in which case we should not insist on the extremes of either. More creative thought is needed here.

Sixth, there has to be a shared **minimum metaphysics** for a world consciousness to emerge. The "oceanic feeling" of sometimes being linked to a transpersonal reality exists from one end of the world to the other. Call it God, call it Brahman, call it Tao. This global metaphysics cannot be based on any existing faith, and the more dogmatic and aggressive aspects of religion would give way to the softer aspects that tend to unite us. Religions such as Buddhism, Quakerism, and the Baha'i faith offer some elements on which to build. The ecumenical approach, searching for similarities rather than differences, provides a model for the future.

THE POLITICAL POWER DIMENSION

Finally there is political power, decision-making power, the command platform for the exercise of other forms of power. Here the participation of any object possibly subject to power becomes crucial. The general formula for that participation is **democracy**, but the problem has been who constitutes the *demos*, the people. Among the hierarchical layers of civilized society only certain classes were admitted to full social membership. In the West, this at one time constituted an elite class of propertied males with laborers, women, and children excluded, and, by extrapolation, animals, plants and the rest of Nature. It seemed as "natural" in earlier ages that merchants, workers, and women should have no voice as it is today that children, not to mention Nature, be excluded. Yet we have gradually broadened participation through time.

Negative peace in connection with political power is identified in Table 15.1 under the heading "internalize national interests." This means, act as much as possible within national borders. If necessary, show some defensive quills toward the outside, but do not try a global reach with military, economic, or cultural tentacles! Learn to satisfy national interests at home, internalize them; do not look to other countries and people as means of satisfying these. Generate policies of military, economic and cultural nonaggression and self-reliance. Each country becomes responsible for its own security, satisfies its own basic needs from its own production factors as much as possible, and derives cultural identity not from missionary expansion, but by creatively perfecting its own culture. There is much to do, some of it pleasant, some laborious, *inside* a country.

Internalizing national interests requires active participation of the whole population. Thus, the democratic agenda should be broadened, first by admitting new layers of beings into the *demos*: adolescents and children, foreigners, and Nature herself. *Homo sapiens* must find ways of representing adequately the nonhuman inhabitants of the world, perhaps through a **Council on Nature**. Second, democracy needs to be less centralized, both geographically and in the way issues are lumped together. An obvious solution is to have decentralized *local* elections at the provincial, municipal, and even neighborhood levels in addition to national elections, and to decide on *issues* at all these levels as well as to select representatives. Nuclear-free municipalities show the way here; local voters decide whether national government shall use *their* territory for potentially aggressive purposes. That could be broadened to decentralize foreign policy generally, challenging the nation-state's monopoly. Of course, cities too may act aggressively—but mostly on a smaller scale than nation-states. Ahead lie numerous problematiques of the political process: tensions between representative and participatory aspects of decision-making; jockeyings among geographically defined constituencies and those composed of more widely dispersed common-interest groups. There is no shortage of challenges. Demilitarized professions—engineers, scientists, physicians, and lawyers—inspired by a Hippocratic peace oath, would help greatly.

But what of positive peace in the political dimension? Somehow national interests have to add up to world interests; "foreign" policies to world policies. We shall need **world institutions for world interests** to complement national institutions for (internalized) national interests. Can democracy be broadened to include the global constituency, and can the United Nations serve as the vehicle? "Yes" on both counts. So far there is a "House of Lords" (the Security Council) and a "House of Commons" (the General Assembly), both composed of one-vote constituencies, the Member States: in short, basically a British parliamentarian framework.

Let us imagine three changes. The Security Council is replaced by a new People's Assembly, with one delegate for each million inhabitants.

Its members could represent territorial or other subdivisions within a nation-state, including parties, but would vote independently for their constituent subgroup. Then add a third Chamber for People's Organizations (nongovernmental organizations) with similar voting formulas. By giving more power to people and less to governments, new subnational and transnational groupings will emerge. If a consultative Upper House is needed, it might be wise to entrust it to intergovernmental organizations, since many of them have been good at developing supranational perspectives. Finally, the transnational corporations might be added in an additional Consultative Chamber.

Models for electing representatives to the new People's Assembly already exist in the European Community, and in the even larger and longer-lasting democratic experiment of India, often overlooked by the chauvinistic West. Despite its size, widespread poverty, and cultural mix, elections somehow work in that subcontinent, with a higher level of participation than in the United States!

If global democracy is possible, so too are **world referenda**, where the entire world population votes on key issues, such as military bases on foreign lands or the existence of national armies. Although political popular participation is often divisive (unless the process continues until consensus), such divisions would generally crisscross humanity, and few things so integrate the larger community as crisscrossing subgroups within it. The danger would be if, instead of crisscrossing, the subgroups aligned regionally, with the whole population in the "northwestern" corner of the world voting against the whole population elsewhere—but this is unlikely for the foreseeable future; the First World has much power, but hardly a global majority.

We could construct an almost endless list of **world institutions**, some of which already exist, albeit in embryonic form, in the United Nations and elsewhere. Because they constrain the actions, particularly of more powerful countries, withdrawals from membership have occurred and indeed are to be expected. Not all nations are ready for participation in world institutions; if they were, the world would not have the strife and conflict it in fact has. Healing takes time.

There are things to do in the meantime. Particularly attractive would be establishing a **World Service** of millions of young people from everywhere, involved in peacekeeping, bettering the environment, and social development. It has often been said that we need the "moral equivalent of war," a drafting of people similar to conscription for military service, but in the service of peace rather than war. This should not be confused with Peace Corps-type organizations that came into existence in the 1960s.

Although addressing the problems of development, they were established to promote the interests of the sponsoring nations more than world interests. A World Service would not be a propaganda institution to enhance the image of particular countries, but more like the international mail service that in fact benefits all without furthering anyone's narrow interests. Imagine millions of youth working together in a world reforestation campaign, or caring for the aged and handicapped, particularly in countries where three-generation families, in which they used to live, have disappeared.

Ideally, world service would be voluntary and open to all people. Countries with conscription, but aspiring to good world citizenship, would give their youth a choice between national and world service, and between military and nonmilitary service. Gradually, national military service would fade into oblivion, retaining only a minor defensive component. Offensive capability would be universally condemned, as slavery now is.

AN EIGHTFOLD PATH

Throughout history, humankind has engaged in social experiments on behalf of humanity as a whole—some successful, some not. We all do this every day in small ways, and deep inside us the Kantian question always lurks: *Is my behavior generalizable? What would happen if everyone in my position did what I am now about to do?* This approach of course can be misused, as when "deviant behaviors" are suppressed as socially disruptive when they are precisely what is needed to overcome unjust social structures. Likewise, one's "position" may be used to justify acts that lesser persons are not permitted: "What *I* do is for *their* own good; when *they* do it, there is anarchy." Nevertheless, there is something to the principle, depending on how one defines "position."

What does "position" mean in a global sense? Many people and countries might claim their behavior is generalizable, but others would immediately object that their action is too clearly marked, even marred, by their age group or gender group, their nation or class, their citizenship or membership, or by the position of their country in the world. We need a clearer conceptualization of what the "human position" or "world citizen" means. What does simply being a member of the human race entail in terms of rights and duties? Which are the human and which the world interests?

The enormous dilemma posed in seeking a definition of world citizenship is the threat to the necessary identities we each derive from seeing ourselves in terms of *our* age, gender, race, nation, and class groupings.

Setting ourselves apart from Nature, celebrating what we think distinguishes us as human beings, is also a part of this relentless search for identity, yet it is destructive of the very Nature on which we depend. Apparently, as we change, we need to nurture, not threaten, our intrinsic human need for identity, seeking new channels through which identity can be attained.

My conclusion is that the key to a peaceful world lies in the celebration of **diversity**, both in the sense of heterogeneity and heterology, and of **symbiosis** in the relationships between those diverse parts, provided the symbiosis is equitable. We may have impeded our visioning by fear of diversity, wondering too much how very different parts—including parts we dislike intensely—can possibly pull together unless they are made more similar. A strong world *government* would tend to reduce diversity, but world *coordination* could retain, even enhance it, and open up even more equitable symbioses. Economic, cultural, and political cooperation among self-reliant partners—as occurs today among the European Community, the ASEAN countries, and the Nordic countries—might ultimately make war look totally redundant.

We *are* on our way! Or, rather, we are on an eightfold path, working on all eight problems—hopefully not falling into the trap of believing that solving one of them will solve the others automatically. Ours is a double agenda: of building more *independent* actors (of **autonomy**), and of building more *interdependent* actors (of **equity**).

That statement seems contradictory: How can simultaneously increased capacities for independence and interdependence produce peace? The answer is simple. It takes defensive independence to live interdependently in a polycentric and highly complex world, without recourse to offensive weapons, whether one's own or those of superpowers. It takes economic independence to live interdependently in a highly interactive world without becoming dependent, exploited, or exploitative. It takes cultural independence not to depend on outside cultural support systems. And it takes political independence to participate equitably with others, without becoming their clients or pawns. Those who are dependent may inadvertently become allies, trade partners, believers and members, concealing the aggression taking place, until the growing resentment finally explodes. Those who are independent cannot.

Abolition of war is similar to what the people fighting slavery and colonialism, abject exploitation, and patriarchy were and are up against. They won, or are winning, their struggles. We now live in their "utopia," which proved after all to be realizable. So is ours: an entirely realizable utopia for peace.

SELECTED BIBLIOGRAPHY

Galtung, Johan. *Nonviolence and Israel / Palestine*. Honolulu, Hawaii: University of Hawaii Press, 1989.

————. *Peace and Development in the Pacific Hemisphere*. Honolulu, Hawaii: University of Hawaii Press, 1989.

————. *Solving Conflicts: A Peace Research Perspective*. Hawaii: University of Hawaii Press, 1989.

16 WHY NOT A SEPARATE COLLEGE OF INTEGRATED STUDIES?

Russell W. Peterson

UNIVERSITIES: SOURCES OF LEADERSHIP

The principal charge of a university is to prepare people for a life of leadership. But there are at least two distinct kinds of "leadership." One refers to "leading" groups of people, and the other, to "showing the way" by expansion of human knowledge through research.

In terms of the latter—research—universities have clearly led the way. As knowledge exploded, they developed ever narrower fields of specialization. This approach has been highly successful in advancing the frontiers of knowledge, and it will no doubt continue to prosper. Recently, our growing need to research the interconnections of people, things, and ideas has also led to an increasing awareness of the inadequacies of training in narrow disciplines. One result has been the proliferation of interdisciplinary research programs that pool the knowledge of specialists from several disciplines. These have been remarkably productive despite the intellectual prejudices that often limit the horizons of specialists, but they are still suboptimal in lacking the services of true generalists who can operate effectively at the interface of several disciplines and whose thinking benefits from a symbiosis among them.

The other kind of leadership—the leadership of people and of institutions—today calls for the broadest of training, not only for understanding the complex world we live in, but also for integrating the increasingly narrow slices of knowledge developed by the disciplines and for making intelligent choices among the alternatives they seem to suggest. My lifetime careers in education, research, industrial management, politics, state and federal government, citizen action, and world conservation and development have provided me, I like to believe, with on-the-job training as a "professional" generalist. During this time I have observed firsthand that more often than not people enter the most influential positions in our society ill-prepared for the breadth of their assignments. This is true for presidents and other political leaders, captains of industry, university presidents and deans, cabinet and military officers, judges, editors and journalists, ambassadors, and heads of citizens' organizations.

Nor are top leaders the only ones who can benefit from a good general education. We all need a broad understanding of the world around us at least as much as we need specialized skills and information. Some people, for example, see environmental issues as merely the concerns of special interests, yet they are issues of the most general interest. They are profoundly related to all quality-of-life issues, including health, poverty, racism, war, economics, and politics. Humankind is an integral part of the biosphere—one of the millions of interconnected species that inhabit it and depend upon each other and upon the air, water, soil, and sun. It is the activity of humans worldwide that most threatens this unique assemblage of life and its delicate balance, so everyone has a stake in environmental issues. And humanists, social scientists, physical scientists, biological scientists, lawyers, physicians, and engineers all have expertise to contribute to resolving environmental problems.

By seeing the connections—environmental, social, and economic—all of us can make choices more favorable to a decent sustainable quality of life for us all. A pediatrician who understands the implications of 40,000 children dying each day in developing countries would be more likely to seize an opportunity to work with the United Nations Children's Fund than someone less informed. A father might better understand his rebellious teenage daughter if he saw the ties between the physical and psychological upheavals of adolescence, his formerly mild-mannered daughter's behavior, and the culture in which she is growing up. A young engineer working on petroleum exploration might welcome the opportunity to work on solar energy, if he or she appreciated the uncertain future of fossil fuels. A mother concerned about her children's future and aware of the global interconnectedness of life might decide to lobby her senators to increase foreign aid, which is currently declining. A broadly educated, comprehending, "generalist" public will spawn good leaders and contribute to their effectiveness.

THE NEED FOR GENERALISTS: SOME CASES IN POINT

The escalating rate of change in the world increases the need for interdisciplinary training and action and for more attention to the future impacts of decisions. We no longer can muddle through, basing our decisions on fragments of specialized information or on this year's profit or next year's election if we wish to avoid cataclysmic disasters. Some examples of our past narrow vision and shortsightedness underscore this point. I begin with environmental awareness, and my own personal experiences in this area.

The recent emphasis on ecology—on the fact that all life, air, water, and land are interconnected and interdependent—constitutes probably the most significant scientific contribution of Western thought in the past century, particularly since it has been coupled with the realization that human interventions in the natural world have long-term consequences. Rachel Carson's *Silent Spring*, Aldo Leopold's *Sand County Almanac*, and J. E. Lovelock's *Gaia* have been landmark publications helping to further this view. In light of their wide-ranging and global implications, I believe that anyone who fails to grasp fundamental ecological principles is inadequately educated.

My personal enlightenment was triggered in 1952 when my ten-year-old son aroused my interest in the study of birds. The birds, good ecological indicators, taught me about the interconnectedness of things and encouraged me, while a Director of Research for the Dupont Company, to learn more of environmental science. As Governor of Delaware, I applied this background in fathering landmark environmental legislation, including the Delaware Coastal Zone Act, which prohibits any more heavy industry in a several-mile-wide strip along the coast. From 1973 to 1976, I served as Chairman of the President's Council on Environmental Quality and then as Director of the Congressional Office of Technology Assessment. These posts involved me worldwide in critical problems concerning the biosphere. I learned firsthand of their environmental, economic, political, technical, and social connections and of the inadequate understanding most decision-makers have about such relationships. Later, as President of the National Audubon Society, I learned how education and citizen action at the local level can affect decisions on global issues at national and international levels. Now, through leadership positions in five international organizations—dealing with peace, population, the environment, resources, and development—and extensive reading in these fields, I find my earlier convictions about the need for more professional generalists strongly reinforced.

The arms race is another case in point. For decades, U.S. policymakers have exhibited a singular narrowness of thought as they pushed military buildup as the "solution" to threats of Communism. Professor John Kenneth Galbraith, a professional generalist as well as a respected economist, put such narrow thinking in perspective when describing the results of a nuclear exchange between the superpowers: "No one, not even the most talented ideologue, will be able to tell the ashes of capitalism from the ashes of socialism."

We must not again wait for thirty-eight years after introducing such a technology before investigating the long-term consequences of its use. Chemists, physicists, and military engineers worked on the bomb, but biologists and agriculturalists essentially ignored it until 1982, when Drs. Paul Crutzen and John Birks suggested in *Ambio* magazine that the fires ignited by a nuclear exchange might loft enough soot into the atmosphere to block sunlight for months, bringing darkness and lower temperatures.[1] This suggestion triggered studies by climatologists and biologists, who in the intervening seven years have argued that the anticipated temperature drop from a nuclear exchange between the United States and the Soviet Union could devastate agricultural production globally, causing more deaths from famine in noncombatant India than suffered from the immediate effects of the exchange in both the United States and the Soviet Union.[2] Yet policymakers still largely ignore this prediction. If the Western Allies faced up to its implications, their current strategy to use nuclear weapons first if necessary in defense of Europe would be widely seen as even more insane.

Similarly, when we turn to the arena of economics, we need to broaden our perspectives. Instead of concentrating solely on the economic miracles wrought by Adam Smith's "invisible hand," we need also to attend to the multiple consequences of the "invisible foot," which has harmed us socially, economically, and environmentally. For example, the development of nuclear energy in the 1950s was projected to provide electricity that would be too cheap to meter; in 1985 one of the world's leading business magazines, *Forbes*, reported, "The failure of the United States nuclear power program ranks as the largest managerial disaster in business history, a disaster on a monumental scale." Its obvious safety and environmental shortcomings led to financial disaster.

During those same years, the dumping of hazardous wastes permitted the production of "better things for better living" at low cost, but now the Office of Technology Assessment says that it will take fifty years and hundreds of billions of dollars to clean up the inherited mess.[3] The accompanying damage to human health and the environment goes unmeasured. It is hard to believe that these debacles would have been allowed to happen if enough professional generalists had been involved in government, industry, and finance.

Another blind spot has been in the area of global justice. While we in the affluent nations celebrate our success in providing an ever higher material standard of living for our people, the number of our fellow human beings living in extreme poverty continues to grow. The Population Crisis Committee's 1987 Human Suffering Index, based on ten quality-of-life parameters, rates seventy-four countries with two-thirds of all people on Earth as experiencing high to extreme human suffering.[4] Dr. M. Swaminathan of India wrote in a 1987 paper on nutrition in Africa, "Hunger is a multidimensional problem. Unfortunately our planning and implementation procedures are predominately unidimensional."[5] By this he meant that hunger is not just a temporary lack-of-food problem of the affected people; it has many components—historical, global, technical, social, political, and economic. Our momentary Western successes can hardly justify ignoring our species' overall failure to provide for its own kind. What is needed to correct this tragedy is a massive sustained interdisciplinary understanding of today's world.

Thus, a broad-based "Renaissance" education is neither intellectually superficial nor appropriate only for a few would-be visionaries standing outside society's mainstream. If we are to solve many of the problems of humanity and take full advantage of life's opportunities, we must develop more interdisciplinary approaches to augment time-tested specialization. Today, however, *no* institution of higher education provides an education adequate to the needs of our planet. It is therefore my objective to propose not only that the general public be better educated, but that there also be established Colleges of Integrated Studies to provide such training: to produce **professional generalists** with bachelor's, master's, and doctorate degrees in integrated studies.

OUR FAILURE TO MEET THE NEED

For several years I served as Vice President of the Council of the International Union for the Conservation of Nature and Natural Resources (IUCN), which works with both government and nongovernment organizations worldwide to provide a decent life for future generations on a sustainable basis. Its members are leaders from all parts of the world; each was educated as a *specialist* but over the years has evolved into a *global generalist*. (Dr. M. Swaminathan, President of IUCN, is an outstanding example. Trained originally as an agricultural scientist, he is today familiar with several cultures and languages, and works in and outside of government, nationally and internationally, on food production, hunger, health, conservation, and other quality-of-life issues.) This distinguished group believes that their biggest obstacle to success is the lack of people in decision-making and advisory positions trained to think holistically and to pursue integrated multifaceted programs.

Nor has this need gone unnoticed here at home. In 1970, Professor F. Kenneth Hare, then of the University of Toronto, wrote in *Science*:

I must stress the incompetence of the established disciplines to tackle many of society's real problems. What we mean by a discipline is an agreed tested body of method—usually analytical—that we bring to bear on problems of our own choosing. The essence of our thinking is that we cannot tackle problems that do not fit the competence of our own discipline. . . . The existing departmental and disciplinary structure of the university is out of kilter with the needs of action-oriented, policy-directed programs.[6]

And in 1983, Professor Lynton K. Caldwell of Indiana University expressed well the need for what he calls metadisciplinary knowledge. He has written:

[T]he need to organize and focus complex bodies of knowledge is a consequence of human inability to wisely and effectively utilize that knowledge in disconnected specialized increments. Unless a better means of integrating and focusing our expanding knowledge is achieved, the advancement of all knowledge may be frustrated by the massive incoherence of increasing specialization. Indeed, the future of reductionist science and specialization may depend upon our ability to relate their components to a hierarchy of knowledge designed to integrate successive levels of complexity dynamically.[7]

Unfortunately, university administrators and department heads, with rare exceptions, have yet to catch up with the need for holistic understanding. They continue to plan and manage their institutions from the reductionist and compartmentalized vantage point of the traditional disciplines. Most courses are still taught within traditional disciplines, and little structure exists to support or promote interdisciplinary study per se. As the famous University of Wisconsin professor, Aldo Leopold, put it: "All the sciences and arts are taught as though they were separate. They are separate only in the classroom. Step out on the campus and they are immediately fused."[8] Since Leopold's time, some faculty members throughout academe have broadened their own education, research, teaching, and outreach work well beyond the normal confines of their disciplines. They are the ones who—against much opposition—have initiated and staffed the promising interdisciplinary courses and programs now extant on many campuses. But though many such interdisciplinary courses and programs exist, for the most part the interested student must find her or his own way through the maze.

Even this slow progress toward integrating the disciplines and establishing more fertile ground for the "Renaissance person" on our campuses has by no means been steady. During the 1980s, interdisciplinary programs were downgraded on university campuses across the United States, so that now there are fewer such programs than in the 1970s, with many existing in name only. Recently I met with 100 leaders of environmental studies programs in 56 universities. All agreed that they were treated as second-class citizens on their campuses. During lean years they received vastly disproportionate cuts in their budgets and in most cases failed to gain approval to grant degrees or provide faculty tenure. Key factors in this downgrading were increasing competition for funding, and faculty members' concerns about intrusion into their academic territories. Furthermore, since interdisciplinary programs are comparatively new, they do not have the same type of institutional power-base as the established disciplines.

Yet, the constant push from concerned faculty—many of whom attended the conference—remains. *The New York Times* (July 19, 1987) reported that the faculty of the Massachusetts Institute of Technology voted in May 1987 to create a minor in the humanities, arts, and social sciences. Samuel Jay Keyser, their Associate Provost for Education Policy and Programs, stated: "Among the engineers, there is a realization that the social and political implications of the technology are as important as the technology itself." The article also reports: "Many educators say that corporations are becoming interested in broadly educated employees rather than those who are well versed in a technology that may soon be obsolete." Clearly the practical and moral importance of breadth is being recognized more and more.

As more people realize the global interconnectedness of all life and life-support systems, as more faculty become dismayed by their discipline's lack of pertinence to the real world, and as more citizens recognize the ineptness of our specialists in coping with today's complex issues, the pressure on our educational system will build until discrete institutions of integrated studies begin to be established.

A HISTORY OF THE PROPOSAL FOR COLLEGES OF INTEGRATED STUDIES

I first proposed the need for colleges of integrated studies in an article in the *L & S Magazine* (Spring 1988) of the University of Wisconsin/Madison.[9] In it, I claimed that there is great interest around the country—indeed, around the world—in such a proposal. This interest, however, exists among a minority of the faculty on any one campus, albeit an enlightened and highly dedicated minority. I personally know dozens of such faculty around the world. They tell me there are thousands like them. They are struggling to make the college curriculum pertinent to the real world. They understand the mounting global crises we, *Homo sapiens*, have created as our global society has blindly moved into the future. They know how we can face up to this global predicament. They are a great asset. We must provide them the opportunity to bring their enlightenment to bear more effectively on teaching and sparking more students, and in providing the ideas needed for humanity's future survival. A separate College of Integrated Studies would provide them the environment and freedom in which they could flourish.

Long before I made this specific proposal, I often experienced profound resistance to the notion of breadth in education, which most frequently arises among members of the traditional disciplines who see the proposed metadisciplinary program impinging on their territory, competing for funds and clashing with the ideology that advanced training is best served by practicing it in ever narrower fields. This was first illustrated for me at a dinner in Cambridge in 1978 when I was Director of the Office of Technology Assessment (OTA). Dr. Jerome Wiesner, the President of M.I.T., had invited me to meet with about thirty department heads and deans from M.I.T. and Harvard. After dinner I suggested that these prestigious institutions set up a new graduate program to produce professional generalists. I pointed out that my experience in industry and government had shown the great need for generalists and the very limited supply. OTA, for example, is charged with advising Congress on the global long-term social, environmental, economic, and political impacts of new technologies—truly an assignment for generalists.

My suggestion triggered a heated debate. One-fourth of the group supported my suggestion; the rest vigorously opposed it. A principal contention was that I, myself, would not now be a generalist (they called me a generalist) if I had not first studied in graduate school the inhibition of air oxidation of vitamin C. The same argument has been presented to me several times since, but I continue to fail to see why one needs to become a Ph.D. **specialist** as a necessary stepping-stone to becoming a **generalist**. On the contrary, there is abundant evidence that Ph.D. specialists, from the narrowness of their training, are blind to the need and opportunities for professional generalists. While specialists argue that breadth implies shallowness, I believe the knowledge required to cope with the problems our world now faces is of a higher order. Rather than requiring less rigor than training in one discipline, training in a metadiscipline (to use Professor Caldwell's term) calls for *more rigor*. Not understanding the interconnections, the specialist looks at a metadiscipline with unseeing eyes.

In reviewing my article in the *L & S Magazine*, Dr. E. David Cronon, Dean of the College of Letters and Science at Wisconsin, stated the following:

Although I am a strong supporter of interdisciplinary studies, I don't share Russell Peterson's enthusiasm for a new college or university of integrated studies, separate from or replacing the liberal arts college. I nevertheless welcome his opening up a discussion of this issue. For myself, I am enough of a traditionalist to retain a strong faith in the resiliency of the various academic disciplines as they now exist (and as some have been developing since classical times).[10]

But Dean Cronon did not get my message. I, too, think liberal arts colleges are very important. I am *not* suggesting that the liberal arts and science colleges be changed or replaced. I am suggesting that a *separate* College of Integrated Studies be established—a pioneering step in academe—providing students with another choice for launching their careers. Providing ever more courses in the Letters and Science school—as Dean Cronon has accomplished at Wisconsin—is good, but it does not necessarily help a student acquire a more comprehensive education. He or she still can select only a few courses from the huge inventory and must do so with little or no guidance and from the limited perspective of a seventeen- or eighteen-year-old. Nor are the courses selected necessarily connected in the sense Dr. Boyer indicated in his keynote address (see Chapter 2).

Instead of such a smorgasbord approach, we need to steer or attract some of our best students into a Renaissance curriculum, such as now occurs at this very same University of Wisconsin in its two-year Integrated Studies Program. Each of its courses is interdisciplinary, drawing on all major fields of study. The courses mesh together and successive courses build on one another, developing deeper and deeper levels of understanding. The courses weave together classic ideas and contemporary problems. This is an excellent beginning, but this kind of program needs to be expanded to a rigorous four- or five-year undergraduate program, situated in a separate college with its own graduate school tailored for the professional generalist.

The Integrated Studies program I envision cannot flower, or even survive, within the traditional Letters and Science school. Most of the administrators and faculty in the traditional disciplines are too strongly opposed. Dean Cronon quoted one of Wisconsin's former deans as saying: "I believe that the man [sic] of broad knowledge would be possible now, as at the time of the Renaissance, if the Renaissance attitude again existed."[11] But I believe the Renaissance attitude *does* exist. The problem is the failure of society—particularly our universities—to provide the means for people with such attitudes to flourish. We diligently funnel students into the narrow confines of the disciplines and inhibit the flowering of any incipient Renaissance attitude. We need the functional equivalent of the Medicis, the popes, and the kings who nourished the Renaissance attitude. A College of Integrated Studies would be one means.

I do not mean to imply that four years, or even eight years, of interdisciplinary schooling will produce a highly educated person. This calls for a lifetime of learning. But a person schooled as a professional generalist, with a love of learning, breadth of knowledge, and skills for integrating knowledge, would enter post–school life from a superior and powerful launching pad. The time will come, I believe, when such training will rank among the most respected that universities provide, when leadership positions in society will be dominated by Ph.D.s in integrated studies.

THOUGHTS ON DESIGN AND IMPLEMENTATION

As already noted, a proposal to create discrete colleges of integrated studies automatically raises questions and objections. Some will ask about administrative structures or scurry to protect long-standing intellectual territories. Others will ask about funding or power. (If we gain this, what will we lose?) Others will resist because of inertia, because change always means hard work and new ways of thinking. Let me briefly touch on these.

A College of Integrated Studies would have its own dean and tenured faculty, selected from among the world's most renowned generalists with a track record of commitment and involvement in rigorous interdisciplinary teaching and research. This structure would attract educators who wish to make this effort their central activity. Most of the courses in such a college would be interdisciplinary, covering material normally taught in several departments. Although a few disciplinary "building-block" courses would be required, such skills as mathematics, writing, and speaking could be incorporated in the interdisciplinary courses. The four-year undergraduate program would be planned as a whole, each course tailored to fill a portion of the overall curriculum. Although the best of today's liberal arts programs could provide the basis of what is needed as an undergraduate foundation to support the more rigorous graduate work required for a professional generalist, much needs to be done to make them more comprehensive and meaningful.

An extensive graduate school curriculum would build on the undergraduate program. Each student would be required to become proficient in one foreign language and to study for six months in one foreign country, and research theses would involve interdisciplinary studies.

Some educators ask who will hire these generalist graduates? My conviction is that once they are available, society will grab them. Today's world of work calls for frequent career changes. Within a few years, most graduates will be working in fields outside that of their major. A graduate from the rigorous program of integrated studies that I envision would have the flexibility and breadth of understanding, mental skills, and values to stand out in the competitive world of work.

Others will ask, how shall such a college be funded? I believe it can emerge without competing directly with funds for existing programs. A Renaissance College of Integrated Studies could be packaged and promoted as a pioneering effort in tune with the blossoming one-world concept and the growing understanding of the interconnectedness of things—a twenty-first century beachhead in academe. I believe major foundations and corporations would support such a demonstration project, especially in a state university, if the governor, legislative leaders and the Board of Trustees all agreed to an additional state matching grant for the purpose.

In a lecture in 1959, C. P. Snow described "two cultures"—that of scientists and that of humanists—and he discussed the gap in understanding between the two. If he were writing today, I believe he would identify the conflict as existing between two rather different antagonists: not between scientists and humanists, per se, but between specialists and generalists. Although the latter two groups may seem to be in conflict, both are essential to the search for knowledge and the solution to societal problems. Today academia favors the "culture of specialists." But clearly, she needs to further the "culture of generalists" as well. The troops to do the job are already available, waiting on campuses only for the necessary leadership and resources to emerge.

NOTES

1. Paul Crutzen and John W. Birks. "The Atmosphere after Nuclear War: Twilight at Noon," *Ambio*, 11 (1982), 115–25.

2. United Nations. *Study on the Climatic and Other Global Effects of Nuclear War* (New York: United Nations, Sales No. E.89.IX.1, 1989).

3. J. S. Hirschhorn. *Superfund Strategy* (Washington, D.C.: Office of Technology Assessment, U.S. Congress, 1985).

4. S. L. Camp and J. J. Speidel. *The International Human Suffering Index* (Washington, D.C.: Population Crisis Commitee, 1987).

5. M. S. Swaminathan, First Annual Arturo Franco Memorial Lecture, Ministerial Session of World Food Council, June 17, 1986. (New York: The Hunger Project, Paper no. 5, 1986).

6. F. Kenneth Hare, "How Should We Treat the Environment?" *Science* (January 23, 1970), 352–55.

7. Lynton K. Caldwell, "Environmental Studies: Discipline or Metadiscipline?" *The Environmental Professional*, 5 (1983), 247–59.

8. Aldo Leopold, "The Role of Wildlife in Liberal Education," *Transactions of the Seventh North American Wildlife Conference* (Washington, D.C.: American Wildlife Institute, 1942).

9. Russell W. Peterson, "Integrated Studies: Education for the Professional Generalist," *L & S Magazine* (Madison: University of Wisconsin, Spring 1988).

10. E. David Cronon, "A View from South Hall," *L & S Magazine* (Madison: University of Wisconsin, Spring 1988).

11. Cronon, "A View from South Hall."

SELECTED BIBLIOGRAPHY

Blank, Robert H. "Toward Better Education in Biopolitics," *Issues in Science and Technology*, Spring 1988, pp. 51–53.

Brown, Lester R. *Building a Sustainable Society*. New York: Norton, 1981.

———, Alan Durning, Christopher Flavin, Lori Heise, Jodi Jacobson, Sandra Postel, Michael Renner, Cynthia Pollack Shea, and Linda Starke. *State of the World 1989*. New York: Norton, 1989.

Caldwell, Lynton K. "Environmental Studies: Discipline or Metadiscipline?" *The Environmental Professional*, 5 (1989), 247–59.

Hare, F. Kenneth. "How Should We Treat the Environment?" *Science*, January 23, 1970, pp. 352–55.

Leopold, Aldo. *A Sand County Almanac*. New York: Oxford University Press, 1949.

Lovelock, John E. *Gaia—A New Look at Life on Earth*. New York: Oxford University Press, 1979.

Meadows, Donella H., Dennis L. Meadows, Jørgen Randers, and William W. Behrens III. *The Limits to Growth*. Washington, D.C.: New American Library, 1972.

National Geographic Society. *Earth 88—Changing Geographic Perspectives*. Washington, D.C.: National Geographic Society, 1988.

Neustadt, Richard E., and Ernest R. May. *Thinking in Time*. New York: The Free Press, 1986.

Peccei, Aurelio. *One Hundred Pages for the Future*. New York: Pergamon Press, 1981.

Peterson, Russell W. "Integrated Studies: Education for the Professional Generalist," *L & S Magazine*, Spring 1988, Madison: University of Wisconsin.

Schneider, Stephen H. "The Whole Earth Dialogue," *Issues in Science and Technology*, Spring 1988, pp. 90–98.

Sigma Xi, The Scientific Research Society. *A New Agenda for Science*. New Haven: Sigma Xi, 1987.

Wolman, M. Gordon. "Interdisciplinary Education: A Continuing Experiment," *Science*, November 25, 1977, pp. 800–804.

V   Developing the New Curriculum

17 CUTTING THE GORDIAN KNOT
SECRETS OF SUCCESSFUL CURRICULAR INTEGRATION

David McFarland and Benjamin F. Taggie

Several critical steps are involved in implementing of integrative curriculum. The most crucial of these are:

1. To demonstrate to faculty that they will benefit personally and professionally by participating in the creation and teaching of such programs;
2. To gain the support of the administration by having them invest resources in such programs; and
3. To sell the program to the university community by convincing such powerful representative political groups as the University Curriculum Committee and the Faculty Senate to support their implementation. This point becomes increasingly vital when incorporating integrative programs into general education.

THE FACULTY

The greatest challenge to the successful implementation of interdisciplinary programs is demonstrating to faculty the benefits of participating in such intellectual and teaching activities. There are several aspects to this issue, the first being that interdisciplinary teaching runs counter to the increasing specialization of our graduate schools. Much of the blame for our current problem may be laid on Martianus Capella, a fifth-century scholar and one of the four great encyclopedists or "Latin transmitters" of classical culture to early medieval Europe. In classical times, the liberal arts formed the basic curriculum appropriate for the training of free men (hence the term "liberal"). By late antiquity seven areas had been established in the curriculum. Martianus authored a treatise entitled *The Marriage of Philology and Mercury*, which began as an allegorical romance and ended as a textbook on the seven liberal arts. It was the beginning of academic specialization. Martianus Capella's treatise, strongly influenced by the writings of his contemporary, Saint Augustine, fixed in the early medieval mind, and later in the curriculum of the medieval university, the number of the liberal arts as seven.

It may seem ludicrous and brutally unkind to indict an obscure North African who lived fifteen hundred years ago for the difficulty of implementing interdisciplinary programs today, but all problems require a scapegoat, and Martianus, in this instance, provides an excellent one. In his treatise the seven liberal arts fall into two groups. One group of three, the trivium, consists of the literary arts: grammar, logic, and rhetoric. The second group of four, the quadrivium, comprises the mathematical or technical arts: geometry, arithmetic, astronomy, and music.

While the relative importance of the seven liberal arts altered from time to time (grammar, for example, lost its preeminence to logic in the first half of the twelfth century), they maintained their eminence as the core curriculum of the medieval university. Students, and hence those who became teaching Masters, studied all seven of the liberal arts, but usually specialized in only one. So it was in the Medieval period, as it is today, that academic reputations were made. By the end of the period, specialization had become increasingly characteristic of the universities.

Those Renaissance personalities, such as Michelangelo, Cellini, and Leonardo da Vinci, whom we so admire today for their intellectual and artistic versatility, might well owe their extraordinary versatility and place in history to the fortuitous circumstance that they never attended a university. Entering our own era, academic disciplines and departments have proliferated. The evolution of new disciplines, such as sociology, psychology, and economics, has been supplemented by the technological and scientific revolution which has given us schools of engineering. These, in turn, generate their own growing areas of specialization, such as petroleum engineering. A product of this growth has been the increasing fragmentation of faculties into individual disciplines, often for administrative convenience. Concurrently, there has been an explosive growth of knowledge. More books have been published since World War II than in all the preceding centuries. It took Harvard University 275 years to acquire its first million books and only five years to collect its latest million.

An even more important factor is the tens of thousands of young doctoral candidates who flooded our graduate schools in the 1950s, 1960s, and 1970s. To accommodate their research needs, increasingly specialized and esoteric research topics were explored. The growing specialization of graduate schools demanded more and earlier specialization at the undergraduate level. For the student intent upon graduate or professional education, little time was left to explore other disciplines and methodologies, or to learn how such disciplines interacted and integrated to create interdisciplinary learning experiences. This problem has been exacerbated by accreditation agencies that have escalated the traditional 30-40 hour major to 70, 80, and even 90 credits. As knowledge expands relentlessly, even specialists find it hard to keep up in their own fields. Specialization, departmentalization, the proliferation of academic disciplines, and the knowledge explosion have all contributed to the fragmentary nature of modern education. It has produced a generation of specialized academics who often find teaching even a survey course in their own discipline a formidable challenge; one can hardly expect them to be inclined or able to give their courses an interdisciplinary perspective. In almost every discipline we find increasing specialization when we are in need of more generalized teaching expertise. It is what Alfred North Whitehead described nearly half a century ago as "the fatal disconnection of subjects which kills the vitality of our modern curriculum."[1]

A good interdisciplinary instructor must be more than a didactic academic specialist. The individual must be prepared to transcend the mere imparting of information in the lecture hall, important as that task might be. It requires a teaching environment where teachers can "educe" a student's opinion in an atmosphere of mutual respect, and where teachers help the student subject those opinions to critical scrutiny while making it clear that the teacher's own notions might be equally partial and in need of scrutiny. Such inquiry cannot be limited by conventional disciplinary boundaries; students and faculty must follow questions wherever they lead, synthesizing insights from various disciplines. As Derek Bok said, "the challenge now is to renew this effort and to seek fresh syntheses that reconcile new insights and needs with more enduring human values in order to bring coherence and diversity into a healthier balance once again."[2]

Interdisciplinary teaching requires one to view a topic (about which one has preconceived notions) through the perspective of another discipline (in which one may have no formal training). In doing so it forces a faculty member to take the same risks—the risks of finding those preconceived notions shallow in a public forum—that students are being asked to take. These risks are themselves intrinsic to interdisciplinary learning.

The risk taking is reduced as interdisciplinary teachers master and assimilate content into their teaching from outside their area of specialization. A good Latin teacher should be more than an expert in declensions and conjugations. If that instructor has a knowledge of Roman history, literature, philosophy, and art, Latin classes can be transformed into quintessential interdisciplinary learning experiences for students. One acquires the skill of interdisciplinary pedagogy by learning and more learning. Educators must be willing to continue to grow as individuals, scholars, and teachers long after they have received their terminal degrees—indeed, to make a lifetime commitment to learning. Once content is mastered, pedagogic expertise comes with practice and experience.

Consider how empty is a history course on twentieth-century America that ignores the works of Arthur Miller, John Steinbeck, and Sinclair Lewis. It does not demand a great imagination to see how enriched students would be to see Willy Loman and Babbitt in an historical context, the products of the idiosyncratic features of American culture. Students could also examine the social values embedded in such literary works to better understand the history of the period. Steinbeck's *Grapes of Wrath* brings a realism to the horror and suffering spawned by the dust bowl that students do not experience from history books alone. Similar examples can be found for many courses.

Combining material from various disciplines into an effective interdisciplinary teaching experience requires commitment and hard work. The would-be interdisciplinary teacher may even seek formal classroom instruction. When academicians evaluate teaching institutions they often cite outstanding libraries, document collections, or scientific research facilities, but they seldom mention the faculty—that great human resource of intelligent, highly trained individuals, all of them expert in something. How unfortunate not to benefit from such a community! Imagine the cogent intellectual experiences administrators could stimulate by rewarding faculty who undertake such activities. More flexible sabbatical leave policies, for instance, would allow faculty to formally study in another discipline. Administrators, of course, must always balance the improvement of instruction with research leading to publication, yet often the seminal activities of teaching and research complement each other. With an aging professorate, the need for faculty renewal becomes even more pressing for the academy. Preparation for serious interdisciplinary teaching can offer restorative experiences to such faculty.

The point is that many faculty are not prepared to undertake the type of serious interdisciplinary teaching that transcends the level of the superficial. By superficial we mean, for example, the historian who by showing art slides in a course assumes that he/she is engaged in interdisciplinary teaching. Real interdisciplinary teaching requires much more. The key to successful interdisciplinary teaching is really very simple. It is the mastery of significant scholarship that is outside the area of specialization and the assimilation of that learning into one's area of teaching.

ADMINISTRATION

Once faculty have been persuaded to buy into interdisciplinary programs, a second challenge must be met—gaining administrative and financial support. That problem is often exacerbated by the fact that the terms "interdisciplinary" or "integrative" cause many educators to equate that pedagogy with the equally effective, but far more expensive, teamteaching.

We must inform administrators that interdisciplinary pedagogy is not *a priori* either a wasteful, excessive expenditure, or even necessarily expensive team-teaching. We do not believe this latter point can be overemphasized. In the minds of too many (including some who appreciate and respect the value of interdisciplinary learning), team-teaching and interdisciplinary teaching are synonymous. This close identification of team-teaching with interdisciplinary teaching is one of the most serious impediments to the development and implementation of interdisciplinary programs. We must acknowledge that a team-taught course can be a vastly rewarding experience for both students and instructors; if properly conducted, it can represent the ultimate interdisciplinary experience. We have taught numerous seminars with partners from various disciplines and have found each experience to be intellectually enriching. We have profited from the knowledge of our colleagues and from the preparation that was necessary to teach such courses. Course evaluations indicated that the students also appreciated, enjoyed, and benefited intellectually from such educational opportunities.

One might wonder, then, how something as good as team-teaching could be potentially hazardous to interdisciplinary courses and/or programs. We have a one word answer—cost. All administrators, from department chairs to university presidents, know how difficult it can be to live within budgets which are, in many cases, being eroded rather than increased. Team-teaching is an extremely expensive activity, unless you have faculty who are willing to participate in it as an overload. This, however, is an unsatisfactory solution. No matter how qualitative a program might be, it must pay its own way in today's education economy. It is regrettable, but true, that team-teaching is a luxury few budgets can support.

In the halcyon days of the 1960s and 1970s the National Endowment for the Humanities was very supportive of interdisciplinary programs, many of which included a team-teaching component. We had the good fortune to receive a pilot grant from the NEH in 1981 to implement several team-taught interdisciplinary seminars. However, built into our proposal was a plan to phase out the team-teaching component, replacing it with individually taught integrative courses. This insured the program's survival beyond the life of the NEH grant. The grant provided release-time for the teaching teams to prepare for the interdisciplinary seminars they would teach. Much of that time was spent by the faculty reading material germane to the discipline of the teaching partner. The grant also provided the opportunity for the seminars to be taught with both members of the teaching team present at all sessions. Our theory was that this intensive preparation and teaching experience would allow one team member to teach the course in the future with only infrequent visits by the second team member. That plan was successful and the courses developed in 1981 are still a viable component of the university curriculum.

Our message is that interdisciplinary programs involve more than team-teaching and do not require resources in excess of any other quality program. To reiterate, the key to successful interdisciplinary teaching is really very simple. It is the mastery and assimilation into one's teaching of significant scholarly content that is outside the area of specialization.

IMPLEMENTATION

Once the benefits of interdisciplinary education have been demonstrated to the faculty and administration, the challenge remains to convince appropriate governing bodies to develop and adopt an interdisciplinary program within general education. One response to this final step will be demonstrated by examining a case study taken from Central Missouri State University.

The primary reason major changes are seldom made in general education relates to the difficulty in winning faculty ownership. Most proposals are cycled through a committee and then given to faculty governance bodies for their approval. At that point general education proposals usually degenerate into battles over credit hours. This process has little chance of accomplishing anything of substance, certainly not something as innovative as including an interdisciplinary studies component in the core. As we describe the process used at Central Missouri State University, you will note that it involved considerable planning and the cultivation of many people through a systematic process. The process focused upon the development of relationships and alliances in informal as well as formal settings. It included scheduled meetings with key individuals, but those same people also were sought out at concerts, receptions, athletic contests, etc. The plan unfolded in a carefully designed manner so that key individuals could develop ownership and carry the plan forward to the general faculty.

The process of developing an interdisciplinary studies component in general education was primarily orchestrated by the Dean of Arts and Sciences and the Provost. These two individuals met at least once a week in an attempt to monitor and keep the plan on track. The Provost played the leadership role, while the Dean orchestrated the logistics.

Initially it was necessary to determine a vehicle through which the issue could be addressed by the faculty rather than the administration. This opportunity occurred late in the spring semester of 1987 when the Governor asked all state-supported universities to submit student outcomes assessment proposals for the following academic year. At that time it was decided by the Dean and Provost that the basic plan would be to use assessment directives to help faculty determine the need to define general education outcomes more carefully. Through the process of defining general education goals, faculty hopefully would be encouraged to add an interdisciplinary studies component. Thus, in concept the plan was very simple. However, the success of any design of this nature is determined by the manner in which the plan is executed. The remainder of this chapter documents many of the detailed steps leading to the final adoption of the framework for an interdisciplinary studies program.

To establish a sense of timing for the case study, we should note the Governor requested the assessment proposal as school was ending in the spring. Consequently, it was difficult to consult with large numbers of the faculty. Broad faculty participation was further inhibited by the Governor's time line of three to four weeks for the submission of the proposal. The Provost requested that the Senate convene an ad hoc faculty committee to aid in the development of the proposal. This strategy also allowed the Provost to be involved in the proposal preparation without appearing intrusive to the faculty, since he was responding to a request from the Governor.

The Provost began by meeting individually with the Senate President and the Committee on Committees' chair to discuss the Governor's request and the possible availability of several hundred thousand dollars in the near future to fund a proposal. The Provost indicated concern about requesting massive funding for something to which the faculty were not yet committed. At the same time, he described the political liabilities of not moving forward with the Governor's request. He also outlined the substantial academic benefits to the University of assessment funding.

Finally, he noted that the challenge for the task force would be to develop a proposal narrow enough in focus to interest the Governor and the legislature, but wide enough in scope to permit the faculty to determine what actually was going to be done.

Before meeting with the ad hoc committee, the Provost drafted a proposal including the following five assessment components:

1. pre-college entrance;
2. midpoint, assessing intellectual skills at the end of the sophomore year;
3. general education outcomes;
4. exit from college;
5. post-graduation follow-up.

The Provost then presented his draft to the ad hoc committee as a starting point for discussion. Although the committee members were encouraged to revise the proposal as needed, they adopted the Provost's draft with few changes and a final proposal was prepared for submission to the Governor. Within a month the proposal was funded. CMSU was granted approximately $300,000 with the caveat from the Governor that the university contribute an additional $100,000 of in-kind resources. Thus, the fall semester began with $400,000 allocated for assessment. The President chose to designate $50,000 of that amount for general education support without restrictions on its use.

During the summer the Provost met formally and informally with each member of the ad hoc Assessment Committee to explore the need to delineate general education outcomes more clearly prior to implementing an assessment process. At that time, the structure of the general education curriculum was distributional or "cafeteria style," with little focus on desired outcomes. The Provost also urged the Assessment Committee to encourage the Senate to integrate the ad hoc group into the Senate structure. As the fall semester began, the Assessment Committee emerged as a regular Senate committee. Concurrently, the Senate instructed the General Education Committee to define clearly the intended outcomes of general education, a task which overwhelmed the five-person General Education Committee.

This situation presented the Provost and Dean of Arts and Sciences with the opportunity to develop a plan to help that Committee deal with its assignment. The General Education Committee previously had viewed general education as a curriculum that would expose students to experiences in the following four categories: (1) basic skills; (2) science and technology; (3) humanities/social sciences and fine arts; and (4) individual development. The program developed by the Provost and Dean retained these four components, but added an "Integrated Studies" component. The Dean and Provost then began to meet individually with the members of the General Education Committee to help them develop ownership in the integrated studies category and to create a process for developing expected general education outcomes.

Given the magnitude of the assignment, it was not difficult to convince the General Education Committee that help was needed. The Provost proposed to the General Education Committee that a portion of the $50,000 assessment grant be used to support the formation of "blue ribbon" task forces to assist the Committee in addressing its formidable charge. The task forces, he suggested, should be composed of faculty with expertise in given content areas and each task force also should be provided with the services of an outside consultant recognized nationally for leadership in general education. The Committee readily accepted the value of bringing in national leaders to assist the task forces. The assignment of one member of the General Education Committee to each task force also won committee approval.

As the General Education Committee developed ownership in the process, it approached the Senate Committee on Committees to ask for assistance in making appointments to the task forces. This was a key step toward the long-term goal of maintaining a sense of ownership on the part of the Senate. The Committee on Committees consented to nominate a pool of faculty from which the task forces could be selected. The faculty were identified based upon the expertise needed by each task force, rather than in terms of university-wide representation. Broader university representation in the discussions was to be provided through the use of symposia, open hearings, and the fact that any final proposal would require approval of the Curriculum Committee and Senate. The actual selection of task force members from the Committee on Committee's pool was made by the General Education Committee Chair and the Provost. As a result, five excellent task forces were assembled and seven outstanding consultants were selected to work with them.

Concurrent with the beginning work of the task forces, the Dean of Arts and Sciences wrote a philosophical statement on general education consisting of five components, matching the five areas to be examined by the task forces. The paper was used as the focus of a four-hour workshop for the Council of Deans. There it was revised and became a position paper for the total Council. The hope was that at a later point in the discussions this white paper signifying philosophical unanimity among the deans would provide helpful administrative "pressure points" through which territoriality could be reduced. Hence, the possibility of support for a strong general education program from all colleges could be increased. The paper was then shared with the General Education Committee as background material, and eventually provided much of the structure for the final general education philosophical statement.

The process of developing a faculty-owned general education philosophical statement through the task force structure was designed so that task forces worked independently as well as collectively. Thirty faculty members were called together for an initial meeting to receive the charge and to discuss the short- and long-term process. Each task force was to develop a statement of philosophy, approximately two pages in length, defining the expected content and goals of their specific academic area. The preliminary drafts of these statements were to be completed before the December holiday vacation. Building upon the work of the individual task forces, the primary assignment was to be completed in plenary session in January prior to the beginning of second semester classes. The salient task of this plenary group was to develop a ten-page document defining the philosophical premises and academic expectations of general education at CMSU. In an attempt to minimize focusing attention on credit hours, a basic ground rule was established specifying that specific courses were not to be debated; only areas of study were open to discussion. Not surprisingly, credit hour distribution was a difficult issue to exclude from the discussions. Nonetheless, the ground rule was diligently upheld.

Once the general plan of action had been accepted by all parties, the actual process began when the consultants were brought to campus for several days early in the fall semester to work with the task forces. First, the consultants met as a group with the Provost and Dean to discuss the process and develop strategies. Two of the consultants were designated as lead consultants and facilitators. These two met individually with every member of the task forces to ascertain the stance of each person, and to work toward broadening the perspective of task force members when needed. The task forces met frequently in plenary meetings to present progress reports. Each task force was challenged to develop an in-depth perspective of its particular academic area, in addition to an abridged philosophical statement. Each group responded with a two-page philosophical statement supported by position papers ranging from twenty-five to forty pages.

As mentioned above, it had been agreed from the beginning that the task forces would meet for a week-long plenary session in early January to develop a composite philosophical statement. Each faculty member was to be paid a $500 stipend for this week. The Chairperson of the Curriculum

Committee, the College Deans, the President, the Provost, and the seven consultants also participated in the plenary session.

The individual philosophical statements from each task force and approximately 150 pages of background material prepared by the task forces were distributed to all participants in mid-December. Each day of the January plenary session began with the group functioning as a committee of the whole for purposes of open discussion. The afternoons provided time for the task forces to meet individually, responding to the particular needs of their specific assignments and reacting to issues raised by the larger group. Each evening the consultants met with the Dean of Arts and Sciences, the Provost, and the Chairperson of the General Education Committee to review the day's progress and develop strategies for the next day.

During the week all sessions were chaired by members of the General Education Committee. In addition a Draft Committee, consisting of one person from each of the five task forces, was given the assignment of writing the final position paper. This committee worked in the evenings and reported on its progress daily. The Provost's secretary took formal minutes, which were distributed and revised as needed at the beginning of each day. Informal discussions were carried on during the daily luncheons. By the end of the week, a working draft of the paper began to emerge and the Draft Committee was given the assignment to complete the revision of the paper within two weeks. The total group was reconvened three weeks later to critique and respond to the draft. The Draft Committee incorporated suggestions in second revision, and the whole group was called back in session two weeks later to make final changes.

At this point, the draft was fairly polished and a symposium was scheduled to focus on the paper. Participants included all deans, department chairs, members of the Curriculum Committee, the task forces, the General Education Committee, the Faculty Senate and the consultants. The draft was distributed in advance, and this group of over 100 people met all day on a Saturday to make revisions and build broader ownership in the document. It was particularly important for the Curriculum Committee and Faculty Senate to develop ownership since these two bodies would eventually be required to take formal action on the final document.

After the symposium, the Draft Committee again made editorial changes and the task forces met in a final plenary session to respond to the changes. It then became the responsibility of the General Education Committee to carry the process further. They proceeded by distributing the document to the full faculty and placing copies of the 150 pages of support materials in the library and in each departmental office. Open hearings on the document were conducted over a two-week period. In addition, a second all-day symposium was scheduled which all faculty were invited to attend. Approximately 175 faculty participated in this second symposium. Based on the open hearings and the second symposium, the General Education Committee made final revisions and forwarded the philosophical statement, along with the 150 pages of background material, to the Curriculum Committee for approval.

By this point it was late spring and the Curriculum Committee was heavily involved in other matters. Thus, the General Education Committee decided to withdraw its proposal from consideration until the fall semester. This gave the Chairperson of the Curriculum Committee, the Provost, and the Dean of Arts and Sciences the summer to work individually with members of the Curriculum Committee and Senate in order to gain their support. It was agreed that a special meeting format under the auspices of the Curriculum Committee be called in the fall. Logic dictated that something as complex as general education be considered very carefully, without unnecessarily protracted discussion. Thus, in early September, the Curriculum Committee, Deans, Provost, President and Vice President of the Senate, resource people from the five task forces, and the two lead consultants traveled to a local conference center and spent the entire day reviewing the proposal. By the end of the day, the Curriculum Committee had passed the entire proposal with only minor changes. The Curriculum Committee met the following week for formal action on the revised document after which the proposal was forwarded to the Senate.

The Senate did not seek further assistance from the consultants because it wanted to remove any further external influence. A meeting was scheduled at which it acted as a committee of the whole, during which no votes were taken and all of the components of the proposal were open for discussion. The discussion was very disorganized and issues included in the discussion spanned the total proposal. This experience served as an object lesson for the Senate, which soon recognized such a discussion could continue indefinitely. Thus, a session was scheduled beginning at the normal 3:15 p.m. meeting time, extending through dinner and into the evening. By the end of this extended Senate meeting, the entire proposal had been approved with virtually no revisions.

It should be noted that the Senate moved to form an implementation committee to deal with specific details that might arise during the implementation of the proposal. It was further decided that the implementation committee would develop a plan for presentation to the Senate. Most importantly, it was agreed that no faculty would be terminated if resulting revisions in general education led to enrollment changes that would require staffing shifts. To avoid terminations a three-to-five-year implementation phase-in time was recommended, thereby allowing staffing changes to be accomplished through resignation, retirement, or retraining.

In summary, the final revision of general education contained many substantial changes including a category of interdisciplinary studies. A change of such scope and significance could never have been made if it had come forward as the idea of the Provost, the Dean, an individual faculty member or even a single committee. It was only possible because a process was used that included broad groups of faculty. As Clark Kerr has aptly observed, "Innovations sometimes succeed best when they have no obvious author."[3]

NOTES

1. Alfred North Whitehead, *The Aims of Education* (New York: Macmillan Company, 1929), p. 123.

2. Derek Bok, *Higher Learning* (Cambridge, Mass.: Harvard University Press, 1986), p. 171.

3. Clark Kerr, as quoted in Bok, *Higher Learning*, pp. 159–60.

SELECTED BIBLIOGRAPHY

Bok, Derek. *Higher Learning*. Cambridge, Mass.: Harvard University Press, 1986.
Whitehead, Alfred North. *The Aims of Education*. New York: Macmillan Company, 1929.

18 HOW DO WE KNOW WHAT WE HAVE DONE?
ASSESSMENT AND FACULTY DEVELOPMENT WITHIN A LEARNING COMMUNITY

James C. Manley and Nancy Ware

PRINCIPLES OF ASSESSMENT—NANCY WARE

When we developed an interdisciplinary general education program, we began with the questions: "What do we want to do and what ought we to do?" Our answer was to make educated persons out of ourselves and our students. About three years into the program, we asked, "How do we know what we have done?" Had we indeed met our goal to change all concerned?

Most often we want to change our students to make them more like ourselves so we can recognize ourselves in them and thus throw ourselves into the future. Have they inherited the culture we value? Perhaps greater gains would come if we recognized their otherness, and the difference between our present and their future. If we related to them as "thou," to use Martin Buber's term, rather than as "it," then perhaps the talk between us that takes place in the classroom now might make some difference in the future.

The danger in assessment is that we distance ourselves from what we are looking at, assuming a superior posture, and then checking off the boxes on our chart. We report back, like nurses to the doctor, the data on our patients' blood pressure, pulse, food intake, and so on. If all goes well we release our patients from the institution, cured of the conditions with which they were admitted.

How can we know what changes we have effected in our students? We *do* care about how they will shape the future, and we assume that how they understand, feel, and act in our classrooms has some bearing on their future lives. We know that it is easy to take credit for changes that would occur without our help. Much that we observe can be attributed to the maturation process, rather than to what we have done. We know that there are kinds of changes we can make boxes for, but we are also interested in the changes that slip through the cracks of our well-reasoned boxes.

Why do we assess our students? Various reasons come to mind: because we are assessed by others; because someone has asked that we do this; because we want excellent students and an excellent university; because we believe it can benefit both ourselves and our students. Perhaps feedback provided by the assessment process can stimulate learning in us all.

For all of these reasons, we at California Polytechnic University, Pomona, decided to pursue the question, "How do we know what we have done?" Under the leadership of Andrew Moss, we set rather wide perimeters on outcomes. The educated person we had in mind was older and wiser than any of us. We recognized that learning is cumulative, integrated, and proceeds by stops and starts; that both students and faculty need to form a "community of learners." We need to set limits on our arrogance. Starting with learning outcomes, we backtracked to subject matter. Once our goals had been set, we had to reconsider curriculum and methods. A degree of trust had to be established among all involved, since faculty and students are wary of taking risks. Students sat on the committees with us.

In the course of a year-long series of meetings, we discovered a relationship between how one thinks of general education and the kinds of assessment that we appropriate to it. We were led to consider the relationships of critical thinking, creative thinking, effective writing, and speaking. We set goals for cross-cultural understanding, talked about the place of values, the arts, historical and social consciousness, and came back again and again to the role our students needed to assume as independent learners.

We wanted our students to develop sturdy and independent characters. If we were lucky, if we got out of our own way, we might do the right things to bring this about. But how do you assess sturdiness and independence? We knew they would follow their own migratory patterns and, if we were lucky, leap from the confines we set. Would we want to measure the energy and distance in their leap? In addition to fostering independence, we wanted students to collaborate and to converse with each other, to satisfy their curiosity, inquire into, formulate, and pursue their own questions. These outcomes are not accessible by the techniques of standardized testing, but they can be assessed nonetheless.

However, we also found we could not talk of assessing students without assessing ourselves as well. In the conversation of the classroom, we are learning to listen as a means of creating a community that generates conversation, including such techniques as having members talk in turn.

We are learning that our role as teachers is changing, that knowledge is a process of continual negotiation and transformation.

The conceptual model of an educated person holistically defined became the assessment model. The outcomes are designed to make students conscious of and responsible for reporting their own growth. We talk with students about certain categories of change at the end of each ten-week quarter. "Readings" are taken at different stages and progress is reviewed throughout their period in the program. Assessments are done by the students themselves, by various faculty teams they work with, and by an outside evaluator. We had to ensure that the outcomes would be appropriate to continuing growth, beyond our two-and-a-half-year program, over an entire lifetime.

The confines of our classroom or our institution are artificial. We want the conversations begun there to extend out into the hallways, into the parking lot, and into the communities where our students live. Though pressed by time, our students do move toward the future in ways that can be observed. Some of their responses to us are not verbal, but can be seen in the way they live their lives.

If we restrict our assessment to the moment, we may look at students reductively, missing the whole. If we measure only their adaptation to our classroom, we may not be seeing the actual growth process. But if we assess ourselves, our curriculum and methods, and consider the leap our students must make into the future, we have a different task. We and they are bound together—as I and thou we move from here into the future.

THE DIMENSION OF FACULTY DEVELOPMENT—
JAMES C. MANLEY

I want to link the question, "How do we know what we have done?" directly to the question, "How can faculty development best proceed?" Within the next twelve years nearly two-thirds of the existing professoriate will retire or leave—at a time when student enrollments will be rising.[1] Since we, the existing professoriate, are responsible for replacing our ranks, it is critical that we renew ourselves, even as we act to find our successors. In this light, faculty development is of the first importance. That is why I want to concentrate on the ways in which our experience has enabled us to foster at least one kind of faculty development, and how that is connected to the assessment question, "How do we know what we have done?"

The Structure of the IGE Program

The Interdisciplinary General Education Program has been in existence at California State Polytechnic University, Pomona, since 1983, even longer if one counts the years of gestation prior to institutional endorsement. This endorsement took the form of a budget and inclusion in the university catalog. Presently some 350 students and 40 faculty are involved in the program.

Our students come from a variety of majors, principally engineering and architecture. A sequence of eight, four-unit courses spanning two and a half years fulfills the humanities and social sciences components of the university general education requirement. These courses are team-taught, an aspect of our program that has special relevance for faculty development and for assessment in general, as I will elaborate below.

A list of the course titles may be helpful.[2] The first-year student begins with "Consciousness and Community: Origins and Development of Human Societies," moving on to "Rationalism and Revelations: The Ancient World" and "Authority and Faith: Feudalism and the Renaissance." During the second year the student takes "Culture and Contact: The Expansion of the West," then "Reform and Revolution: The Age of Enlightenment," concluding with "Individualism and Collectivism, Competing Ideologies: The Industrial Age." Finally, during the third year, two courses stressing independent work are taken—"Promise and Crisis: The Modern World," and "Connections Seminar: Exploration and Personal Expression."

Associated with these courses is an Arts Events package, which enables students to see events as disparate as the Garth Fagan Bucket Dance group and Professor Leonard Pronko describing and demonstrating the art of Kabuki. In addition, we have a coordinated series of lectures devoted to value issues. For example, this past year Roy Woodruff and Roger Beajolois spoke on why they took actions as whistleblowers, despite knowing that doing so might end their careers.

The Faculty Component

The IGE Program began with about 100 students, doubling within three years. During this time it received widespread commendation from sources both within and beyond our university.[3] The California State University Chancellor, Ann Reynolds, praised the program as follows: "Integration of disciplinary approaches and active involvement of students in the learning process, as they have apparently been achieved in the

Interdisciplinary General Education Program, put into practice key recommendations of 'Involvement in Learning,' the 1984 report of the Study Group on the Conditions of Excellence in American Higher Education."[4]

What are the reasons for these successes? One reason is that, over the past decade, our faculty has had the opportunity to be involved in successive and overlapping learning communities. In particular, the learning community that evolved into the IGE Program has learned how to adapt to a "shared curriculum," which has implications for both assessment and faculty development.

In the late 1970s and early 1980s, several of our faculty participated in a California State University system-wide task force charged with devising curriculum in the area of Ethics, Values, and Technology. Its two dozen members represented most of the CSU campuses, and came from a variety of different disciplines, primarily within the humanities and social sciences. Participation in the task force allowed them to enjoy positive experiences in working with colleagues outside their own disciplines on a topic of mutual importance. While the aim of changing existing "values" curriculum within the CSU system was not realized, another important aim was, namely, that of creating constructive working relationships among colleagues from different fields and campuses.

The basic format of group meetings was a retreat attended by some three dozen faculty, each prepared to enter into a series of talks, workshops, and discussions over a two-day period. The prototype retreat was held at Cal Poly in 1979 under the theme "Searching for Civilization." It focused on the public/private tensions in citizenship and climaxed twenty-seven weekly presentations on this same theme given during the regular academic year.[5]

The practice of weekly presentations on a common theme during the academic year has continued on our campus as the Campus Forum. The practice of having yearly retreats also has continued, although these have evolved into IGE retreats rather than Campus Forum retreats over the course of five or six years. This transition was very smooth since the membership of the two groups overlapped considerably. The focus simply shifted to strategies for achieving a shared curriculum in IGE rather than continuing the discussion of the Campus Forum topics.[6]

In contrast to the ambience of many disciplinary bodies, this past decade has seen an unusual amount of activity on our campus in structured discussion—cross-disciplinary, voluntary, and supportive. This experience was particularly important this past year, when, to strengthen the IGE curriculum, a task force was formed to determine how certain cross-disciplinary outcomes within its eight courses could best be met. These outcomes, articulated three years ago by members of the IGE learning community, provide additional ways to create a shared curriculum. They are:

Communication skills and critical thinking

Development of historical and social consciousness

Multicultural understanding

Understanding and appreciation of aesthetic experiences

Understanding and articulation of values

Independent integration of knowledge and experience through active student learning.

Each outcome is a node drawing together members from different disciplines. For example, the "Communication skills and critical thinking" outcome can bring together teachers of philosophy, rhetoric, communication arts, and composition in on-campus workshops. Or the "Multicultural" outcome can bring together history, philosophy, English, and arts faculties in public workshops. These activities facilitate faculty development, but, because they are public, they lead to assessment in the best sense—review by one's peers. Hence, they provide a realistic benchmark by which we can measure our work.

Models of Development: Individual Teaching vs. Team-Teaching

I now turn to some factors that can impede the sort of success I have described. I shall argue that a primary impediment is an individualistic model of faculty development and research. Although there are changes afoot, this traditional model of faculty development and research is still very much in place. In this model, research is primarily solitary until there is public testing in a setting far removed from the home campus. The faculty member researches a topic, writes a paper or a book, and then presents or defends that paper or publication in a disciplinary forum.

As a philosopher, I might, for example, write a paper on aesthetics and present it at a professional meeting. The topic likely would be dictated in part by what is current, or "hot," in the field. If well-received, the paper might subsequently be published. That in turn would be documented in my retention, tenure, and promotion file. Traditional professional reinforcement proceeds in this way. The problem here is that the conduct of inquiry tends to reinforce disciplinary pursuits undertaken in isolation. Moreover, these pursuits need not be directly associated with teaching.

Team-teaching is an excellent way to move away from the individualistic model of scholarship and research. In teams composed of faculty from different disciplines, those involved find their intellectual life much enriched. The success of the IGE Program, in my opinion, is directly connected to the willingness of our institution to support team-teaching. It is difficult for me to imagine the same kind of learning community developing in a context where team-teaching does not occur.

Consider team-teaching's alternative model for research and scholarship within a learning community focused on a shared curriculum. Ideas, suggestions, proposals are made by members of the community in regard to strengthening the curriculum. Some ideas fly, others do not. The ones that do may later be written up for publication—even the "null cases" may have value. However, in all probability such research will not appear in disciplinary publications. Scholarship does occur in a learning community, but it is not of the traditional kind. Yet it is no less worthy than traditional scholarship and should be reinforced in any institution that seeks to emulate the success of the IGE Program.

The two questions, "What does a faculty member gain from participation in a program like the IGE Program?" and "How do we know what we have done?" are really closely linked. My own experience over the past year, as a faculty member teaching in the Program, serves as an example. My primary academic training is in philosophy. In teaching with Nancy, an English instructor and poet, the course on The Ancient World, I had the opportunity to explore myth and poetry in ways that otherwise would not have occurred. As a member of the Task Force on IGE Outcomes, I attended—and learned from—workshops led by colleagues from each of the outcome areas. They included such topics as the Aesthetic Dimension, featuring the aesthetics of Chartre Cathedral and of Bernini's St. Teresa; Communication Skills and Critical Thinking, where the importance of writing for a particular audience was indelibly modeled; and Historical and Social Consciousness, in which we deconstructed the simplistic histories of high school texts, in order to replace them with something more substantial, albeit more complex.

There were several sequential workshops on the Multicultural Aspect of our eight IGE courses, during which I saw the development of new sets of arguments about the importance of not seeing the world through Eurocentric or gendered filters. In the Workshops on Values and the Independent Integration of Knowledge and Experience through Active Student Learning, I saw, first, the enormous difficulties associated with the teaching of values along with some hope for securing consensus regarding a family of values and, second, the articulate linking of independent work in the classroom with the independence required of a good citizen.

We videotaped workshops in an attempt to provide a snapshot of work-in-progress on the outcomes. These turned out to stimulate extremely productive conversation, and served as an introduction to new ways of using technology to further inquiry. The arts performances provided stimuli for working with the students. In addition, there were the course-planning meetings for the various courses, which provided still another forum where faculty from the several sections assembled and interacted.

Conclusions

I am now in a position to state my thesis more clearly—really, a set of theses. First, success in developing a shared curriculum is associated with the presence of a learning community, which is indispensable to a shared curriculum. Moreover, in our experience team-teaching by faculty in different disciplines is an extraordinarily important part of creating a learning community.

Furthermore, a learning community is an extraordinarily important part of the conditions facilitating faculty development. The curriculum in the eight IGE courses is itself a reflection of a substantial part of our intellectual heritage. What better way to stay intellectually alive than to become a part of what Robert Hutchins called the Great Conversation? It is only within a learning community that we can answer the question, "How do we know what we have done?" We must test ideas in public, yet the forum for this public testing precisely constitutes a learning community. The development of curriculum, faculty development, and assessment ideally all proceed hand in hand in a learning community. The curriculum is strengthened by suggestions, proposals, and examples presented in a public forum.

Assessment begins with one's peers and in the context of the faculty's own intellectual development. Questionnaires and other such evaluative instruments have been used; we have undertaken longitudinal studies of our alumni; we have used outside evaluators. All of these measures have been strongly supportive of our program. But the most crucial measure has been the supportive, but diligently critical, scrutiny of our colleagues in workshops, planning sessions, retreats, public presentations, and in the context of team-teaching. We know what we have done because we engage in a continuing, public conversation about what matters in our curriculum and what that curriculum maps, namely the great issues in public life.

How can we best renew the two-thirds of all college professors now teaching who are slated for retirement in the next twelve years? It seems that the only choice is to renew ourselves, by providing an intellectual environment where we can continue learning.

I will conclude with these observations by my colleague, Dick Jacobs, on the "exportability" of programs such as the IGE Program:[7]

The need to reform general education should emerge from an informed and concerned faculty and not be imposed from the top down on the faculty.

Each college and university must create its own institutional and intellectual world. The pride of authorship and the process of deliberation cannot be short-circuited by the import of another program. At the same time, the inevitable insularity of the individual institution can be diminished by the investigation of other viable models. The IGE Program would serve as a valuable resource and model in this regard.

There must be a group of faculty, with broad intellectual interests, who can broker and mediate the proprietary interests of departmental and disciplinary concerns.

The emphasis should be on the significant issues, paradigms, and concepts of the human experience, with an open-ended and problematic approach. This helps to avoid looking at curriculum as turf, to be divided up according to some fixed scheme.

Methods may be developed to activate faculty as authentic learners, sufficiently secure and adequately supported, to pursue the possibilities for professional renewal and institutional reform. . . . The definitions of professional responsibility must be extended beyond subject specialization to include an obligation to the level of excellence and sum total impact of the entire university and college experience on the students.

The first step in the initial process of consideration should not be practicable or even reasonable, taking into account institutional resources, past traditions, and the immediate disposition of faculty. Rather, the first step should be the visionary projections of the ideal curriculum for young people about to step into the twenty-first century. Global questions that incorporate normative and intellectual goals and aspirations can form a motivating and inspirational basis for stimulating intellectual reflection.

NOTES

1. Jack H. Schuster, "The Changing Academic Workplace and the Future of College Teaching," Lilly Conference on College Teaching-West, March 17-19, 1989.

2. For complete titles and course descriptions, contact the IGE Office, California Polytechnic University, Pomona, 3801 West Temple Ave., Pomona, CA 91768. The IGE Guide also is available from this source.

3. Included among these awards was a citation for Undergraduate Education from Brown University (1985); recognition from the Association of American Colleges, in 1986, for an outstanding model program; and a citation in the G. Theodore Mitau Award competition for Innovation and Change in Higher Education in 1987. Articles have also appeared in publications of the Association of American Colleges and of the Meiklejohn Education Foundation.

4. Letter from Chancellor Reynolds to President Hugh LaBounty, dated October 20, 1985. See also Joseph S. Johnston, Jr., Susan Shaman, and Robert Zemsky, *Unfinished Design: The Humanities and Social Sciences in Undergraduate Engineering Education* (American Association of Colleges, 1988), pp. 46–47.

5. The entire series, including the retreat, was partially funded by a grant from the California Council for the Humanities, authored by Richard Jacobs and David Levering of Cal Poly.

6. The Center for Normative Studies was created in the early 1980s as an institutional umbrella for the Campus Forum, retreats, and small institutes, continuing today. The IGE Program subsequently emerged as its own administrative unit within the College of Arts.

7. Richard Jacobs has been the Director of IGE since its inception in 1983. He has taught extensively in the program and lectured widely on its success. These comments are from an internal position paper, "The Interdisciplinary General Education Program," March 6, 1989, Cal Poly, Pomona, pp. 13–14.

SELECTED BIBLIOGRAPHY

"California State Polytechnic Pomona," *The Forum for Liberal Education*, 8, no. 4 (March 1986), 6–8.

Johnston, Jr., Joseph S., Susan Shaman and Robert Zemsky. *Unfinished Design: The Humanities and Social Sciences in Undergraduate Engineering Education*. American Association of Colleges, 1988.

Markgraf, Phil, David Reinhard, Robert Ruscitto, and Pei Wang. "This Program Creates 'Better Human beings.' " *Voices of Youth*. Meiklejohn Education Foundation, Fall 1986, 36–37.

Romer, Karen T., ed. *Models of Collaboration in Undergraduate Education*. Providence, R.I.: Brown University, 1985.

19 WHAT TO DO NEXT
STRATEGIES FOR CHANGE

William H. Newell

MY VISION

A real possibility exists within American higher education for establishing a symbiotic relationship between the reductionist academic disciplines and holistic interdisciplinary study. While a long-time advocate of interdisciplinary education, I have become convinced that the disciplines and interdisciplinary study need each other: neither can stand alone.

The disciplines need interdisciplinary study at both the societal and individual levels. Much of our failure to deal with the increasingly complex societal and global problems we have faced in the twentieth century is attributable to our reliance on expertise grounded in disciplines that are better and better at analyzing smaller and smaller pieces of large complex issues. It is becoming increasingly obvious that we need to educate experts in the process of integrating those valuable, but limited, discipline-based insights into a holistic understanding of the larger issues. To use Bill Reckmeyer's language, interdisciplinary study offers our best hope for managing the "messes" in which we find ourselves.

At the level of the individual, the narrow foci of disciplines have proven dangerous as well as ineffective. They have contributed to the sense of isolation and communal detachment that increasingly characterizes individuals in modern societies, especially a society as large as the United States. Some of the blame for the glorification of selfishness and irresponsibility symbolized by the recent Reagan administration perhaps should be assigned to the reductionist mode of disciplinary thinking taught in our colleges and universities. Certainly, the liberal education provided by most colleges and universities did little to counteract that perversion of individualism.

But interdisciplinary study needs the disciplines as well. More and more of us are coming to appreciate that interdisciplinary study is founded upon the disciplines: they provide the insights that we integrate. We may even find it fruitful to think of the disciplines and interdisciplinary study as existing in a Yin-Yang relationship, as two complementary modes of thinking that not only play off one another, but taken together form a complete understanding. It has been my experience that interdisciplinary courses that ignore disciplinary insights—or recognize the insights but ignore how they were arrived at—tend to be intellectually shallow. In the process they give other excellent interdisciplinary courses a bad name.

I am less severe than Robert Costanza, Richard Rubenstein, Hazel Henderson, and others in my criticism of the disciplines, and less heartily in favor of transdisciplinary education. It may turn out that on a particular topic or problem area, such as Rubenstein's example of conflict resolution, the disciplines are so intellectually impoverished that they have nothing to contribute. Nevertheless, I believe that for each problem area we should follow Rubenstein's lead by trying an interdisciplinary approach *first* to see if the disciplines do in fact offer only falsehoods. If they do, then a transdisciplinary approach is in order. However, my experience has been that, for most problems, the disciplines *do* have some useful insights, at least in a limited sense, and consequently an interdisciplinary approach is appropriate.

Having recognized the essential complementarity existing between the disciplines and interdisciplinary study, how can we embody it in the curricular and institutional structure of American undergraduate education? I set forth such a vision in 1981 when I argued for an extensive reorganization of American higher education.[1] At the time I envisioned *all* liberal arts students taking a curriculum starting with broad interdisciplinary general education courses, moving on to disciplinary theory courses, and ending with problem or issue-focused interdisciplinary courses that draw upon their disciplinary training. I proposed that faculty teaching those interdisciplinary courses be housed in a department of interdisciplinary studies. Much discussion turned on the pragmatic issues of how to bring about the requisite curricular and organizational reform in institutions that we all know to be highly resistant to change, especially if change is perceived as a threat to departmental turf.

Note that my focus has been on integrative courses rather than on an integrated curriculum. The coherence of the curriculum is, I believe, a concern for administrators more than faculty or students. Naturally I am interested in the coverage and sequencing of the courses students take, but I am much more interested in what goes on within each course—the kind of thinking it encourages, the skills, values, habits of mind and action it promotes. My primary focus thus is on educational outcomes.

Leaving aside temporarily the question of implementation, let us look at the vision itself. Interdisciplinary general education courses should be designed to give entering students the opportunity to explore the "big questions," so that the enthusiasm for learning, which stimulates many to attend college in the first place, can be sustained. If these courses are developed skillfully, they also can effectively present introductory concepts, theories, and methods from various disciplines by comparing their relative strengths and weaknesses. In the process, disciplinary expertise will be demystified as students learn that "any one discipline is a powerful but limited tool whose insights must be taken with a grain of salt because it captures only one aspect of reality."[2] Students also will learn which disciplinary worldview provides the most comfortable fit for them, permitting a more informed choice of a disciplinary major.

Disciplinary courses bear the task of giving students an in-depth exposure to a body of theory, concepts, and modes of analysis, along with some facility with that discipline's perspective on the world. While for a few students interdisciplinary study itself can become their major, most can be expected to select a traditional academic major.

Upper division should give students an opportunity to apply their new-found disciplinary expertise to large issues or problems, while reminding them of its limitations, of the value of other disciplinary perspectives, and of the need to integrate those perspectives by means of the interdisciplinary process. Each upper division course should have substantial disciplinary prerequisites. A course on modernization, for example, might require coursework in economics, political science, and sociology, replacing existing courses in economic development, political modernization, and the sociology of development.

Students should graduate with roughly equal training in analytic and synthetic modes of thinking. They should appreciate the limitations as well as the strengths of their expertise and be prepared to contribute to the holistic understanding of large-scale societal issues in a way that is not now possible. On a personal level, they should be more receptive to alternative ways of thinking, more tolerant of ambiguity or paradox, more creative or unconventional in their thinking, and more sensitive to bias (whether disciplinary, ideological, or religious). Being more aware of communal and public issues, they would be better equipped to see how those issues relate to their lives, and more confident of their ability to understand and evaluate those issues. Thus, students with this educational experience would feel more empowered and less alienated.

The impact of this restructuring of American higher education would not be limited to students, however. I suspect it would alter the very disciplines in ways that can only be applauded. It is easy to act as though your narrow disciplinary perspective is the only right one when it is not systematically and publicly subjected to comparison with more holistic perspectives, and when the goal is to compete with other narrow perspectives for new adherents. But when all potential majors are taught to see the limitations along with the strengths of each disciplinary perspective and its underlying assumptions, disciplines will be forced to see themselves as their potential majors see them, namely from the vantage point of a holistic perspective. When they do, I predict they will start to reexamine their more restrictive assumptions, which eventually should lead to a broadening of the worldview of the discipline. They also should come to think in terms of how their contributions to more comprehensive analyses can complement those of other disciplines.

The consequences of this vision for American society are potentially enormous. It prepares students to grapple with the complex real world societal problems they will face as citizens. After all, "interdisciplinary study is holistic in its vision, issue-oriented in its curricular structure, and empowering in making judgements on complex technical issues."[3] By critically contrasting the formulation of issues by different disciplines, interdisciplinary training helps citizens identify the fundamental, underlying issues. By providing training in the integration of insights from several disciplines, interdisciplinary education prepares citizens to deal with complexity. In fact, they should be uncomfortable with single-cause explanations and simplistic solutions. They should become quick to question the interpretations of political authorities or disciplinary experts regarding the nature of and solution to our global problems.

Interdisciplinary education breeds tolerance of diversity through the ability it develops to look at an issue from multiple perspectives. More importantly perhaps, practice in integrating the insights generated develops respect for the contributions of each perspective, and a corresponding breadth of vision. As our country becomes ever more culturally and racially pluralistic, and our world more interdependent, these mental habits can help replace impending social upheaval with cohesion.

But the impact of this vision is not limited to our citizens. We can expect a whole new category of experts to form—interdisciplinary experts. They would synthesize the specialized insights of disciplinary experts into a comprehensive understanding of large-scale societal or global problems and their solutions. Thus, for the first time since the Germanization of

American higher education in the nineteenth century, we will be able to establish a balance between methods of analysis and synthesis.

I am *not* seeking a balance between specialists and generalists here. In fact, I intentionally avoid the label "generalist" used by others, because the problems faced by our society and our planet are too complex for any one person to understand them all. Instead, I seek a more appropriate *scale* of specialization, one that respects the broad scope of contemporary issues. I seek a more holistic perspective that respects the interrelatedness of those issues. In the context of academic politics, it is one thing to advocate a change in the appropriate scale of specialization, but quite another to attack specialization itself. I believe the interplay of disciplinary and interdisciplinary education sketched above offers our best hope for producing the kind of experts we so desperately need.

WHAT HAS BEEN DONE?

When I first developed my vision a decade ago, it seemed futuristic indeed. The era of widespread experimentation in higher education appeared to have ended. The '60s, with their interdisciplinary colleges and cluster colleges, seemed far removed from the conservative '80s. Those of us teaching in what we thought of as the few remaining interdisciplinary programs felt we were in the rear guard, surrounded by Philistines.

We had organized the Association for Integrative Studies in 1979 in the hope that it would become a national voice on behalf of interdisciplinary studies, as well as a professional haven for interdisciplinarians. Still, the vision of interdisciplinary studies as a profession seemed unrealistic. No recognized professional literature, journal, or theoretical base existed, and there was not even any agreement on the meaning of interdisciplinary study. In the eyes of the disciplinarians we had no legitimacy. Only a handful of people in higher education even knew of our existence.

Unbeknownst to us, forces were already at work even a decade ago leading to a renaissance in interdisciplinary study. Although many of the cluster colleges and freestanding interdisciplinary institutions of the '60s are gone, rather than disappearing from American higher education interdisciplinary study has moved from the radical fringe into the liberal mainstream. Intellectuals who were students in the '60s were becoming faculty themselves, and began reasserting their control over the curriculum. Colleges and universities were beginning to rethink their general education requirements and were revising them to incorporate interdisciplinary components. Today these trends are so pronounced that when the latest addition to Ohio's system of state universities proposed a general education distribution requirement, the Ohio Board of Regents told them to replace it with an interdisciplinary general education core.

Honor programs also have been revitalized over the past decade, and that trend has been accelerating as "excellence" becomes the watchword of legislatures and overseers of American higher education. The National Collegiate Honors Council goes so far as to assert that "honors" and "interdisciplinary" are synonymous! Interdisciplinary majors, senior capstone courses, humanities courses, and women's studies programs all have contributed to a tremendous resurgence of experimentation in four-year colleges and universities. Community colleges likewise have been active in developing interdisciplinary programs.

The results of this nationwide burst of activity are quite extraordinary for established interdisciplinary programs. At my home institution, Miami University in Ohio, the School of Interdisciplinary Studies was a controversial program a decade ago with an uncertain future. Today, the same program is seen as one of the jewels in Miami's crown. In the past four years we have won four awards for academic excellence: one from the state, two Academic Challenge grants from the university, and a three-year grant from FIPSE. The climate for implementation of my proposal to restructure undergraduate education has never been better.

Our progress can be measured by more than an improved climate, however. The outline of an interdisciplinary studies profession has begun to emerge. Membership in the Association for Integrative Studies grew from 35 charter members to its current 300. AIS now publishes a quarterly newsletter and an annual journal, as well as hosting annual conferences with as many as 150 participants. A directory of undergraduate interdisciplinary programs was published by the Association in 1986, stimulating an awareness of their widespread existence. Within a year a bibliography of professional literature on interdisciplinarity will be available on-line, with plans underway for computer access to the entire literature.[4]

AIS members, who serve as consultants to colleges and universities initiating or expanding interdisciplinary general education programs, exert a profound influence on the thinking of more and more innovative faculty and administrators beyond the Association. When I made presentations on interdisciplinary studies a decade ago, I was appalled by the surrounding intellectual confusion. "Interdisciplinary study" meant almost anything, and too often boiled down to a lack of intellectual substance. Today it is a rare committee report, working paper, or speech on interdisciplinary studies that does not reflect at least some understanding of the consensus developed within the AIS. Hence, the level of discourse on interdisciplinarity has been raised substantially, and with it respect has been gained among disciplinarians.

When we recognize the widespread experimentation with interdisciplinary study within both general education and honors programs, combined with the creation of an embryonic interdisciplinary studies profession and improved understanding of interdisciplinarity, we can begin to appreciate how much progress has been made toward the vision which only a decade ago seemed a pipe-dream.

WHAT REMAINS TO BE DONE?

Much of what remains to be done is nuts and bolts activity—hammering out agreements with Commissions for Higher Education, for example, on standards for evaluating proposals for new interdisciplinary programs. These activities are not very glamorous, nor very exciting to discuss, but many are now underway.

Two further steps need to be taken. The first is a need for high-quality Ph.D. programs in interdisciplinary study, graduate programs that prepare students to teach in the new interdisciplinary general education programs as well as conduct interdisciplinary research. Without a continuing flow of students from graduate schools into teaching and from undergraduate education into graduate schools, interdisciplinary undergraduate education cannot be maintained. Only a limited number of discipline-trained faculty are willing to undertake the major professional retraining necessary to teach interdisciplinary courses. Without high quality Ph.D. programs to provide faculty *trained* in interdisciplinary study, these programs will soon grind to a halt and a golden opportunity will have been lost.

The second step is strategic—convincing honors programs that their future lies in upper division interdisciplinary courses. As more and more institutions establish lower division interdisciplinary general education courses for *all* students, the distinctive mission of honors programs is being eroded. If these programs take up the challenge of developing interdisciplinary courses for juniors and seniors drawing upon, while transcending, their disciplinary major, those students will have a liberal arts education very close to what I have envisioned.

Colleges and universities tend eventually to adopt for all students innovations pioneered by their honors programs, since they want an excellent education for all. This tendency explains some of the current trends towards interdisciplinary general education programs as a university-wide requirement. If honors programs are successful in developing interdisciplinary upper division courses, and if we can train enough new

Ph.D.s in interdisciplinary studies to teach those courses, then a decade from now the vision may begin to be fulfilled.

In facing the reality of entrenched academic disciplines, be assured that you are not alone. Many others in and out of higher education share these same concerns and values. There are literally hundreds of genuinely interdisciplinary undergraduate programs, and thousands of interdisciplinary faculty throughout the United States, and their numbers are rapidly growing. We are, indeed, part of a national movement that holds out the promise of transforming American higher education in the early twenty-first century.

NOTES

1. William H. Newell, "The Role of Interdisciplinary Studies in the Liberal Education of the 1980s," *Liberal Education*, 69:3 (1983), 245–55.

2. Newell, 247.

3. William H. Newell and Allen J. Davis, "Education for Citizenship: The Role of Progressive Education and Interdisciplinary Studies," *Innovative Education*, 13:1 (Fall/Winter 1988), 32.

4. Julie T. Klein, *Interdisciplinarity: History, Theory, Practice* (Detroit: Wayne State University Press, 1989).

SELECTED BIBLIOGRAPHY

Klein, Julie T. *Interdisciplinarity: History, Theory, Practice.* Detroit: Wayne State University Press, 1989.

Newell, William H. "The Role of Interdisciplinary Studies in the Liberal Education of the 1980s," *Liberal Education* 69, 3 (1983).

———, and Allen J. Davis. "Education for Citizenship: The Role of Progressive Education and Interdisciplinary Studies," *Innovative Education* 13, 1 (Fall/Winter 1988).

INDEX

ABOUT THE
CONTRIBUTORS

ALBERT A. BARTLETT is Professor Emeritus of Physics at the University of Colorado, Boulder. Although active in scientific research (he began his career at Los Alamos during World War II), his greatest love has been teaching, for which he received national recognition in 1981 when the American Association of Physics Teachers honored him with the Robert A. Millikan Award. For the past dozen years he has devoted himself to alerting the public to the obvious—yet utterly ignored—consequences of exponential growth.

ERNEST L. BOYER is President of the Carnegie Foundation for the Advancement of Teaching. His eclectic career spans virtually every discipline and every role in education, including faculty member, dean, chancellor of the State University of New York (the nation's largest), and U.S. Commissioner of Education. In addition to holding nearly one hundred honorary degrees, he has received international recognition as an educator, and is widely known for such books as *High School* and *College: The Undergraduate Experience*.

GEORGE BUGLIARELLO is President of Polytechnic University, Brooklyn, New York. An engineer by training, his scientific career has spanned civil engineering, biomedical engineering, fluid mechanics, and computer languages. He has acquired both national and international recognition as an educator and consultant in the area of technology as it affects society, development, and public policy, and is well-known as an advocate and interpreter of the role of science and technology in human affairs.

MARY E. CLARK teaches biology at San Diego State University. In addition to her research on the molecular aspects of water stress, she has had a long-standing interest in teaching about global problems. Her introductory textbook, *Contemporary Biology*, was the first to incorporate applications of biological information to everyday life. She then developed a widely known interdisciplinary course, "Our Global Future," and in 1981 was named the first National Professor of the Year. She was co-organizer of the conference, "Rethinking the Curriculum."

ROBERT COSTANZA is Associate Professor in the Coastal and Environmental Policy Program, Chesapeake Biological Laboratory of the University of Maryland. Trained as a wetlands ecologist, he long ago expanded his interests into ecological modeling and, more recently, into ecological economics, in an attempt to describe the interface between the natural world that supports us and the abstract theoretical overlay we humans bring to our understanding of the planet we inhabit. Currently, as Chief Editor of *Ecological Economics*, he seeks to establish dialogue between those who understand Nature and those who make major economic decisions.

CHARLES WEI-HSUN FU is on the faculty of Temple University in Philadelphia. A graduate of National Taiwan University, he received degrees in philosophy in the United States and has taught Buddhism and Western philosophy at several universities both here and abroad. He has been a prolific scholar and author of numerous books and articles on Asian and Western philosophy and religion, and has made several tours of Asia as a lecturer and conference speaker. He maintains a deep interest, not only in interpreting Asian worldviews to the West, but in seeking a fertile fusion of the best aspects of both in humankind's future.

JOHAN GALTUNG is currently Professor of Peace Studies at the University of Hawaii. Born and raised in Oslo, he earned advanced degrees in mathematics and sociology before embarking on an international professorial odyssey that has included Europe, South America, Japan, Africa, Southeast Asia, and North America. Galtung's vision of "peace" encompasses not merely arms reduction and cessation of hostilities, but significant changes in our economic, political, and social thinking. In 1987, he received the Right Livelihood Award in Stockholm, Sweden.

HAZEL HENDERSON is an independent futurist/economist and social entrepreneur. She is an invited lecturer at universities, an advisor to governments and corporations in more than thirty-five countries, a fellow of numerous environmental/futuristic organizations, and author of *Creat-*

ing Alternative Futures (1978) and *The Politics of the Solar Age* (1981 and a new 1988 edition) as well as of hundreds of articles. Her current goals are to explode the myths of contemporary "economics" and to continue building models of ecologically sustainable, equitable, people-centered development in all human societies.

FRANCES MOORE LAPPÉ is co-founder and director of the Institute for Food and Development Policy in San Francisco. In graduate school she suddenly recognized the inappropriateness of much of "higher education" to global problems, choosing instead to educate herself, particularly on the subject of hunger. Like structural violence, she found global hunger is more a human invention than a natural occurrence. Her best-known books are *Diet for a Small Planet, Food First: Beyond the Myth of Scarcity*, and, most recently, *Rediscovering America's Values* (1989.) In 1987, she received the Right Livelihood Award in Stockholm, Sweden.

ROBERT W. MALONE is Professor of Philosophy at Brock University in St. Catharines, Ontario. His recent concern with global issues led him to organize the previous conference on the theme "Sanity, Science and Global Responsibility" held on his campus in July 1988. As co-founder of Responsibility International, a society dedicated to global networking among concerned academics and others, he is continuing his efforts to focus attention upon survival issues as they relate to all humankind.

JAMES C. MANLEY is Co-Associate Director of the Interdisciplinary General Education Program at California State Polytechnic University, Pomona. His specialization is in aesthetics, with particular emphases on the East and on cinematic art. He has been a central figure in developing the now internationally recognized Interdisciplinary General Education program and its progenitor, the Cal Poly Campus Forum, since their inception nearly a decade ago.

DAVID McFARLAND is President of Kutztown University, Kutztown, Pennsylvania. An aeronautical engineer, he was a stress analyst for Boeing before entering academic life, where he soon took on administrative responsibilities. Prior to his moving to Kutztown he served as provost at Central Missouri State University, where he initiated and developed a highly successful integrated general education curriculum, the subject of his conference presentation.

MARY MIDGLEY, formerly Lecturer in Philosophy at the University of Newcastle-upon-Tyne, England, was trained in what she has dubbed "the arid garden of British moral philosophy." Retired since 1980 in order to devote full time to her writing, she is author of *Beast and Man, Heart and Mind, Animals and Why They Matter, Women's Choices* (with Judith Hughes), *Evolution as a Religion*, and *Wisdom, Information and Wonder*. She has written numerous articles, including a popular series, "Body and Soul," in the *Manchester Guardian*, and is in constant demand as a speaker at international meetings. She also functions on several national councils in Great Britain.

WILLIAM H. NEWELL is Professor of Interdisciplinary Studies at Miami University, Oxford, Ohio, and a charter faculty member in the Western College Program, a four-year integrated liberal arts degree program. While maintaining an active interest in his field, economic history, he has been a national leader in the development of interdisciplinary education, serving as the founding president in 1979 of the Association for Integrative Studies, in which he remains an active officer.

RUSSELL W. PETERSON has a doctorate in chemistry and worked twenty-six years in industry before entering public life as Governor of Delaware. Concern for the future led him to help create the Global Tomorrow Coalition, the Center on the Consequences of Nuclear War, and the Better World Society. He is a former president of the National Audubon Society, chair of the President's Council on Environmental Quality, vice-president of the International Union for the Conservation of Nature and Natural Resources, and director of the Office of Technology Assessment. He is currently involved in numerous national and global organizations dealing with energy, population, and conservation of the environment.

WILLIAM J. RECKMEYER is Professor and Chairman of the Department of Anthropology and Cybernetic Systems at San Jose State University. A Russian historian by training, he has spent the past fifteen years as a systems educator, scholar, and consultant helping develop more integrative approaches for handling complex organizational and societal issues. He is past president of the American Society for Cybernetics, serves as editor of *General Systems Yearbook*, represents the United States on the US-USSR Project on Cybernetics and Systems, and is currently a Kellogg National Fellow working on "Leadership and Public Policy for the Twenty-first Century."

RICHARD E. RUBENSTEIN is Director of the Center for Conflict Analysis and Resolution at George Mason University. He holds degrees in political theory and the law and has long been concerned with the coercive aspects of social order and the causes of political violence. Previously he has taught at the Antioch School of Law in Washington, D.C. He is author of *Rebels in Eden: Mass Political Violence in the United States* and *Alchemists of Revolution: Terrorism in the Modern World.*

HUSTON SMITH is perhaps America's best know religious philosopher. He is Thomas J. Watson Professor of Religion and Distinguished Adjunct Professor of Philosophy Emeritus at Syracuse University, and held prior positions at Washington University in Saint Louis and the Massachusetts Institute of Technology. His six books include *The Religions of Man* (which has sold over two million copies), *Forgotten Truth*, and *Beyond the Post-Modern Mind.* His documentary films on world religions have garnered international acclaim and awards.

BENJAMIN F. TAGGIE is currently Provost and Vice President for Academic Affairs at Millersville University, Millersville, Pennsylvania. A Spanish Medieval historian by training, he began teaching in the public schools of Michigan, later joining the faculty at Central Michigan University, then moving to Central Missouri State where he became Dean of the College of Arts and Sciences. It was there that he helped develop the highly successful integrated general education curriculum that is the subject of his and Dr. McFarland's contribution to the conference.

NANCY WARE is Co-Associate Director of the internationally recognized Interdisciplinary General Education program at California State Polytechnic University, Pomona. Her training is in the humanities, with an emphasis in English literature. Prior to joining the faculty at Cal Poly, she was in secondary school education. She has been a central figure in the development of the Interdisciplinary General Education program virtually from its inception.

SANDRA A. WAWRYTKO is on the faculties of Philosophy and Asian Studies at San Diego State University. She has been involved in several international professional organizations, including executive roles in the International Society for Chinese Philosophy, the World Congress of Logotherapy, and the International Society for Philosophy and Psychotherapy. Her specialization is in comparative East-West philosophy, with an emphasis on China. Her numerous books and articles include a forthcoming series of volumes of commentary and translation of key classical Chinese texts. She was co-organizer of the conference, "Rethinking the Curriculum."

TERRENCE H. WHITE is President of Brock University, St. Catharines, Ontario, host of the 1988 conference, "Sanity, Science, and Global Responsibility." His degree in sociology has led him to study organizations, the quality of working life, and the nature of corporate boards of directors. In conjunction with these, he also serves as a consultant for industry and government in the areas of human resource management and organizational design. He is author of *Power or Pawns: Boards of Directors in Canadian Corporations*.